Marketing Management in Practice
2003–2004

Marketing Management in Practice 2003–2004

John Williams and Tony Curtis

AMSTERDAM BOSTON HEIDELBERG LONDON NEW YORK OXFORD
PARIS SAN DIEGO SAN FRANCISCO SINGAPORE SYDNEY TOKYO

Butterworth-Heinemann
An imprint of Elsevier
Linacre House, Jordan Hill, Oxford OX2 8DP
200 Wheeler Road, Burlington MA 01803

First published 2003

British Library Cataloguing in Publication Data
A catalogue record for this book is available from the British Library

ISBN 0 7506 5960 2

For information on all Butterworth-Heinemann publications
visit our website at www.bh.com

Typeset by Integra Software Services Pvt. Ltd, Pondicherry, India
www.integra-india.com
Printed and bound in Italy

Contents

preface
welcome to the CIM coursebooks

An introduction from the academic development advisor

In the last two years we have seen some significant changes to the CIM Professional Series initiated by the Chartered Institute of Marketing. The changes have been introduced on a year-on-year basis, with Stage 1 (Certificate) changes implemented last year in 2002, and the Stage 2 (Advanced Certificate in Marketing) being implemented this year. It is anticipated that next year in 2004 the Stage 3 (Postgraduate Diploma) changes will be implemented.

As a result the authoring team, Butterworth-Heinemann and I have aimed to rigorously revise and update the coursebook series to make sure that every title is the best possible study aid and accurately reflects the latest CIM syllabus.

The revisions to the series this year included continued development in the Stage 1 and Postgraduate Diploma Series, and complete re-writes at Stage 2 to align with the radical overhaul of the CIM syllabus. There are a number of new authors and indeed Senior Examiners in the series who have been commissioned for their CIM course teaching and examining experience, as well as their research into specific curriculum-related areas and their wide general knowledge of the latest thinking in marketing.

We are certain that you will find these coursebooks highly beneficial in terms of the content and assessment opportunities and a study tool that will prepare you for both CIM examinations and continuous/integrative assessment opportunities. They will guide you in a logical and structured way through the detail of the syllabus, providing you with the required underpinning knowledge, understanding and application of theory.

The editorial team and authors wish you every success as you embark upon your studies.

Karen Beamish
Academic Development Advisor

How to use these coursebooks

Everyone who has contributed to this series has been careful to structure the books with the exams in mind. Each unit, therefore, covers an essential part of the syllabus. You need to work through the complete coursebook systematically to ensure that you have covered everything you need to know.

This coursebook is divided into units each containing a selection of the following standard elements:

- o **Learning objectives** Tell you what you will be expected to know, having read the unit
- o **Syllabus references** Outline what part of the syllabus is covered in the module
- o **Study guides** Tell you how long the unit is and how long its activities take to do
- o **Questions** Are designed to give you practice – they will be similar to those you get in the exam
- o **Answers** (at the end of the book) suggest a format for answering exam questions. Remember there is no such thing as a model answer – you should use these examples only as guidelines
- o **Activities** Give you a chance to put what you have learned into practice
- o **Debriefings** (at the end of the book) shed light on the methodologies involved in the activities
- o **Hints and tips** Are tips from the senior examiner, examiner or author which are designed to help you avoid common mistakes made by previous candidates and give you guidance on improving your knowledge base
- o **Insights** Encourage you to contextualize your academic knowledge by reference to real-life experience
- o **Key definitions** Highlight and explain the key points relevant to that module
- o **Definitions** May be used for words you must know to pass the exam
- o **Summaries** Cover what you should have picked up from reading the unit
- o **Further study** Provides details of recommended reading in addition to the coursebook.

While you will find that each section of the syllabus has been covered within this text, you might find that the order of some of the topics has been changed. This is because it sometimes makes more sense to put certain topics together when you are studying, even though they might appear in different sections of the syllabus itself. If you are following the reading and other activities, your coverage of the syllabus will be just fine, but don't forget to follow up with trade press reading!

About MarketingOnline

With this year's coursebooks, Butterworth-Heinemann is offering readers free access to MarketingOnline (www.marketingonline.co.uk), our premier online support engine for the CIM marketing courses. On this site you can benefit from:

- o Tutorials on key topics every two weeks during the term, comprehensive revision support material and access to revision days from Tactics – the highly acclaimed independent trainer for CIM courses
- o Fully customizable electronic versions of the coursebooks – annotate, cut and paste sections of text to create your own tailored learning notes
- o Instant access to weblinks related to the coursebooks
- o Capacity to search the coursebook online for instant access to definitions and key concepts.

Logging on

Before you can access MarketingOnline you will first need to get a password. Please go to www.marketingonline.co.uk where you will find registration instructions for coursebook purchasers. Once you have got your password, you will need to log on using the onscreen instructions. This will give you access to the various functions outlined below.

Using MarketingOnline

MarketingOnline is broadly divided into four sections which can each be accessed from the front page after you have logged on to the system:

1. *The coursebooks* Buttons corresponding to the three levels of CIM marketing qualification are situated on the home page. Select your level and you will be presented with the four coursebook titles for each module of that level. Click on the desired coursebook to access the full online text (divided up by chapter). On each page of text you have the option to add an electronic bookmark or annotation by following the onscreen instructions. You can also freely cut and paste text into a blank word document to create your own learning notes.
2. *Revision material* Click on the 'Revision material' link and select the appropriate CIM level and coursebook to access revision material.
3. *Useful links* Click on 'Useful links' to access a list of links to other sites of interest for further reading and research.
4. *Glossary* Click on the 'Glossary' button to access our online dictionary of marketing terms.

If you have specific queries about using MarketingOnline then you should consult our fully searchable FAQ section – again, this is accessible through the appropriate link on the front page of the site. Please also note that a **full user guide** can be downloaded by clicking on the link on the opening page of the website.

unit 1
management and marketing roles

o To describe the nature of relationships with other functions in organizations operating in a range of different industries and contexts (1.1)

o To explain the importance of developing and maintaining effective relationships with people in other functions and disciplines (1.2).

The learning objectives are only partly covered in this chapter and they are a theme throughout the book. Other chapters will also be concerned with these objectives , particularly, the chapters that focus on the use of teams and communications.

Key definitions

Accountability – The extent to which individuals and managers are held responsible for the outcome of the decisions they make.

Autonomy – Independence to make decisions within a decentralized working environment, where decision-making is passed down from the top of the organization to the lower levels.

Fads – Fashions that enter quickly, are adopted with great zeal, peak early and decline very fast.

Flat hierarchy – An organizational structure that provides a wide span of control within only a few layers of organizational hierarchy.

Global firm – A firm that by operating in more than one country gains R&D, production, marketing and financial advantages in its costs and reputation that are not available to purely domestic competitors.

Global organization – A form of international organization whereby top corporate management and staff plan worldwide manufacturing or operational facilities, marketing policies, financial flows and logistical systems. The global operating unit reports directly to the chief executive, not to an international divisional head.

International division – A form of international marketing organization in which the division handles all of the firm's international activities. Marketing, manufacturing, research, planning and specialist staff are organized into operating units according to geography or product groups, or as an international subsidiary responsible for its own sales and profitability.

Marketing database – An organized set of data about individual customers or prospects that can be used to generate and qualify customer leads, sell products and services and maintain customer relationships.

Market research – The process of 1) analysing marketing opportunities; 2) selecting target markets; 3) developing the marketing mix; 4) managing the marketing effort.

Marketing mix – The set of controllable tactical marketing tools – product, price, place and promotion – that the firm blends to produce the response it wants in the target market.

Market segment – A group of consumers who respond in a similar way to a given set of marketing stimuli.

Market segmentation – Dividing a market into distinct groups of buyers with different needs, characteristics or behaviour, who might require separate products or marketing mixes.

Study Guide

The whole of the coursebook is targeted at assisting you to pass the Marketing in Management Practice examination. The main focus of the CIM Advanced Certificate Course Marketing Management in Practice is on the development and implementation of marketing plans at an operational level in organizations. A key aspect of this is working within a team to develop plans and managing teams, through marketing activities and projects, to implement the plan. The syllabus is covered in eight units and these cover the main areas that contribute to effective marketing management. A marketing oriented company needs to align its distinctive competencies with market opportunities but to do this effectively requires a team effort.

Customer focus needs to be shared by the whole organization and is not the responsibility of the marketing department in isolation. Achieving an organization-wide sense of shared values and beliefs can take a long time as it may mean changing the structure and culture of the organization. Front line staff are often the public face of the organization and, as customer service providers, they possess useful information. A key element of a market orientation is intelligence-gathering about customer needs and preferences and what influences them. This should involve people throughout the organization but channelled for analysis towards a particular part of it. This is often a marketing department in larger organizations.

The structure of an organization can be a barrier to success if it separates one department from another. In some organizations, sales, marketing and customer service are organized as a team but finance, human resource management, research and development, production, purchasing and management all affect the marketing effort. To ensure that everyone is working to the same broad objectives as a team requires good communication and an awareness and respect for each other's contributions. The book looks at these key issues. The first chapter introduces the broad subject of management in the context of marketing and marketing management. The diverse roles of marketing management and the various ways in which the marketing function is organized are discussed. Guidance on examination preparation will focus on the examination techniques that will maximize your probability of passing.

Management

Introduction to the book

The Marketing Management in Practice module focuses on marketing at an operational level but requires an awareness of the strategic context. The module:

○ Provides the *final assessment* of your ability to *create* an operational marketing plan. It forms an important measure of your ability to meet organization's requirements of an operational marketer

○ Seeks to *integrate learning* from the Stage 2 syllabus.

Managing people and teams

This element provides the underpinning knowledge required for the selection, development and maintenance of effective marketing teams. Marketing teams are operating in an organizational and global context and how different organizations adopt different approaches to marketing depends on their context and culture. Key Skills – 'Working with others' and 'Improving one's own knowledge and performance'.

Managing marketing projects and activities

Managing the planning and performance of a marketing task by a team requires skills in planning, scheduling, directing, motivating and monitoring. The techniques of project management equip marketing managers to manage marketing activities and projects effectively.

Managing knowledge and delivering market research projects

Knowledge management is about people. People need to be motivated and enthused to share and exchange knowledge. This cannot be done by simply presenting them with a piece of IT equipment. It requires a cultural norm of open communication, informing and sharing knowledge, and motivating and rewarding knowledge-sharing that benefits the business.

Developing and implementing marketing plans

This element requires effective teamwork, and a good understanding of the marketing planning process and techniques to produce successful outcomes.

Studying management

Key issues to bear in mind when studying management are: firstly, although it is possible to identify trends that are occurring in some large well known companies, this doesn't necessarily mean that they are occurring everywhere in all sizes and types of companies.

Awareness of similarities and differences

Examples from one sector may not always be appropriate for understanding what happens in other sectors. There are stereotypes about what happens in both the 'private' and the 'public sector' from within each sector. It is important to go beyond the stereotypes to look for similarities as well as differences. Not all private sector management is good and public sector management bad and vice versa.

Culture

What happens in one country may not be easily applied in other countries because it is difficult to transplant all the social and cultural conditions that make a particular initiative or innovation a success. In recent years, there have been many attempts to use Japanese management techniques with varying degrees of success. Much management writing is based on what happens in companies in the USA and the UK, so it is important to be aware of cultural differences and how other countries do things. What works in one context may not work as well in a different context.

When Parker Pen devised advertisements for its ball point pen they were meant to say 'It won't leak in your pocket and embarrass you'. However, in Spanish 'embararzar' means pregnant, not embarrassed and the advertisement was translated as 'It won't leak in your pocket and make you pregnant'. In Chinese, the name Coca-Cola was translated as Ke-kou-ke-la to make it sound similar to the original. However, after printing its signs, the company discovered that, in at least one dialect the phrase means 'female horse stuffed with wax'. In Taiwan, the slogan 'Come alive with the Pepsi Generation' was translated as 'Pepsi will bring your ancestors back from the dead'.

Fads and fashions

Writing about management is prone to fads and fashions with management gurus often very influential in disseminating ideas about what seems to be working. However, not all popular management ideas are effective. Some management ideas have had a negative effect on some organizations. In the early 1990s, the Chief Economist of Morgan Stanley argued strongly in favour of downsizing, saying that it was a cure for companies' problems. By 1997 he had changed his mind and argued, on the contrary, it could be a recipe for disaster. In 1982, Tom Peters wrote *In Search Of Excellence*, a book that identified 43 successful companies and gave reasons for their success over 20 years. However, many of the companies, including the computer company IBM (see Case Study, p. 10) ran into problems not long after the book was published. Peters apologized, saying that 'there are no excellent companies' and now says of his writing 'Some of my stuff is wrong. Some stuff is right, but I hope all of it is provocative'.

Reading 1.1 Boddy, D. (2002). *Management: An Introduction*, pp 30–32, conventional and critical perspectives and studying management.

What is management?

Management is an inclusive term that is used in a variety of ways. Generally, it is the process of planning, organizing, leading, co-ordinating and controlling aspects of an organization's resources to achieve organizational goals. Different managers have different styles that are formed by their past experience, the nature of the tasks they have to undertake, the context they work in, and the expectations, capabilities and motivation of the people they work with. Studies of management behaviour show that there are wide variations both for the same manager from one week to another and between managers in similar jobs. There are also wide differences between managers' jobs in the same country as well as across countries. Individual influences such as gender, age, ethnic background, education, career experience and personality may also have an impact but there is no conclusive evidence about whether and how these factors influence management behaviour. Rosemary Stewart recommended a three-part classification for the analysis of management jobs. She identified:

- ○ job demands (what you must do)
- ○ job choices (the freedoms you have to decide what to do)
- ○ job constraints (the limit on what you can do)

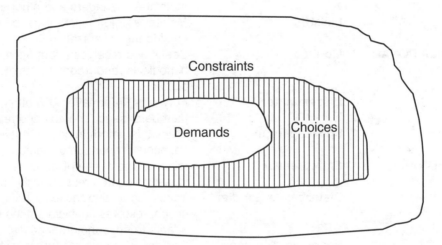

Figure 1.1 The reality of management
Source: Stewart, R. (1963)

 ## Activity 1.1

How would you draw the diagram to represent opportunities, constraints and demands on your own job?

1. *Job Demands* – What job activities must not be neglected? What are the targets that you must meet? Who or what defines these demands? – Your manager? Your peers in the organization? People outside the organization? You – your standards or ambitions? Rank them again according to how much attention/time you allocate to each of them. Do these rankings reflect their importance?
2. *Job Constraints* – What factors limit you in what you would like to do in your job? Attitudes or expectations of your manager? Your colleagues? People outside the

organization? Your organization's policies or procedures? Shortage of other resources? Technology? Your own skills, relationships with other functions in the organization?

3. *Job Choices* – What choice do you have over the work that is to be done? When it is to be done? How it is to be done? The standards to which it is to be done? The results that are to be achieved? Over who does the work?

Management roles

Henry Mintzberg analysed the nature of managerial work and concluded that management consisted of a mass of fragmented activities, constant interruption, pressure for immediate answers and reliance on word-of-mouth messages. Managers value 'soft' information, often acquired through gossip, hearsay and speculation. Consequently, important information for the organization is held not necessarily in the memory of its computers but in the minds of its managers. Mintzberg offered a view of management based on 'roles'.

INTERPERSONAL	Figurehead	Performs ceremonial and symbolic duties such as greeting visitors, signing legal documents.
	Leader	Sets the strategic direction of the organization, motivates managers and other staff.
	Liaison	Maintains information links both inside and outside the organization.
INFORMATIONAL	Monitor	Seeks and receives information, scans periodicals and reports, maintains personal contacts.
	Disseminator	Forwards information to other organization members, sends memos and reports.
	Spokesperson	Transmits information to outsiders through speeches, reports and memos.
DECISIONAL	Entrepreneur	Initiates improvement projects, identifies new ideas, delegates responsibility to others.
	Disturbance Handler	Takes corrective action during disputes or crises, resolves conflicts among subordinates, adapts to environmental crises.
	Resource Allocator	Decides who gets resources, scheduling, budgeting, sets priorities.
	Negotiator	Represents department during negotiation of contracts, sales, purchases, budgets.

Figure 1.2 Mintzberg's managerial roles
Source: Mintzberg, H. (1973) *The nature of managerial work*, London, Harper Row

Each of the ten roles cover a different aspect of managerial work. The ten roles form an integrated whole but different managers are likely to give greater prominence to different aspects of the job. For example, sales managers tend to spend relatively more time in their interpersonal roles, while production managers tend to give relatively more attention to the decisional roles. Mintzberg found that the amount of time spent in the three sets of roles varied with the level of the manager. For example, first-line supervisory positions are likely to have more decisional roles (at a day to day operational level). Senior managers spend more time on interpersonal roles. Middle managers tend to be more occupied with informational roles. Roles will also change with culture and organizational size.

Activity 1.2

Write some brief notes summarizing what you think 'management' means. What is your experience of management? – As someone who has been managed or when you have managed something or someone. Think of the best manager that you have encountered – what characteristics did they possess? Who was the worst manager you have encountered and what were their characteristics? What conclusions do you draw from this exercise about what makes an effective manager?

Reading 1.2 Boddy, D. (2002). *Management: An Introduction*, pp 21–24, the process of management.

Activity 1.3

This activity asks you, first of all, to try to make a note of everything you do on your next day at work and how long you spend doing it. Draw up a chart with the following headings:

- ○ Time begun
- ○ Nature of activity
- ○ Who was involved?
- ○ Whether planned or unplanned but occurring as the result of your taking advantage of an opportunity
- ○ Completed/not completed/deferred/referred elsewhere.

Consider the following questions:

- ○ How typical a day was this?
- ○ How much time did you actually spend on what you regard as managerial tasks? You might express this as an approximate percentage of your day at work
- ○ What approximate percentage of your time was spent dealing with trivial matters that you feel need not have concerned you?
- ○ What was the longest period of time you spent on any one task?
- ○ How many interruptions did you suffer during the day?
- ○ How many of the things you had intended to do during the day did you actually complete?
- ○ How long did you spend at your place of work?
- ○ How much time did you spend on interpersonal roles? decisional roles? informational roles?
- ○ Which of Mintzberg's ten management roles do you perform? What are the most common situations when you would enact these roles?

Marketing management

CIM's definition of marketing is 'The management process which identifies, anticipates and satisfies customer requirements profitability. This process varies depending on factors such as the size of the organization, the sector in which it is located, the type of work role performed by the manager and the career experience that the marketing manager brings with them. Generally speaking, the smaller the organization the more multifaceted are the roles of the marketing manager.

Marketing titles

Marketing titles and positions vary considerably along with the particular responsibilities that accompany them. They span a range of positions, including marketing director, marketing manager, sales manager, advertising manager, promotion manager and public relations manager. A marketing director is responsible for directing overall marketing policy. Marketing managers work with service or product development, market research and others to develop detailed marketing strategies.

Sales and marketing

As mentioned above, sometimes Sales and Marketing are combined in one department, section or job description so as to avoid the damaging splits that can sometimes occur when they are separate. Sales and marketing teams should work together creating opportunities for new business, identifying new markets and gathering competitive intelligence. However, they may work quite differently. Sales managers direct the efforts of sales professionals by assigning territories, establishing goals, developing training programs, and supervising local sales managers and their personnel. Sales teams need immediate information to close sales quickly whereas marketing teams are often focused on longer-term results. Differences in philosophy and work style can create barriers to sharing information and make it difficult to close sales.

Working across organizational boundaries

Marketing management has an important role in working across organizational boundaries to help prepare managers to develop strategies for their products and services, and incorporate marketing into the corporate strategy. This means that marketing managers need to work with, for example, colleagues from Human Resources and Finance to deal with recruitment and the reward of staff as well as securing and monitoring budgets and expenditure. If a company has introduced a human resource management approach as opposed to a 'personnel' approach, a manager may find that many of the responsibilities that used to belong to the personnel department have been pushed across to line managers. The following Case Study describes how marketing management process works in the railway industry. It highlights the need for a marketing orientation across the organization.

Case Study

An overview of the Marketing Management process in a railway environment

In railways, departments that play a role in service delivery – Operations, Mechanical Engineering and Civil Engineering – affect the quality of the Seven Ps and have an important influence on the marketability of the railway product. They also have a 'Marketing' role but the Marketing Department has primary responsibility for translating the needs of customers into service requirements and communicating them to service providers. It must also ensure that customer needs are met. The wants and needs of the organization's target customers is the main factor influencing the process of Marketing Management. The development of a strategy to meet the needs of the target market must also adapt to distribution channels, suppliers, competitors and publics. It must also adapt to demographic, economic, political, legal, technological, physical and social forces. Marketing Management must take into account all the actors and forces to develop its strategy to serve the target market.

The Case Study illustrates the point that a marketing orientation requires all the parts of an organization to work interdependently because they can all have an affect on the marketability of the service. Sometimes, a narrow focus on the demands of particular functional requirements with no regard for the customer or end-user can be bad public relations. For example, the scheduling and duration of maintenance work needs to take into account the impact on the travelling public. Releasing stories about the 'wrong' kind of leaves or snow having an adverse affect on the rail network might be technically accurate but a disaster in public relations terms. For example, as part of an English language programme, the German radio station Bayern Radio carried a story entitled 'Leaves on the track: The story of Britain's railway system' and described a comedian's patter:

'a leaf grows on a tree. It's very small. It's harmless. You can stick one in your mouth and chew it. But when a leaf falls on a railway line, it can stop the biggest train and make it thirty minutes late. One leaf! And now we have the wrong kind of snow. I mean, what is the wrong kind of snow? Nobody knows, but watch the weather forecast. If it's the wrong kind of snow, do not get on a train' (Bayern Radio, 1999)

This might be a parody of the technical difficulties experienced by Railtrack but it does show the need to make sure that technical issues are presented in a way that understands the potential impact on public relations.

The following diagram shows an example of a structure for a marketing-oriented organization and the typical marketing roles.

Figure 1.3 Departmentalism by function

In smaller organizations, where these roles exist, they may be carried out by one or two people. The following case study describes how IBM needed to change the structure of its organization to enable people to work together and become more focused on the needs of customers. When you read it, reflect on your own organization and the way that different parts of it work together. Are there any particular arrangements that contribute to successful or unsuccessful collaboration? For example, does the use of IT help or hinder? Is there room for improvement?

Case Study

Changing IBM's focus

In the 1990s, IBM faced a difficult competitive environment with demand for its products declining. IBM was used to developing systems and then looking for customers with a problem who would fit the 'solution'. However, it was recognized that helping customers use technology effectively was the critical success factor. 'Solution selling' required a good understanding of the company's capabilities and the ability to integrate these from the different parts of the organization. At IBM, product chiefs and the geographic region heads were the powerful players. IBM's organizational structure stood in the way of providing solutions to customers. Since resources needed mobilising across product and country organizations, there were conflicts. New co-ordinating processes were developed. The sales force had to change from being order takers to becoming consultants and they were re-organized along industry lines. IBM also understood the importance of aligning structure with strategy and encouraged various IBM units to work together.

Source: Adapted from Kumar, Nirmalya, The path to change, *Financial Times*, 6 December 2002.

The Case Study identifies the need for organizations to ensure that their structure fits the strategy that the company is pursuing rather than working against it. It also highlights the importance of being able to draw on resources from across the organization, and to identify and remove any barriers that stand in the way of this. This might involve confronting vested interests and it is important to make sure that solving one problem doesn't cause another problem somewhere else in the organization. This is looked at in more detail in the unit 'Managing Change'. The functions of marketing vary in different sectors. The following case study is based on marketing legal services and is interesting because sometimes established professions need a lot of convincing that marketing is necessary.

Case Study

Marketing legal services

The leading London-based firms have remarkable marketing departments, with extensive budgets, sophisticated technical equipment and talented marketers. Their marketing departments may be broken down into myriad areas including: publications, conferences, desktop publishing and graphics, public relations, internal and external communications, business research, Internet marketing web and Intranet, and database management. British firms also have additional practice development specialists. The departments are growing in size and results are being tracked to enable the management to see the benefits that the marketing department provides. Marketing departments need to be viewed as knowledge centers and marketers seen as assets and not cost centres.

Source: 'Growing Your Marketing Department into a Knowledge Management Team: Aim to Hire Assets Not Overheads' by Linda Sedloff Orton, http://www.llrx.com/features/market.htm.

The Case Study illustrates the importance of trying to assess the value of marketing rather than seeing it exclusively as a cost. This is likely to require a proactive approach to measuring value but there are a wide range of activities that fall under the marketing umbrella. Many people are likely to be surprised at the extent of marketing activity in legal practices. Another issue that is important for considering working relationships is how the function relates to professionals. Professionals tend to value autonomy and having control over their working life. It isn't always easy to incorporate them into marketing activities. Throughout the 1980s and 1990s, there were major changes to public sector organization and management. A key aspect of this change was the emergence of a 'new managerialism', i.e. the importation of modern private sector management techniques which challenged some established principles and practices within the public sector. It was seen as a threat to the traditional dominance of professionalism and professionals.

The digital economy

Communication and information processing technologies are an important tool in many organizations. Company intranets provide an interface for sharing company-wide information and people can access information, collaborate and distribute results anywhere, anytime. High-speed networking capability and software innovations allow work teams to collaborate at a distance, and the growth in the use of ICT also means that the skill mix that people need to perform their jobs is changing.

Organization benefits are:

  o New promotional media
  o Access to richer and more targeted research data

     ○   Enhanced employee and customer communication
     ○   Ability to customize promotions.

Activity 1.4

Visit the *Lord of the Rings* film website www.lordoftherings.net that supports the film and then go to the *Spiderman* movie website www.spiderman.sonypictures.com/ that supports that film.

Compare the two sites:

○ What are the ways used to involve the web viewer and to generate interest in the respective movies?

○ What are your views about the potential of this kind of promotional effort?

○ How effective is each promotional strategy, given what you have seen?

○ What are the types of merchandise each site is selling as part of its merchandising strategy?

○ Which site do you think is more effective in marketing terms? What criteria are you using to judge?

○ What channel(s) of distribution are being promoted here to purchase this merchandise?

Reading 1.3 Boddy, D. *Information systems and the process of management*, pp 550–563.

New work practices and implications for management

With the rapid advancements in technology, acceptance of new forms of working from home is set to increase considerably in the future. Teleworking is seen as a way of creating new jobs and increasing flexibility and is now a mainstream form of employment in Europe and the USA. One employee in 20 in the UK is now a teleworker. However, the UK lags behind other parts of the EU where the practice is growing more rapidly. A number of multinational companies have set up teleworking operations around the world and 70 per cent of large companies recognize teleworking. Teleworking is growing rapidly in The Netherlands, Finland and Italy. The public sector is using teleworking, for example in Social Services, Leisure and Environment departments.

Charles Handy wrote *The Age of Unreason* (1991) and predicted a time when new working patterns such as outsourcing, telecommuting and the rise of knowledge workers would become widespread. A number of organizational forms would emerge in an age of unreason.

The shamrock organization is one that is based on a core of permanent workers supported by outside contractors and consultants used for specific time-limited inputs and part-time help brought in and laid off to cope with peaks and troughs in demand.

The federal organization is a form of decentralisation that combines the autonomy of individual parts with the economies of scale that occur because the centre co-ordinates, advises, influences and suggests rather than directs or controls.

The Triple I organizations such as universities and research organizations will try to create value out of knowledge, specifically Information, Intelligence and Ideas. Handy also predicted the growth of Portfolio working which would include paid work and 'free' work encompassing homework, gift work and study work. Paid work is for time given, free work is for results delivered, homework includes the range of tasks carried out in the home. Gift work is work undertaken for charities, neighbours or for the community. The idea of study work is self-explanatory and can take place in and out of the home. A balanced portfolio would comprise elements of each of these types of work in differing proportions for different people.

Activity 1.5

Write a report which explains the likely problems of new work practices for managers and employees. Include the main implications for the business, such as impact on business operations and implications of setting up teleworking. (Adapted from CIM June 2001 Exam Paper)

The role of marketing in the organization

Insight

A survey on Marketing in British organizations by McKinsey & Co. found that the role of marketing was at its most sophisticated in the Business to Consumer area (B2C) and the lowest in the Business to Business area (B2B). The primary role of marketing for a quarter of all sectors' respondents was promoting sales. But B2C gave greater weight to building brands (28 per cent). Many organizations ran a marketing function without a specific department – 47 per cent for B2C and B2B, and 39 per cent for 'Both'. A specific marketing department was found in 41 per cent of B2C organizations, but in only 15 per cent of B2B and 29 per cent of 'Both'. Almost a third (31 per cent) of all B2B respondents combined marketing with sales or other functions, compared with 23 per cent of 'Both' and only 6 per cent B2C. Less than 10 per cent of respondents stated that marketing does not really exist as a function within their organizations.

Just over half the respondents showed that the most critical change required in their organizations was the need for enhanced collaboration between marketing and other functions. Nearly half of each sector stated that marketing worked with other functions 'most of the time' (45 per cent B2C, 47 per cent both, 46 per cent B2B), and slightly less specified 'all the time' (32 per cent B2C, 29 per cent both, 29 per cent B2B).

Source: McKinsey Marketing Practice, 2002.

The extract from the survey shows that there is a lot of work to be done to improve cross-organization working and, in particular, the way that marketing works with other functions in the organization. This is looked at in greater depth in Unit 3 'Developing the Team'.

Question 1.1

How is marketing activity organized in your organization? How would you describe collaboration? Is it successful? If so, what factors contribute to its success? If not, how could it be improved? The following extract written by a marketing manager shows some of the diversity that exists in marketing jobs.

Insight

I am a marketing manager in a services company. There is a flat hierarchical structure, with a CEO, a layer of senior management and then the rest of us. We are a small team of self-managers and are encouraged to manage our own career-development. We are not issued with job descriptions to demonstrate that the role is dynamic and evolving. We are also encouraged to develop our roles individually rather than have our workload dictated by the management. Our jobs have 'breadth' rather than 'depth' which makes us less specialised but more able to handle ad-hoc enquiries across different areas and we are each required to turn our hand to whatever situation arises.

Question 1.3

Do you have a job description? – Is it useful or does it gather dust? – Does it accurately reflect what you do? Is it reviewed regularly? – If you do not have one are there any problems that arise because of it?

Organization culture

Charles Handy reporting the work of Harrison suggests that organizations can be classified under four cultures. He felt that every organization was a different mix of the same four basic cultures.

Power culture
Handy describes this as the Zeus Culture, after the head of the gods, and is an organization dominated by the personality and power of one person, often the owner. The visual image is of a spider's web with power residing at the centre controlled by a single owner or a small group. Power and influence spread out from a central figure or group. The organization is dependent on the ability and judgement of the central power base.

Role culture
Handy calls this the Apollo Culture, after the god of harmony and order, and represents a culture dominated by rules and procedures. Work within and between departments is controlled formally by procedures, role descriptions, lines of authority and well-defined systems. Matters for decision have to be taken up the line and co-ordination is at the top by the senior management group. Role cultures tend to develop in relatively stable environments. The civil service and the IBM of the late 1980s are examples of a role culture.

Task culture

This is called the Athena Culture, after the warrior goddess. It is a culture that is suited to project work and is typical of consultancies and advertising agencies. The visual image used by Handy is a net with its vertical and horizontal lines and, not surprisingly, network and matrix organizations are examples of this kind of culture. People with the necessary skills, sometimes from different levels of the organization, are brought together to work on specific projects. The teams can be formed for specific purposes, disbanded, reformed and reconfigured according to the nature of the work that needs to be undertaken.

Person culture

Handy calls this the Dionysius Culture, where the individual has the freedom to develop their own ideas in the way they want such as in an artists' studio, or a traditional university. In this type of culture it is difficult to manage individuals since there is very little structure and individuals are relatively autonomous to carry out their work in the way that they want. Some consultants, barristers' chambers and universities are examples of such a culture. Typically, individuals work on their own but they do find administrative support useful.

Every organization is different from each other but they are all a mix of the same four basic cultures. The problem is that some organizations get 'stuck' in one of them instead of mixing all four.

Objectives of an organizational structure

Organization Structure refers to the pattern of relationships among positions in the organization and among members of the organization. The purpose of structure is to divide work among members of the organization and co-ordinate their activities so that they are directed towards achieving the goals and objectives of the organization. Structure defines tasks and responsibilities, work roles and relationships, and channels of communication. It should embrace:

○ accountability for the areas of work undertaken by groups and individual members of the organization
○ co-ordination of different parts of the organization and different areas of work
○ effective and efficient organizational performance, including resource utilization
○ monitoring the activities of the organization
○ flexibility in order to respond to changing environmental factors
○ job satisfaction of members of the organization.

An organization's structure is said to have two major components, these include formalization and centralization. Formalization is the extent to which rules and regulations are used to regulate behaviour. This is affected by the size of the organization because a small shop will not have as many rules as a hospital or an oil refinery. Centralization refers to where decision-making powers lie within an organization. In highly centralized organizations, most decisions are made at the highest level of management and these are communicated to other members. In a decentralized organization, the authority to make decisions is more widespread at all levels of management. Most organizations use a variety of these forms and may combine aspects of both for different parts of the organization.

Hierarchical models of organizations

- o Responsibilities and duties are clearly laid down –strong on formalization and strong on centralization
- o Specialized rather than generic roles
- o Vertical rather than horizontal communication
- o Decision-making is strongly centralized at senior levels of the organization
- o Clear lines of accountability between different levels of the hierarchy
- o Clear rules of procedure written down.

Collegial models of organizations

- o Authority is generally through expertise and knowledge rather than necessarily through position
- o Weak on decentralization
- o 'Bottom–heavy' – large numbers with the same pay and conditions
- o Common goals and purposes – people work together in teams
- o Formal and informal opportunities to participate in the development of initiatives
- o Employees are autonomous individuals needing a minimum of rules.

Handy's model of organizational culture can be put together with the formalization and centralization dimensions to form a matrix as shown in the diagram below:

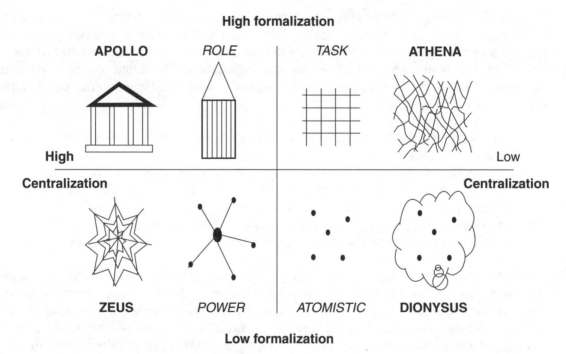

Figure 1.4 Models of organizational culture

The following case study identifies what is needed from an organization structure and culture in a fast moving airline industry that can be strongly influenced by external social, political and economic forces.

Case Study 1

Singapore Airlines

The Group needs a flexible structure that enables people to work with one another in a co-ordinated and co-operative way. Issues associated with decentralizing a business include: *maintaining lines of communication* – so that people know how other parts of the enterprise are working; *staff motivation* – the structure must provide job satisfaction and be capable of motivating all employees; *achieving goals* – employees need to know the goals set for them; *thinking globally whilst acting locally* – responding to local needs but remaining conscious of the global environment. A flatter organizational structure creates a more dynamic and flexible business, empowering people to make decisions in response to customer needs and to the changing nature of the Group's activity.

The case of Singapore airlines identifies a range of issues that need to be addressed, particularly, the need to balance a range of factors such as knowledge of local markets but also being able to see the 'bigger picture' and the autonomy to make decisions whilst also requiring greater collaboration and co-ordination amongst people. Potentially, these trends could work against each other which is why managers need to be alert and guard against it.

Activity 1.6

Using the key factors identified in the Case Study above – Communication, motivation, achieving goals and, if appropriate, acting locally and thinking globally – analyse the structure of your own organization from the point of view of enabling people with a marketing role to work with one another, and with other people in the organization in a co-ordinated and co-operative way.

Types of organizational structure

Functional

This type of structure groups major functions, e.g. information, finance, personnel and marketing. The advantages of this kind of structure are that it increases the utilization and co-ordination of groups of people with technical/specialized expertise. It can encourage sectional interests and conflicts, and make it difficult for an organization to adapt to product/service diversification.

Figure 1.5 Traditional organization of marketing departments

Product/Service

This is where there is grouping by service/product. For example, in the Health Service, the structure could have groupings around specialisms such as orthopaedic, surgical, psychiatric, etc., rather than medical, nursing, and paramedical functions.

Figure 1.6

The following provides an example of a large marketing-oriented organization chart. In this kind of structure, marketing is represented at Board level and a Marketing Manager co-ordinates the marketing activity in the organization.

Geographical

A nationalized service develops regions or areas; for example, in the NHS there are District Health Authorities, Health Authorities, Primary Care Groups, Hospital Trusts, Primary Care Trusts and Strategic Health Authorities covering regional and local organizations. Such a structure should mean greater responsiveness to local/ regional issues and different cultures, national/state laws, etc. A potential disadvantage is the possibility of localities/regions conflicting with each other. The following two Case Studies are both examples of very different organizations with a geographical organization structure.

Case Study

The Seventh-day Adventist Church is organized with a representative form of church government. This means that authority in the Church comes from the membership of local churches. Four levels of Church structure lead from the individual believer to the worldwide Church organization.

1. The local church made up of individual believers
2. The local conference, or local field/mission, made up of a number of local churches in a state, province, or territory
3. The union conference, or union field/mission, made up of conferences or fields within a larger territory (often a grouping of states or a a whole country)
4. The General Conference, the most extensive unit of organization, made up of all unions in all parts of the world. Divisions are sections of the General Conference, with administrative responsibility for particular geographical areas.

Figure 1.7 Departmentalism by territory

Singapore Airlines uses a geographical structure because it perceives that this makes it easier to customise services to local markets and enable greater responsiveness to customers.

Case Study

As a global business with operations in more than 80 countries, Singapore Airlines has also divided up its overseas business by geographical area. For each region, it has created a senior vice president with authority for that region. Being organized geographically makes it easier for a large company to:

o   respond quickly to local issues and problems
o   build up knowledge of specific markets
o   tailor its strategies to local conditions, laws and customs.

Within this structure, general managers for each country have the independence to make their own decisions, allowing the organization to respond more quickly and appropriately to market conditions.

Geographical structures

Geographical structures traditionally developed as companies expanded their offerings across territories. There was usually a need to be close to the customer, and to minimize the costs of travel and distribution. Today, the economics of location is important but information technology is making it less important in certain industries. The use of geographical structure depends on the industry. In service industries where the service is provided on-site, geography continues to be a structural basis for many companies. Sales forces and knowledge services like consulting were traditionally managed out of local offices, based on personal relationships and knowledge of the region. However, industry knowledge and expertise are becoming more important. Geographical structures are occurring in industries where the technology is creating a smaller efficient scale and flexible plants and where customers demand just-in-time delivery.

Swedish match company

Figure 1.8

North Europe Division, markets snuff, cigars, pipe tobacco, matches and lighters in the Nordic countries. Headquarters in Stockholm.

North America Division markets the company's products in North America. The division also manufactures cigars, pipe tobacco, snuff and chewing tobaccco. Head Office is in Richmond VA.

Overseas Division markets the company's products in South America, Australia, Asia and South Africa. The Division manufactures cigars, pipe tobacco and snuff. The head office is in Rio de Janeiro, Brazil.

Continental Europe markets the company's products in Europe with the exception of the Nordic countries. The Division manufactures cigars, pipe tobacco and lighters. The head office is in Valkenswaard, The Netherlands.

Match Division manufactures matches in Sweden, Brazil, Spain, Hungary, Turkey, Bulgaria, Indonesia and India. The matches are marketed globally through the four geographic divisions: North Europe, Continental Europe, North America and Overseas. The head office is in High Wycombe, Great Britain.

Divisional structure

This is where the organization is divided into divisions with devolved responsibility for the conduct of their business and financial performance. The grouping of services and/or geography and functionality (but often with functions such as finance, personnel, planning retained at headquarters). This can be suitable for international companies that are highly diversified, working in more than one country, e.g. a pharmaceutical company with divisions in each country producing and marketing products developed by the parent company. Divisional structures can be tight or loose, i.e. with varying degrees of central control and common service (finance, personnel, computing, etc.). Examples of this kind of structure are General Motors and GEC (UK).

The divisional structure is often developed in response to the difficulties associated with the functional structure. Divisions or business units are set out, each being regarded as a profit centre. Often the divisions are decided upon according to processes, geographic region, product type, or sometimes some combination of two of these. There is often diversity within a division which can be combated by subdivisions (e.g. product divisions further divided according to geographic region), or by having a functional structure within the division. The main advantage is that each division can be managed almost as if it were a separate company, which helps to deal effectively with different products or markets. This division of the company can however lead to wasteful duplication of services. This structure is suited to companies which are able to very clearly distinguish between different divisions. When there is confusion as to which division should be responsible for something, it can lead to considerable managerial difficulties. Advantages include improved decision-making, accountability for performance and better co-ordination of functions. The disadvantage is that economies of scale can be lost and rivalry among divisions might be fostered.

Singapore police training command

As the Police Force is operating in an environment that is changing rapidly, training and continuous learning play an important role in enabling officers to cope with change. Therefore, there is a need to have training capabilities, that enable the organization to monitor and control operational doctrines and translate them into training contents.

Figure 1.9

Matrix

To make use of both marketing and product know-how, modern companies establish a matrix organization. It should combine product and marketing know-how in a flat hierarchy that is flexible towards market requirements. The matrix approach involves organizing the management of a task along lines that cross normal departmental boundaries so that the ability of product managers and functional managers to communicate with each other is crucial. For example, a new product development team might be formed from an engineer, a research chemist, a marketing manager and a designer. In the matrix individuals have two or more 'managers', e.g. a sales manager will report to the marketing director and the product manager. Once the project has been finished, the team may be disbanded, with the individual members being drafted into other teams or absorbed back into the organizational structure. This kind of structure should ensure the project is better co-ordinated than with four or five departments contributing occasionally. If many different project teams are organized, it gives more people an opportunity to use their capabilities. It emphasizes that project aims are all-important. The disadvantage is that individuals may suffer if both managers make heavy demands on them and there can be conflict between the project leader and the functional leader. Sometimes there can be a failure to provide clear lines of accountability.

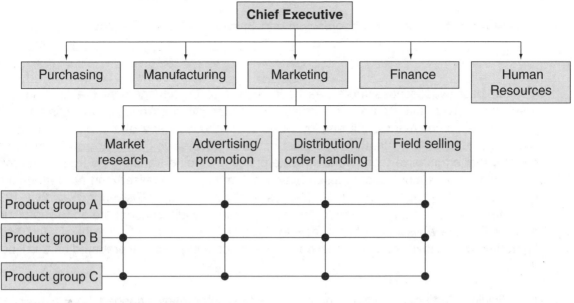

Figure 1.10

The problem with all forms of organization structure is how to encourage people to feel that not only do they belong to their part of the organization but also to the whole organization. The Singapore Airlines Case Study provides an example of how managers are encouraged to have a company-wide focus. Do you have any similar policies in your organization? Do they work? Do they cause unanticipated problems, for example, loss of expertise?

Case Study 2

Singapore Airlines

A problem that can result from organizing by function is that people know one part of the business but have no experience of the business as a whole. Singapore Airlines has a policy of moving key staff around to provide managers with cross-functional expertise and knowledge of the business as a whole. At the same time, the Group wishes to retain a sense of common purpose. Wherever they work, every employee within the Group is united in a number of other ways, through the Singapore Airlines song, through wearing similar uniforms and through sharing a common business culture, philosophy and goals.

To what extent do you feel that these examples are culturally specific, or would they work anywhere? Obviously, your organization may be too small for this to be a factor but does your own organization have any particular ways of making people feel that they belong to the 'whole' organization ?

Question 1.2

Does your organization do anything specific to encourage employees to understand the business as a whole and develop a sense of common purpose?

Reading 1.4   Boddy, D. *Organization and Culture*, Ch 8, pp 233–260.

Over the past two decades there has been a change in management practices in many organizations. This shift is based on a greater focus on customers' needs and aspirations, and engaging the commitment of all employees to meet those needs effectively. Typically, the organizational boundaries that used to exist between people are being replaced with internal networks that emphasize team working. Enterprises are being transformed from hierarchical organizations with simple jobs, to less hierarchical, more decentralized and network-oriented organizations, with more complex jobs. Charles Handy in his book, *The Empty Raincoat* (1990) has written about the future 'Shamrock' organization that would concentrate on fewer full time people at the core whilst others had to develop 'portfolio' lives, a mix of different bits and pieces of part-time work. However, he felt that people were not being properly prepared for this kind of future.

The following Case Study shows how a well-known company changed from a traditional functional structure to one based on cross-functional teams. Interestingly, one of the benefits is a cross-company marketing culture.

Case Study

Elida Faberge from 'Marketing Department' to 'Marketing Company'

In 1992, Elida Faberge started to bring about a change of approach to meet the needs of a changing environment. The typical organization prior to 1992 was based on a functional structure with the key functions being Marketing, Sales, Commercial, Technical and Personnel. The business was re-organized as a process-based organization. Traditional departments like 'Marketing' were abolished. Work is now planned and implemented by cross-functional teams. New process-based systems of strategic planning and control have been created, which ensure customer requirements are given priority. The cross-functional approach has resulted in a pan-company marketing culture. Training days per employee significantly increased from 7 to 10. Productivity per employee rose by 50 per cent. Numbers of managers reduced by 30 per cent between 1992 and 1994, and then kept at the same level.

Managing yourself

Managing effectively requires knowing yourself and effective managers understand how their behaviour affects others. They are able to adapt their style to the context in which they work. Personal management skills are common to all management jobs at whatever level. The Charities Aid Foundation (CAF) has identified competences in four clusters: managing self, managing others, managing work and technical competences. CAF has identified job competences from level 1 to 5 and, as can be seen below, the position requires competences mainly at level 3. It is unusual for organizations to use this level of detail in identifying the characteristics needed to perform a particular role effectively but the following are the 'managing self' competences required by CAF for a Marketing Co-ordinator position.

Communication	**Level 3**

Takes account of the audience when making presentations. Conveys complex and/or technical information in a clear, concise way. Contributes complete sections of Departmental documents. The job requires provision of written data within the department.

Creativity	**Level 3**

Rapidly absorbs facts and evidence, and makes considered decisions under pressure. Decisions cover a range of activities where information may not always be available. Awareness of the impact of decisions on others and the business overall.

Motivation	**Level 2**

Adapts approach to meet objectives and pursues key result areas. Looks to recover from setbacks to regain position. Works with a sense of urgency to ensure targets are met and is encouraging to others in the team.

Sharing Knowledge	**Level 3**

Establishes procedures that encourage sharing of good practice across the organization. Formally researches to ensure all information and data is accurate before used by self, team and others. Probes for additional information on clients and issues.

Interpersonal	**Level 3**

Judges and makes inferences about the concerns of others, predicts likely responses and prepares accordingly.

Integrity	**Level 3**

Able to give constructive feedback in a difficult situation and resolve minor discrepancies. Areas of serious concern are relayed to above level. (*Source*: CAF)

Figure 1.11 Managing self job competences

Managing people

The belief that people are the most important asset that an organization has is based on some key assumptions:

- o People make the difference and need to be treated as assets, not costs
- o In the light of the importance of people, their management is an issue of strategic importance
- o Managing human resources is too important to be left to personnel managers – it must be an activity undertaken by all managers
- o Managing people, policies and practices needs to be fully integrated with the other aspects of the organization's strategy.

HRM is supposed to represent a more strategic approach to the management of people, and its main purpose is to ensure that all people management policies are integrated, coherent, mutually reinforcing and supportive of the strategic direction of the organization. This is why performance management is an important issue – it provides a way of linking individuals and groups with organizational priorities. Central to this is the role of managers who are expected to be much more active in managing the staff in their unit or department to contribute to the organization's effectiveness.

Key marketing roles and tasks

Marketing titles and positions can vary among different organizations and sectors of the economy along with the responsibilities that accompany them. The marketing function can also be organized in different ways depending on factors such as size, management philosophy and type of business.

Activity 1.7

Look for marketing jobs and positions on the Internet and make a note of the skills and working relationships required. See the example below.

Advertisement for ePaper Marketing Manager, May 2002

General responsibility: Define regional strategy for enterprise and ePaper marketing.

Develop **annual and quarterly plans** in line with company planning cycles.

Deliver on plans in conjunction with rest of team.

Line manage local ePaper marketing executives (to include provision of input on regional marketing objectives, reporting of results and sharing of best practices) and **regional marketing managers,** in a **matrix environment** as dotted line with local MD will exist.

Manage budget

Interface with ePaper product **marketing team** in US, and peers across Europe.

Act as **spokesperson** for enterprise and ePaper.

Relationships

Advertising agencies, PR agencies, marketing services suppliers.

Enterprise and mainstream press.

Corporate Marketing for development of regional marketing strategies, programmes and sales and marketing tools in line with worldwide Enterprise strategy.

Product Marketing for development of regional marketing strategies, programmes and sales and marketing tools in line with worldwide ePaper marketing strategy, and provision of local input and feedback.

Sales to ensure integrated campaigns in line with sales objectives.

Regional country managers and marketing managers to ensure consistency of campaigns throughout region as appropriate.

Field Marketing colleagues for field implementation of programmes, collaborating with **functional marketing managers** for delivery of campaigns.

Finance for budget planning and management.

As the advertisement demonstrates, the role of a marketing manager can be multifaceted. A summary of some of the main marketing management roles is shown below.

Marketing manager

One of the main responsibilities of a marketing manager is to identify the target market for products and services, devise strategies and select media that will reach and attract the target market. A marketing manager needs to work with a range of people inside and outside the organization on all aspects of marketing. Inside the company the marketing manager may work with the sales force, promotion manager, product development teams and market research. Outside the company this may involve advertising agencies, consultants and market research organizations. This means that marketing managers need to have good people skills. A marketing manager's responsibilities include large-scale customer relationship management, utilizing skills in customer segmentation, customer loyalty, customer satisfaction, database marketing and direct marketing. These jobs may require market research skills or they may be the responsibility of a market research manager.

Advertising

Advertising managers may oversee account services, creative services and media services departments. Planning and managing advertising campaigns and briefing and managing advertising agencies are a key part of the role, particularly in larger organizations. In larger firms, advertising managers oversee in-house accounts, creative and media services departments. An account executive manages the account services department, assesses the need for advertising and, in advertising agencies, maintain the accounts of clients. The creative services department develops the subject matter and presentation of advertising. A creative director oversees the copy chief, art director and their respective staffs. A media director oversees planning groups that select the communication media – for example, radio, television, newspapers, magazines, Internet, or outdoor signs – to disseminate the advertising. Assessing the effectiveness of advertising is often undertaken in conjunction with market researchers. In a small firm, managers may serve as a liaison between the firm and the advertising or promotion agency to which many advertising or promotional functions are contracted out.

Brand management

Brand managers design and enhance the brand image to support the marketing strategy and plans. They identify the issues to explore with consumers about their brand experiences, and they build the research capabilities to gather that intelligence. Then, with help from each of the company's functions, product development, manufacturing, marketing and sales, they translate this learning into specifications for product development and process design. They also fund the development of brand-building capabilities and track the performance of the functions they oversee. The following two extracts show the developments that are occurring in brands and their management. The developments have implications for the kinds of management skills needed to be a successful Brand Manager and the trend towards interactive and more customized marketing.

Extended knowledge

The New Brand Management – Traditional brand managers are responsible mainly for managing promotions, advertising and relations with the trade. Often, they have neither the authority nor the skills to articulate the strategic, cross-functional, long-term perspective that is required. It takes someone with the power, skills, perspective and access to information necessary to drive the development of new products and the design of new business processes. What might the new brand-management function look like?

Category Brand Management – Category managers patrol the boundaries and relationships among brands ensuring that a company's brands are not competing with each other.

Corporate Brand Management – A manager must have a holistic perspective on the consumer's experience and on the entire business system that defines a brand. The levels of managerial expertise are higher, and the stakes involved in launching, maintaining and evolving a brand are also higher today compared to the past.

Does this match up with your experience of brand management and brand managers ?

Labels like Nike are out of favour on Wall Street, – and losing their cool on the high street. On both sides of the Atlantic, the story is the same: It's not easy for a global company whose trainers are on every high street to remain fashionable. Young people like brands that are (a bit) rebellious and Nike is perilously close to being the establishment. A decision was taken in the mid-Eighties to turn the business into 'a marketing-oriented company'. Nike stopped making anything and became a kind of shell, branding and distributing products. An assumption grew up that all products were the same because technology made goods so easy to copy. Values, though, were different. You couldn't copy 'Just do it'. Brands that are seen to be too big and homogenized need to diversify. McDonald's has bought Prêt a Manger, and Coca-Cola hedges its bets by buying up or creating sub-brands. The future for the big brands is to get customers more involved. Megabrands aren't offering what consumers want. Now the challenge is how to involve the consumer and individualize the product.

Source: Geraldine Bedell, Sunday, 19 January 2003, *The Observer*.

Customer relationship management

This is an area of marketing that has been influenced considerably by the availability of IT solutions, particularly large interactive databases to enable companies to gather and maintain large amounts of data about individual customers and enable more individualized marketing. Customer databases and database marketing are the key to Effective CRM.

Database uses include:

- ○ Identifying the best prospects
- ○ Matching offers to customers
- ○ Strengthening customer loyalty
- ○ Re-activating customer purchasing.

Relationship marketing sees the concept of ongoing customer loyalty at the core of its customer relationship marketing strategy. The key aims are to ensure existing customers continue to purchase from them on a life-long basis, i.e. achieving lifetime value to both the customer and the organization, rather than just one-off transactions. Sometimes, organizations concentrate solely on their customers, but there are other important relationships that should be considered. Typically, these groups are known as the stakeholder audience and include the following:

- ○ *Internal markets* If employees are treated as customers it should be possible to improve levels of customer service and quality throughout the organization
- ○ *Influence markets* These are any bodies or groups that influence or have the potential to influence the organization's operations. This includes government and regulatory bodies
- ○ *Employee markets* The recruitment, retention and succession of skilled staff are important to the continuing success of the organization and companies need HR strategies to address this
- ○ *Supplier markets* In recent years, there has been a lot more emphasis on partnerships and alliances, and the synergy that is created from different forms of co-operative relationship
- ○ *Referral markets* This is where organizations refer potential customers to third parties, for example, banks may refer mortgage customers to insurance companies and vice versa.

In order to implement successfully the ethos and culture of relationship marketing, the organization will need to look at internal markets – i.e. the employees and management of the organization. This aspect is considered in more detail in Unit 3 'Developing the Team'.

Activity 1.8

Visit CRM Update at http://techupdate.cnet.com/enterprise/0-6133427-724-20156564.html and answer the following questions:

1. The site contains information about CRM. How could a CRM manager benefit from the site?
2. Read one of the related articles on CRM found on the site and describe how a company can benefit from the information you found.

Direct marketing

This develops the direct marketing strategy, ensuring it complements the overall marketing strategy. It requires an understanding of the various channels through which customers can be reached directly. It requires building, developing, maintaining and using large databases. Campaign results and trends need to be analysed and presented to senior management. External agencies need to be briefed and managed.

Internal marketing

Internal marketing is based on the premise that all customer contact employees, supporting service people and the whole organization need to develop a marketing orientation and work as a team to provide customer satisfaction. If employees are motivated, this has positive benefits for the employee–customer relationship. The areas that companies need to pay attention to are: recruitment and training of staff, levels of remuneration, delegation of decision-making to give customer interfacing staff greater discretion to respond to customers, developing and/or introducing systems and technology that are designed to have a beneficial impact on customer service and reducing any mismatch between supply and demand.

Market analysis

Markets and current and future demand for products and services needs to be understood and this flows from analysis. Marketing managers need to analyse their markets and customers before they undertake the development of marketing plans. Identifying, collecting and analysing information about a company's current and potential markets, including the activities of competitors and suppliers is central to anticipating and adapting to changes in the external environment.

Market research

Virtually every company in the UK uses market research and it is one way of keeping the company in touch with its customers. It is often commissioned from external agencies. The main purpose of market research is to provide information about actual and potential customers to support marketing decisions. A marketing manager's responsibilities include large-scale customer relationship management, encompassing the key customer approach and utilizing skills in international marketing, customer segmentation, customer loyalty, customer satisfaction, database marketing and direct marketing. These jobs may be very intensive in market research skills or may be the responsibility of a market research manager. Within market research firms or consulting firms, marketing research managers might specialize in market strategy (including new products and markets), customer satisfaction and customer segmentation (customer care in many consulting firms), service marketing, database or direct marketing and emerging technologies such as e-commerce.

Marketing strategy

In line with a company's mission this is the broad direction in which the company needs to travel in order to achieve objectives and ensure its competitiveness. It is concerned with the longer term positioning of the company in relation to its markets and includes segmentation, decisions about entering or withdrawing from markets, maintaining and developing products and services, and allocating resources and responsibilities.

Not-for-profit marketing

Marketing is often criticized for promoting materialism and unnecessary consumption. However marketing can be good or bad depending on who uses it and to what use it is put. Many not-for-profit organizations routinely use marketing to further their mission and goals. Not-for-profit organizations have more 'key publics' that they need to consider compared to commercial organizations. These can be classified as:

- o *Beneficiaries* – People who benefit directly from services.
- o *Funders* – Funding may be offered and received from many sources. The people providing the funding may have different motives which may raise ethical issues when deciding whether or not to accept funds.
- o *Internal Staff* – These may be mostly volunteers who undertake the work for a variety of reasons and motivations. This can alter the manager-employee relationship and, for example, volunteers may not want to undertake certain tasks. The manager may not have much leverage beyond personal influence and persuasion. This may be an issue if levels of customer service are compromised by an unwillingness to undertake certain tasks.

Public relations

Public relations managers conduct publicity programmes and supervise the specialists who implement them. They provide advice about pitfalls to avoid and opportunities to pursue. A key part of the role is to monitor and assess PR activity to ensure that it is effective, for example, evaluating advertising and promotion campaigns to see that they are compatible with public relations efforts. Adverse publicity needs to be managed, and media coverage needs to be archived and distributed to managers so that they are aware of what is being written about the company. Keeping track of competitor activity, as reported in various types of publications, is also an important part of the role. Public relations managers may specialize in a specific area, such as crisis management, or in a specific industry, such as health care. They may produce internal company communications such as newsletters and liase with financial managers to produce company reports. They can also have a role in drafting speeches, arranging interviews and maintaining other forms of public contact.

Product or service management

The original purpose in creating product or service managers was to have someone who would take full responsibility for an individual product or a portfolio of products or services. This meant that the role was there to ensure that important issues weren't overlooked. Product management involves monitoring the performance of a specific product or service group in the market place. This makes it possible to avoid having a marketing department that focuses only on a few favoured products or services. The potential benefits of product and service management are:

- o expertise and know-how is acquired about all aspects of a product or service group
- o new product or service development is better oriented towards market requirements
- o a more cost-effective marketing mix for the product group can be developed
- o changes in the market place that are relevant for the product or service group can be identified more quickly and acted upon
- o someone is responsible and accountable for the profit generated by the service or product group.

The product manager needs to co-ordinate all activities relating to the product and service. One of the problems often associated with the role is the lack of direct authority compared to functional department heads. This cross-departmental role means that a product or service manager often needs to work by persuasion rather than through direct authority to champion the product internally as well as externally. A service marketing manager's role is often parallel to that of a product manager. For example, on the service side of a computer manufacturer's business, the ongoing servicing of the product and customer over several years may be a much larger piece of business compared to the initial sale.

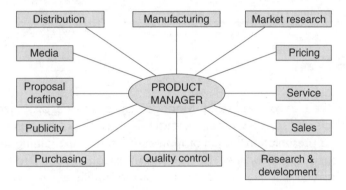

Figure 1.12 The cross departmental role of the product manager

Promotion management

Promotion managers direct promotional programmes that combine advertising with purchase incentives in order to increase the sales of products and/or services. They direct promotion programmes combining advertising with purchase incentives to increase sales. In an effort to establish closer contact with purchasers, dealers, distributors or consumers, promotion programmes may involve direct mail, telemarketing, television or radio advertising, catalogues, exhibits, inserts in newspapers, Internet advertisements or websites, in-store displays or product endorsements and special events. Purchase incentives may include discounts, samples, gifts, rebates, coupons, sweepstakes and contests.

Social marketing

Social marketing involves the application of marketing principles and techniques, developed in the private sector, to social issues. It has been defined as 'the design, implementation and control of programmes calculated to influence the acceptability of social ideas and involving considerations of product planning, pricing, communication, distribution and marketing research' (Kotler and Zaltman (1971)). They argue that every organization performs marketing-like activities and that marketing has evolved from an economic discipline to one concerned with the relationships of organizations in the broadest sense.

Activity 1.9

Go to the Ben & Jerry's USA home page. Click on 'Company Information' on the menu. Read 'Ben & Jerry's Philanthropy'. Click on the 'Ben & Jerry's Foundation' and read about its mission. How is this web site used to identify social causes?

What links are provided to non-profit organization(s) promoting social causes?

How are Ben & Jerry's using its site as a marketing tool to promote and sell its products ?

Go to the Ben & Jerry's UK site – What differences do you notice? – How would you account for the differences?

Activity 1.10

You are employed as a Marketing Manager by a service organization that supplies cleaning products and services to commercial premises. Your Managing Director has asked you to prepare a presentation for junior marketing recruits explaining the characteristics of services marketing and how they apply to your organization. Draft a document which details the areas you will need to cover in your presentation.

Summary

- ○ Marketing Departments can be organized by:
    - ○ Function
    - ○ Geographic area
    - ○ Products or brands
    - ○ Matrix
    - ○ Corporate divisions
    - ○ Global aspects.
- ○ A marketing manager needs to work with a range of people inside and outside the organization on all aspects of marketing
- ○ The marketing manager is involved in a wide range of activities, particularly in small organizations

o The marketing function is organized in different ways in different organizations, depending on factors such as size, geographical spread, management philosophy, and type of business

o A matrix structure is suited for collaborative working focused on projects that cross normal departmental boundaries.

o Managing effectively requires knowing yourself, and effective managers understand how their behaviour affects others and are able to adapt their style to the context in which they work. Personal management skills are common to all management jobs at whatever level.

Further study
Book

Kolter, P. (2000). *Marketing Management: Analysis, Planning, Implementation, and Control*, 10th Edition, Englewood Cliffs, NJ: Prentice Hall.

Websites

1. Management Learning website: http://managementlearning.com/art/culttsoc/index.html.
2. Reports, books, newsletters or websites on permission-based e-mail marketing: http://www.email-marketing-reports.com/report_imt1.htm.
3. Connected in Marketing – A site dedicated to e-marketing: http://www.cim.co.uk/ece/cfml/index.cfm.
4. What's New in Marketing Newsletter? http://www.wnim.com/issue13/pages/index.htm.
5. Free articles http://www.marketingprofs.com/intro.asp.
6. Free marketing articles http://www.bizweb2000.com/articles.htm.

Hints and Tips

o Where possible, include examples from the marketing press, textbooks, journals and Internet to support your examination answers. This is one way of demonstrating your wider knowledge and understanding to the senior examiner.

o Marketing is a practical business so examples that illustrate the way that theory relates to practice will demonstrate your broader knowledge and understanding of marketing.

o Reports from examiners are published regularly and are available to students. These reveal that there are similar concerns and problems occurring frequently across all subject areas. The most common mistakes are caused by a lack of exam technique and examination practice.

o **Not answering the question set**
Examiners are looking for both relevant content and its application in an appropriate context. You must be able to work flexibly with the material you have studied, answering different questions in different ways, even though the fundamental theory remains the same.

○ **Presentation and style**
These skills are important to a marketing practitioner. The examiners expect work to be presented in a well-written, professional manner. 'Report' style, using sub-headings and indented numbering for points, etc. looks much more credible than an essay style. This approach allows you to break the work up, highlight the key points, and structure your answer in a logical way. Take care with your grammar and use of language; small errors can change the sense.

○ **Timing**
The scarce resource in an examination is time. You must control your time carefully. Read the instructions carefully, identify what has to be done and how the marks are allocated. Spread your time proportionately to the mark allocation. Allow a few minutes at the end to read through your work.

○ **Theory without application**
The examiners expect relevant theory to be illustrated with practical examples and illustrations. These can be drawn from your own marketing experience observations, or your reading. A theory paper without evidence of practical appreciation is unlikely to be successful.

Bibliography

Bayern Radio (1999). http://www.bronline.de/imperia/md/content/bayern/collegegrad/englisch/7.rtf.

Boddy, D. (2002). *Management: An Introduction*, pp 30–32, conventional and critical perspectives and studying management.

The Charities Aid Foundation (CAF) Job Competences, www.cafonline.org.

Christopher, M., Payne, M. and Ballantyne, D. (2001). *Relationship Marketing: Creating Shareholder Value*, London, Butterworth-Heinemann.

ESCAP: Guidelines for Development of Railway Marketing Systems and Procedures, www.unescap.org/tctd/pubs/marketingtoc.htm.

Geraldine Bedell, (2003). The Changing Face of the Brand, 19 January, *The Observer*, http://www.observer.co.uk/review/story/0,6903,877476,00.html.

Handy, Charles, (1976). *Understanding Organizations*, Penguin.

Handy, Charles, (1991). *The Age of Unreason*, Business Books.

Handy, Charles, (1995). *Gods of Management: The Changing Work of Organizations*, London: Arrow.

Harrison, R. and Stokes, H. (1992). *Diagnosing Organizational Culture*, San Francisco: Pfeiffer.

Kotler, P. and Zaltman, G. (1971). Social Marketing: An Approach to Planned Social Change. *Journal of Marketing*, **35**, pp 3–12.

Kumar, Nirmalya, The path to change. *Financial Times*, 6 December 2002.

Linda Sedloff Orton, (2002). Growing Your Marketing Department into a Knowledge Management Team: Aim to Hire Assets Not Overheads, http://www.llrx.com/features/market.htm.

McKinsey Marketing Practice, Creating Leading-Edge Marketing Organizations, http://www.mckinsey.com/

Mintzberg, H. (1973). *The Nature of Managerial Work*, London, Harper Row.

Paraguayan, A., Zeithaml, V.A. and Berry, L.L. (1988). SERVQUAL: A Multiple Item Scale for Measuring Consumer Perceptions of Service Quality. *Journal of Retailing*, **64**, pp 13–37.

Peters, T. and Waterman, R.H. (1982). *In Search Of Excellence*, New York, Harper and Row.

Stewart, R. (1963). *The Reality of Management*, London, Heinemann.

Sample exam questions and answers for the Marketing Management in Practice module as a whole can be found in Appendix 3 at the back of the book.

unit 2
recruiting the team

Learning objectives

○ Describe the functions, roles of marketing managers and typical marketing jobs and the nature of relationships with other functions in organizations operating in a range of different industries and contexts (1.1). This objective was also partly covered in the previous unit

○ Identify and explain the key challenges of managing marketing teams in a multi-national or multi-cultural context (1.3)

○ Explain how you would use the techniques available for selecting, building, developing and motivating marketing teams to improve performance (1.4)

○ This last objective is partly dealt with in this unit and also in the following unit. In this unit, the focus is more upon selecting the team.

Key definitions

Cultural empathy – An understanding of and a true feeling for a culture.

Cultural environment – Institutions and other forces that affect society's basic values, perceptions, preferences and behaviours.

Cultural universals – Cultural characteristics and attributes that are found in a wide range of cultures: that is, features that transcend national cultures.

Culture – The set of basic values, perceptions, wants and behaviours learned by a member of society from family and other important institutions.

International division – A form of international marketing organization in which the division handles all of the firm's international activities. Marketing, manufacturing, research, planning and specialist staff are organized into operating units according to geography or product groups, or as an international subsidiary responsible for its own sales and profitability.

International market – Buyers in other countries, including consumers, producers, resellers and governments.

Team selling – Using teams of people from sales, marketing, production, finance, technical support, and even upper management to service large, complex accounts.

Teams

Introduction

A number of factors are contributing to an increasing emphasis on teams, including the increasing availability and affordability of Information and Communication Technology (ICT) and demands for making work more flexible by reducing its dependence on location. Many organizations have flattened their structures and delegated responsibility in order to cut costs and to utilize the skills of the workforce more effectively. Shifting authority and responsibility down the organization allows teams to take over roles and functions previously performed by management. There are also changes in relationships – among employees, between employees and employers, and between all kinds of organizations and their customers and business partners. Companies that formerly developed products solo are now forming development alliances with suppliers, customers, contractors, consultants, and even competitors.

Most teams are created to increase productivity, maximize co-operation and communication, and minimize conflict. Work teams, which are part of larger systems like managerial or production systems, perform a wide array of activities within the organization. Teams often have well-defined boundaries, and norms or rules governing interaction and behaviour.

The internal leader may be a full-time team member. Management may appoint an external leader, who serves as co-ordinator, facilitator or mentor. The leadership role may also be shared by several people, or the leader may perform several functions. Teams differ in many ways, including size, purpose, type of work performed, structure, leadership, influence and decision-making ability.

Types of teams include:

- natural work group
- management
- project improvement
- process redesign or re-engineering
- cross-functional, e.g. design and production include people of various skill levels from throughout the organization
- new product and service design teams.

More and more work is performed in new ways, so as to exploit the possibilities of co-operative work across national boundaries and time zones. Many tasks are too complex for individuals to handle alone and teams are potentially more effective in solving problems and learning more quickly than individuals. When a team works well, it can improve problem-solving, become more creative and generate acceptance, support and commitment. However, teams can also be inefficient, indecisive, frustrating and, ultimately, inferior to what a collection of individuals working on their own can accomplish. Equally, some people are more comfortable working on their own than they are in a group. A key characteristic of a team is that the members have a common purpose and the following case study is an example of how teamwork extends to board level.

Tesco now plays a team game

Tesco has moved from domination by the family of an entrepreneur to management by a team of professionals working closely together. At board level, directors never vote on anything. Instead, they have a discussion and come to a consensus. This is an important part of the teamwork management culture. By visiting stores unannounced, senior executives have close contact with customers and staff, which helps them understand the marketplace. The creation of a management culture based on teamwork comes with the following recommendations:

o discuss and come to a consensus on major boardroom issues
o deal decisively with corporate succession; retire senior executives at 60
o clearly identify your exact business goal and follow this single-mindedly
o understand the retail market in which you are working; never lose touch with your home market
o drive the business with research and marketing
o keep close to customers and staff; reward customer loyalty.

Source: Maclaurin, I., 1999, 11 *Strategic Direction*.

The team ideal

Robbins and Finley (2001) in their provocatively entitled book *Why Teams Don't Work: What Goes Wrong and How to Make It Right* maintain that in the 1980s the functional or specialist team worked in its organizational 'silo' in parallel rather than with other teams. These teams included, for example, accounting, finance, advertising and marketing who spoke their own functional language and didn't really communicate across their functional boundaries. In contrast, today there is more variety and a cornucopia of different types of teams. For example, there are teams where everyone has the same skills but people perform different tasks, teams where people with different expertise each tackle a different part of a task, functional teams, cross-functional teams, inter-organizational teams and intra-organizational teams. Some teams work together for long periods of time while others form for a week or two then dissolve. There are self-managed teams, leader-led teams and teams where leadership is distributed within the team so that everyone leads. Clearly, what is meant by the concept of a 'team' can vary considerably and cover various organizational arrangements. However, teams are not the answer to all organizational ills and used inappropriately they can mean that less, rather than more, is achieved.

Insight

The great sin of the age of teaming is to ask teams to do everything. A job done by a team is better than a job done by a single individual. You get that synergy going, you know, all that shared information. The truth is that teams are inherently inferior to individuals, in terms of efficiency. If a single person has sufficient information to complete a task, he or she will run rings around a team assigned the same task. There are no handoffs to other individuals. No misunderstandings or conflicting cultures. Beware. Teaming can be bad. Sometimes managers prefer teaming because it spreads accountability around, makes blaming more difficult. Or it means hand-picking team members. The saddest thing we hear is 'We were told we had to do everything as a team.' The CEO is all ga-ga about teams, so now unless you do something as a team you're a pariah in your organization. It is team tyranny and people resent it. (Robbins and Finley, 2002.)

Types of marketing teams

Examples include

Sales teams which can consist of one or a mix of the following:

- o Field sales people
- o Sales engineers
- o Sales technicians
- o Office sales staff
- o Sales manager
- o Export sales force.

Marketing research teams which can consist of one or a mix of the following:

- o Market analysts
- o Market researchers
- o Interviewers.

Product management teams which can consist of one or a mix of the following:

- o Research and development engineers
- o Design engineers
- o Packaging and design.

Activity 2.1

Identify key stakeholders and their expectations

- o Stakeholders in this exercise are individuals and groups with whom you work to achieve your work objectives. This can include other teams in the organization, for example, support functions such as Finance, HR or suppliers.
- o Who are your key Stakeholders and what do you need to do together to produce your product, service, etc.?
- o What are your key Stakeholders' expectations of your team and how do you know?
- o What is your team's purpose and role in the organization?
- o What products and/or services do you provide?

> o What skills and capabilities does your team contribute to customer value?
> o Who are your customers?

However, if teams are comparatively inefficient they should be more effective because they enable the collective talents of people to be brought to bear on issues, problems and situations. They can also ensure that the organization presents a consistent and coherent face internally and externally and that plans are developed to make the best use of organizational resources. There are synergies that can be derived from working together that can produce efficiency and effectiveness. Few people could deny that a marketing campaign is more effective if people in the organization are working together to ensure that it is integrated with schedules for production, operations, sales and merchandising.

All parts of an organization should have a common focus and work together purposefully to pursue the organization's overall objectives. In practice, however, relationships between different parts of an organization can be characterized by rivalry and distrust. This can affect all types and sizes of organization and give rise to what is often referred to euphemistically as office politics, or 'the informal and sometimes emotion-driven process of allocating limited resources and working out goals, decisions and actions in an environment of people with different and competing interests and personalities' (Dobson, D. and Dobson, M. (2000)). Sometimes conflict arises from differences in view about what is in the organizations's best interests; sometimes it is from trade-offs between what is seen to be best for the organization as a whole against what is best for a particular part of it and sometimes it arises from stereotypes and prejudices about the relative worth of different functional specialisms. In organizations staffed by professionals, the conflict can sometimes occur around who feels that they know best about what is in the interests of the customer. The customer might be a patient, a parent, a client or other service-user but in the tradition of paternalistic public services, the professional may feel that they know much better what is best rather than managers, customers or clients.

The wisdom of cross-functional teams

Don H. Lester, an operations manager for Hoechst developed criteria for staffing cross-functional new product teams.

- o What team leadership style and level of expertise is required?
- o What team member skills and expertise are needed?
- o What is the level of interest in the particular product concept? – is there a Champion? – is there a high level of ownership and commitment?
- o Motivation – What will motivate individuals to want to take part in the product development project?
- o Diversity of team members? – The greater the diversity, the greater the range of viewpoints represented.

Source: Lester, Don H., 1998

The role of the Manager

The role of the Manager is important in creating, co-ordinating and maintaining the team. This requires an understanding of the specific skills and abilities of team members, and their ways of working. Managers need to understand their staff and use their influence over the way the team works, transforming them from a group of individuals to a team that is able to work together. It is also the manager's responsibility to oversee the assimilation of new recruits into a team.

Most teams are created to increase productivity, maximize co-operation and communication, and minimize conflict. Work teams that are part of larger systems like managerial or production systems, perform a wide array of activities within the organization. The manager may be a full-time team member. Management may appoint an external leader, who serves as co-ordinator, facilitator, mentor, encourager, cheerleader, or consultant, but not as a foreman or supervisor. The management role may also be shared by several people, or the manager may perform several functions. Teams differ in many ways, including size, purpose, type of work performed, structure, leadership, influence, and decision-making ability. The following diagram gives an indication of the range of stakeholders with whom a product manager may need to interact, although the extent to which this might be called a meaningful team is questionable. More realistically it is likely that the product manager and his or her team need to relate to these other teams in the organization and/or, the product manager forms a middle management team with other managers from other functions.

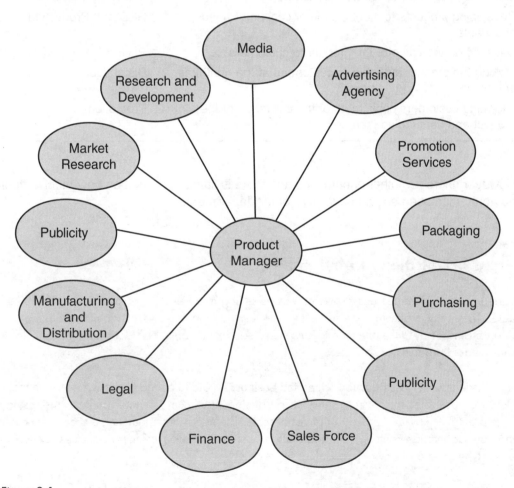

Figure 2.1

Relations between departments in an organization

Managers see teams as a way of accomplishing some or all of the following:

- Providing a structure where people with a range of technical skills, functional specialisms and different perspectives can come together, exchange ideas, learn from each other and, ultimately, provide a better service to internal and external stakeholders
- Providing a forum in which issues or problems can be aired and dealt with
- Encouraging acceptance and understanding of a problem and a proposed solution
- Enable people to develop their roles.

Each part of an organization can have an impact on customer satisfaction. If it has a marketing orientation, all departments should focus on the customer or service-user and work together to meet needs, wants and expectations. An organization with a marketing orientation sees the needs of customers and consumers as central to everything and, depending on size, may have something like the following structural characteristics:

Activity	Function
Identifying customer/consumer needs and wants	Marketing research
Developing products to meet customer/consumer needs and wants	R&D and Production
Deciding on the value of the product to customers	Pricing (sales and marketing)
Making the product available to customers at the right time and place	Distribution
Informing customers/consumers of the existence of the product and persuading them to buy it	Promotion

However, there are other orientations and there is little agreement on how much influence and authority marketing should have over other departments.

Different orientations to the market

Sales orientation – When the need is perceived as selling more of a product or service that is already available. They may make full use of selling, pricing, promotion and distribution skills but a sales-orientated business pays little attention to customer needs and wants, and does not try particularly hard to create suitable products or services.

Production orientation – A production-orientated business is said to be mainly concerned with making as many units as possible. By concentrating on producing maximum volumes, such a business aims to maximize profitability by exploiting economies of scale. The needs of customers are secondary compared with the need to increase output. This approach works best when a business operates in high growth markets or where there are few opportunities for economies of scale.

Product orientation – This is a business that focuses exclusively on its own products. They may even be rather arrogant about how good they are. However, a failure to be kept up with developments in the external market or with changing consumer preferences means that it loses business to its competitors.

Kotler, P. (2003) has identified the differences and conflicts of interest that can exist between different functions in an organization. Left to their own devices, departments can interpret organizational goals from their own viewpoint rather than the interests of the whole organization. There is no suggestion that the following descriptions are typical of all organizations but they do occur in some contexts. They should be thought of as worst case scenarios.

R&D

The drive for successful new products is often hindered by weak working relations between R&D and marketing. This can arise because of different professional and organizational cultures meaning that they operate with different priorities. R&D scientists and technicians may pride themselves more on scientific curiosity and detachment whereas marketing and sales personnel are likely to have a more practical set of concerns and look for products and services with features that can be promoted and sold in the market place. In some companies, R&D and marketing share responsibility for market-oriented innovation. R&D staff take responsibility for innovation and product launch, and marketing staff must take responsibility for new sales features and for correctly identifying customer needs and preferences.

Engineering and purchasing

Engineering is responsible for finding practical ways to design new products and production processes. Engineers, who may be focused more on technical quality and manufacturing simplicity, may be in conflict with the marketing function if they are asked for products with slightly different features, adding to manufacturing complexity. Purchasers want to obtain materials and components in the right quantities and quality at the lowest possible cost. They may have a perception of marketers as people who want products with small quantities of many components rather than large quantities with fewer components. They can also be critical of the forecasting inaccuracy of marketing personnel.

Manufacturing and operations

They may see marketers, stereotypically, as people who complain about delays in production, poor quality control and poor customer service. They may also see marketers as providing inaccurate sales forecasts who promise a higher level of service than is reasonable. Marketers are seen as not particularly interested in production problems but focused much more on the problems of customers who need goods and services quickly, who may receive defective merchandise, and who do not receive the service they need. In marketing-driven companies, the company will do all it can to satisfy its customers but this can result in high and fluctuating manufacturing costs. Organizations that have a balanced orientation ensure that manufacturing and marketing jointly determine what is best for the organization. Managing operations in service industries is concerned with service levels, and it is necessary for marketing and operations to work together. Marketing people must fully understand the capabilities and mindset of those delivering the service, and continuously try to improve attitudes and capabilities.

Finance

Financial executives evaluate the profit implications of proposed business activity. Marketing executives ask for substantial budgets for advertising, sales promotions and the sales force, without being able to prove how much this expenditure will contribute to the bottom line. They believe marketers are too often tempted to reduce prices to win orders instead of pricing to make a profit. However, marketers can see finance as conservative, risk-averse and the cause of lost opportunities because of a failure to invest in long-term development.

Accounting

Accountants may not be very keen on the special deals sales people make with customers because these require special accounting procedures. Marketers may dislike the inflexible way that accountants allocate fixed-costs to products and services. They would also like accounting to produce special reports on sales and profitability by segments, important customers, individuals and products, channels, territories, order sizes and so on. Marketers may feel that credit standards are too high and when they do find customers, they may not be able to sell to them because of a low credit rating.

Achrol and Kotler

The marketing 'department' will become a functional silo, the creator and repository of the firm's marketing skills and knowledge base. It will operate the firm's market information system, databases and analytical models, conduct research commissioned by its process teams or market units and be responsible for environmental scanning. It will be the base for marketing specialists assigned to various teams or units. It will have the opportunity to lead the training and education of technical and non-technical members of the organization in marketing. Its most important function will be to create marketing know-how that operational levels of the organization will find invaluable to their success.

Source: Achrol, R. and Kotler, P., 1999

Benefits of working in teams

o Links individuals' skills, abilities and knowledge to create innovative, cost-effective services and products, customers, partners, suppliers and others in the supplier – user chain
o Synergy results when the complementary skills of group members are directed to solve problems
o Helps achieve common purposes by establishing consensus and building commitment throughout the organization.

Concerns about working in teams

o Few companies know how to properly implement a team process. Many managers lack the necessary skills to provide strong leadership in a team environment
o Managers too frequently select people in their own image
o Managers do not understand the strengths of their team members and do not allocate work appropriately
o Members of unbalanced teams often feel that their particular talents and abilities are not being used to the full. Managers do not know how to motivate people because they do not understand individual needs
o Groupthink drives out critical judgement, e.g. illusion of invulnerability, illusion of unanimity, self censorship.

What are effective teams?

Mike Woodcock identified a number of characteristics in his Team Development Manual, as follows:

Openness and confrontation – Where the team is working well, people can express themselves openly and confront mistakes, confusions or frustrations. Such feedback can be received without recrimination and act as feedback to team members and management.

Support and trust – Trustful working relationships stem from positive orientations to others. In reality there is often too much at stake between people at work (personal rivalry, politics). Concerns such as being helpful, endeavouring to understand the perception and difficulties of others are important for team leaders responsible for giving feedback to members whose actions generate difficulty within the team.

Co-operation and conflict – Helpful competition can stimulate ideas and energy but unhelpful competition and conflicts, hidden agendas and stereotyping of people and problems need to be avoided.

Sound procedures – Effective teams need sound procedures for calling meetings, drawing up agendas, managing meetings, ensuring that follow-up action is implemented. Sound procedures include, e.g. chairing skills, briefing, summarizing, questioning and exploration skills. Decision-making arrangements also need to be clear. Should the team vote on issues? Does the Chair have the final say?

Appropriate Leadership – The team leader has to focus on the task, the team and the needs of individuals, ensuring that the team works effectively and efficiently, and achieves its aims and objectives. The range of styles that a leader or manager can use has been captured by Tannenbaum and Schmidt.

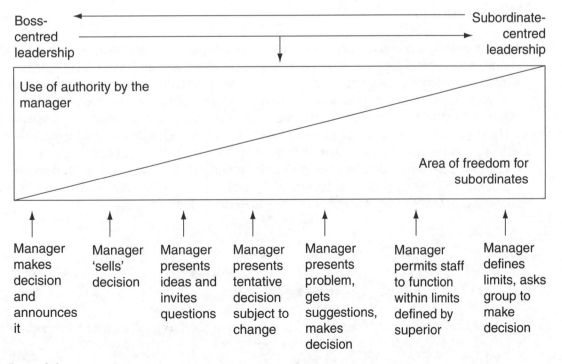

Figure 2.2

There is no one best style to adopt, rather it depends on the nature of the context, the type of work tasks undertaken and the people who make up a team and the relative importance of the decision. Styles are also contingent on factors such as timescales for making a decision. Therefore, fitness for purpose means that different approaches might be used according to how this range of factors varies.

Regular review – A team regularly reviews where it is going and focuses on issues such as: Are we achieving our objectives? Are we being effective? How well are we working together? How can we improve?

Individual development – Members' needs for growth, all-round ability, satisfaction of needs, opportunity and experience need attention.

Sound inter-group relations – Effective teams have good relationships with other departments/ teams. Each values and respects the other. The respective leaders themselves comprise an effective team. Inter-group processes require shared information and an open approach to problem-solving.

Activity 2.2

- ○ Choose a team in your organization
- ○ What is its function?
- ○ What are the key considerations to take into account in building the team?
- ○ How would you rate its effectiveness using Woodcock's criteria, above?
- ○ What, if any, are the key barriers to effectiveness in your chosen team?

Virtual teams

A virtual team is a group of people who are working together, even though they are not all in the same geographical location. The team members use communication technologies such as e-mail, video-conferencing and telephone more often than face-to-face meetings to communicate with each other. Common reasons for forming virtual teams are to integrate expertise from different locations, to save on travel time and travel costs, and to build relationships, shared understanding and shared identities across workplaces or organizations. Virtual teams face both the same challenges that traditional teams do and some unique ones such as those relating to communication technologies and working at a distance. The dispersion of team members can make it difficult to establish a strong team identity, and it can be more of a challenge for the team members to work towards a common goal.

Seven things virtual teams can do to work better:

1. Have face-to-face meetings with all the members as soon as possible after the team is formed
2. Find ways of building trust between the team members
3. Clearly define goals, roles and tasks
4. Ensure all team members are trained in cultural awareness and interpersonal skills

5. Encourage informal communication between team members
6. Set standards for responding to communications frequency, and acceptable times to call those in different time-zones.
7. Rotate the team members.

Leaders of virtual teams need to be proactive in building the team, and should anticipate and resolve misunderstandings and conflicts before they are allowed to develop. Difficult areas for dispersed teams include co-ordination and collaboration, and dealing with conflict and performance problems when team members cannot be observed directly.

Managing diversity

The trend towards a global economy is bringing people of different ethnic and cultural backgrounds together. The development of greater intercultural understanding should be an important element in all organizations because of the nature of the societies in which we live, the markets in which organizations operate, and the customers and clients that are served. Organizational culture encompasses the shared values, beliefs, behaviour and background of people, and includes race, gender, sexual orientation, age, or disability. Ethnocentricity is the inclination for majority group members to view their beliefs, behaviours and values more positively than those of other minority 'out' groups and to evaluate the latter's beliefs, behaviours and values negatively from the perspective of the majority group. The members of virtual teams often include people from different countries, cultures, disciplines, or organizations. Such differences mean that people have different expectations, for example, about how things should be done or said, or how people should behave. This can make it difficult to build and maintain trust and personal relationships between the team members. Bringing the team together for face-to-face meetings can help here, but one of the most important things is to ensure that team members have a good degree of cultural and interpersonal awareness and are prepared to give each other the benefit of the doubt and thus avoid a blame culture.

People of different ethnic backgrounds do not always share the same attitudes, values and norms. The contemporary organizational trend is to acknowledge, accept and value the differences among diverse groups. This raises interesting questions about how best to manage people in a workforce which becomes increasingly diverse.

Insight

The term Latino covers some two dozen nationalities, and includes a variety of cultures, physical types and racial backgrounds. Cuban, Mexican, Puerto Rican, Dominican, and other Central and South American groups are included under the Latino umbrella. It is the fastest growing minority in the USA and presents some major challenges to marketers. However, there are also common elements such as strong family values, product loyalty and a concern for product quality. Spanish language TV is the best medium for reaching Latinos, who tend to watch more TV than their American counterparts. (Wynter, Leon E., 1997)

One area that has been researched extensively is the contrast between individualism and collectivism. Compared to individualist cultures, collectivist cultures emphasize the needs of the group, social norms, shared beliefs and co-operation with group members. In general,

Asians, Hispanics and Blacks have roots in nations with collectivist traditions, while Anglos have roots in the European tradition of individualism. Groups composed of people from collectivist cultural traditions tend to exhibit more co-operative behaviour than groups of people from individualistic cultural traditions.

Geert Hofstede developed four different axes for measuring cultural factors and found considerable differences from one nation to the next.

Individualism dimension Individualism and the collectivist approach. This considers whether or not a culture allows scope for individual or group-centred issues to be addressed

Power distance dimension High or low power distance. Whether or not the culture encourages 'superiors' to dominate and exert power and authority

Uncertainty avoidance dimension Strong uncertainty avoidance – Weak uncertainty avoidance. Here the focus is about the ease with which the culture copes with novelty and change

Masculinity dimension Are gender roles clearly differentiated, or is it an equal status country?

Hofstede's data revealed an Anglo culture of management based on high individualism, low to medium power distance between bosses and their subordinates, low to medium uncertainty avoidance and high masculinity. However there are also considerable differences within Anglo cultures. Of the 52 countries in his study, Australians were the most likely to say that leaving staff alone to get the job done was the attribute that made for a good manager. Canada ranked next, while the United States was not far behind. In relationships with suppliers, Europeans are more likely to develop a long-term relationship based upon ideas of partnership, whereas both Americans and Australians perceive contracts with suppliers as 'deals'.

How managers see their working lives

Figure 2.3

International Marketing activities are usually organized in three ways: through export departments, international divisions or a global organization.

○ A global strategy looks upon the world as single market
○ A multinational strategy treats the world as a portfolio of national opportunities
○ A 'global' strategy is based on standardizing some aspects and localizing other aspects of a Company's products and services.

Source: Bartlett, C.A. and Ghoshal, S., 1989

Hofstede's seven dimensional model
This model looks at another set of cultural issues

Universalism versus particularism Here there is consideration of the rules versus relationships. Does the cultural emphasis on living by the rules – respect for law, etc. take precedence over personal relationships.

Communitarianism versus individualism Consideration of groups versus individuals. Cultures, for a variety of reasons, either tend to value self-orientation or group orientation. This can affect the decision-making process and from a negotiating perspective it is vital to understand the culture.

Neutral versus emotional (affective) This reflects the range of emotions that people are able to express openly. This could have a considerable impact upon the way in which products are promoted, and how relationships are established with customers and the organizations in which they operate.

Specific versus diffuse This reflects how people will adjust their behaviour in different settings (specific). However, diffuse reflects the consistency of a person's relationships regardless of their situation. This has implications for managing staff, i.e. 'once the boss, always the boss', as opposed to specific where 'the boss is the boss in work and friend out of work'. This has a number of complexities, particularly for international working relationships.

Achievement versus ascription This relates to how status is accorded. Status is achieved via years of experience, service, education and age. In other words 'respect your elders' scenario.

Sequential time versus synchronic time This is essentially the difference between a sequence of events or simultaneous events. It is a question of being able to juggle a lot of balls in respect of time, or needing to operate in a sequence to differentiate activities. This can indicate a lot about an individual's ability to work individually, within a team, on a self-motivated basis, or on a delegated activity basis.

High context and Low context High context behaviour will have a form of ritual behaviour in everyday life. Priorities, status, etc. will be important. Low context will see little in the way of ritual behaviour and can generally cope with a number of events happening at any one time.

Fons Trompenaars and Charles Hampden Turner (2001) interviewed 15,000 managers in 28 countries to explore the cultural differences between what they called universalist societies and particularist societies. In Universalist societies people follow the rules and assume that the standards they support are the correct ones. Further, they believe that society works better if everyone conforms to them. Particularist societies believe that particular circumstances are more important than general rules, and that people's responses depend on circumstances and on the particular people involved. In Universalist countries written contracts are taken seriously. Teams of lawyers are employed to make sure that a contract is correctly drafted, and once signed it must be policed to ensure it is kept. Particularist countries think that the relationship is more important than the contract and that a written contract is not always necessary – the particular people and the particular situation matter more than the universal rules. Different cultures have different ways of coping with life, a different set of responses to the same underlying dilemmas. In Far Eastern cultures, books start 'at the back' and are read from right to left in vertical columns. To Westerners, this seems a reversal of normal practice. Managers need to display cross-cultural competence and reconcile cultural differences. Successful leaders are those that are flexible, sensitive and skilled enough to be able to ride what they call 'the waves of culture'.

The following Insight illustrates how different cultures look upon teamwork and the difficulties associated with its use in India.

The magic of teamwork missing in India/Asia
(Sam Pitroda, Chairman & CEO of World Tel)

Lack of teamwork and co-operation
This is a problem in India and wherever Indians work worldwide. if someone is trying to climb higher and achieve more, others drag him down. The signal sent out is, 'I couldn't do it; I wouldn't let you do it and, if by chance you start succeeding, we will all gang up and make sure that you don't get to do it.' Where does this attitude come from?

Hierarchical system
We've had a feudal and a hierarchical social system in which whoever is senior supposedly knows best. However, today, a young computer-trained person may have more answers for an accounting problem than a senior accountant has. Until we are able to leverage this diversity of experience, we will not be able to create and fully utilize the right kind of teams. Because of our background, we often don't learn how to exercise and accept leadership – to lead and to follow simultaneously. In teamwork, everyone needs to be able to do both.

People in India tend to focus on achieving total agreement, which is almost always impossible. They should say 'OK. This is what we agree on, so let's start working on this. What we don't agree on, we will resolve as we go along.'

Activity 2.3

- Do you have experience of working with international organizations, or does your own organization have international divisions? – If not, try to find out about the business culture in a very different country from the one in which you work.
- What are the key differences in culture between each country that have an impact on working life, for example, are there different approaches to team-work, team leadership, management style, delegation, making mistakes?
- What do you think will be the key differences that would have an impact on the manager's role?

Role of the HRM function

All large organizations have developed HRM departments, and their managers can rely upon the existence of clear personnel policies and back-up through every aspect of concern to personnel management. For many managers, however, there is likely to be little formal support and it is for them to recruit, select and manage. Even for managers with HRM support, there is a need to understand fully the systems and procedures so that they have sufficient understanding to be able to exert control as needed. In this, the relationship with HRM is exactly the same as with any other specialist function.

Recruitment and selection

The process involves clearly defined stages and the use of a systematic approach should ensure that you don't overlook anything important and, significantly, it will reduce the area of subjective judgement where people's biases, prejudices and weaknesses can creep in. This is important for several reasons. Firstly, on grounds of natural justice, there is the obvious point that everyone needs to be treated fairly and equitably. One of the most depressing situations that can arise in organizations is when people are denied opportunities for reasons beyond their personal control such as their age, ethnicity, disability or gender. This may deny the organization the opportunity to appoint the best candidate. Other weaknesses in the recruitment process can mean that weak or unsuitable people may be appointed on superficial criteria. There are also legal, recruitment and poor public relations consequences that can follow if a recruitment process is flawed. Who is the best candidate for a post depends on the nature of the job, the people with whom the person will need to work with and interact, and the context in which the work is carried out. It is a matching process between the existing strengths and weaknesses of team members, future requirements of the role, and the qualities and capabilities of the prospective candidates.

Recruiting externally

Businesses could choose to search using the following media:

- Advertising in papers, magazines or locally
- Employment agencies
- Executive 'Head-hunters'
- Job centres
- Colleges/universities
- Careers fairs.

These are all useful, but there are some disadvantages:

- Companies might be overlooking and frustrating talented internal candidates
- External recruitment can be expensive.

Internal recruiting

Internal recruiting has traditionally been done by a manager appointing or promoting people. Some organizations use formal internal advertising to find the best candidate. They will advertise on noticeboards, via intranets or newsletters.

Not everyone agrees with formalized internal recruitment:

- Employees may think it is an empty exercise, believing decisions are already made
- Some managers anticipate problems in succession planning if they must use open internal markets.

To avoid problems, businesses can bring someone impartial – managers from other departments, someone from HR – into the procedure. Internal recruitment can be efficient because:

- o The person and the firm know each other
- o Savings on commercial advertising rates for recruitment can be made
- o Employees are motivated because they can see the possibility of progression.

Whilst there is a cost in building on existing skills internally, this can be more reliable and less expensive than external recruitment. On the down side:

- o Good people outside could be overlooked
- o Unsuccessful internal candidates can feel slighted
- o Entirely new skills may need intensive training.

Advertising and the use of agencies

Advertising is a major marketing activity and marketers use agencies regularly. The concepts of positioning, segmentation and targeting apply just as much to recruitment as to any other form of advertising. The agency's job is to translate your needs into short-listed candidates. The aim is to design an advert so that only those who have a realistic chance of being successful apply for the position. It is as important for unsuitable candidates to rule themselves out as it is to encourage eligible people to apply. Having a large field of candidates is of little use if many of them would stand little chance of being appointed.

Question 2.1

What are the recruitment methods used in your organization for:

- o administrative
- o sales
- o professional
- o managerial jobs?

Applications

After the closing date, a long-list of possible candidates can be drawn up. From the long list you can use your personnel specification to compile a short-list. It is good practice to respond to all applicants, but some organizations feel they cannot afford it. Applicants are consumers in the market place so it is important to create a favourable impression.

Discrimination: what the law says

There are a number of Acts of Parliament which are relevant to the recruitment of staff. The main provisions are the Sex Discrimination Acts of 1975 and 1986, the Race Relations Act 1976, the Race Relations (Amendment) Act 2000 and the Disability Discrimination Act of 1995. These Acts seek to promote equality of opportunity and to ensure that no person is treated less favourably than another person on the grounds of disability, colour, race, nationality, ethnic or national origins, sex or marital status. The Disability Discrimination Act 1995 gives disabled people the right not to be treated less favourably than other job applicants, unless the employer can justify objectively such treatment.

Discrimination

Under the Sex Discrimination Act 1975 and Race Relations Act 1976, the main forms of discrimination are:

Direct discrimination, i.e. where a woman is treated less favourably than a man or vice versa, a married person is treated less favourably than a single person or vice versa, or someone is treated less favourably on grounds that they are intending to undergo, are undergoing or have undergone a gender reassignment. Direct discrimination can occur where someone is treated less favourably on the grounds of their sexual orientation.

Indirect discrimination, i.e. applying a requirement or condition which, although applied equally to all groups, is such that a considerably smaller proportion of a particular racial group, sex or married persons can comply with it and which cannot be shown to be justifiable. Possible examples are unjustifiable age limits which could discriminate against women who have taken time out of employment for child rearing and rules about clothing or uniforms which disproportionately disadvantage a particular racial group.

Both types of discrimination are unlawful irrespective of whether there has been any intention to discriminate.

Disability discrimination While legislation covering discrimination on grounds of race and sex makes discriminatory conduct unlawful, the Disability Discrimination Act 1995 goes further by requiring employers to make 'reasonable adjustments' to the workplace where that would help to overcome the practical effects of disability. Failure to carry out this legal duty amounts to discrimination unless an employer is able to justify it. People with disabilities who feel that they have been unfairly discriminated against can seek redress through the Employment Tribunals.

Equal Pay

The Equal Pay Act 1970, as amended by the Equal Pay Regulations, covers all contractual conditions of service, not only pay. It gives both sexes the right to an 'equality clause', which means that if any term in their contract is less favourable than that in a contract of the opposite sex it must be modified to make it equitable.

i.   'Like work', i.e. work of the same or a broadly similar nature
ii. Work rated as equivalent under a non-discriminatory evaluation scheme
iii. Work of equal value in terms of the demands made, e.g. under such headings as effort, skill and decision-making.

Job description

A job description is the focus of any employee's relationship with the employer. In establishing what the job is, the manager provides the foundation for all the stages of recruitment, selection, training and appraisal that follow. The job description describes the tasks and responsibilities which make up the job. As well as being a pre-requisite to the recruitment process, it provides a standard against which the performance and development needs of the post-holder can be assessed. It also enables the department to focus on the characteristics of the post rather than those of the previous occupant. Job descriptions have several standard components, provided in greater detail as needed:

Job title Accurate titles reflecting the function and level of the job – modest duties should not have grand titles. 'Engineer' should only describe a qualified engineer

Position Stating the job title of the person to whom the employee is responsible as well as those who report to the job holder

Areas of responsibility Stating the overall purpose of the job – the principle role of the job holder and the expected contribution to achieving objectives

Main tasks Identifying the tasks, grouping together related ones. Includes the objective or purpose of each task but not how it is done

Description of tasks In short numbered paragraphs, with no more than two sentences per description. Gives details of measures of work involved and proportion of time involved for any task. Descriptive headings to group together related tasks: organizing or planning

Special requirements Equipment, tools, special skills

Location of the job and travelling needed

Special circumstances Lifting, dangerous or unpleasant conditions, night work, overtime, weekend working

Challenging aspects of the job This can be useful in attracting applicants

What is the overall purpose of the job? Describe in one sentence, e.g. 'to assist the Head of Department in the efficient running of the departmental office'

What are the main tasks of the job? Try to use active verbs, e.g. 'producing', 'planning', rather than vague terms such as 'deals with', 'handles'

What are the main responsibilities involved? 'Responsibilities' define the scope of the job, e.g. for managing staff, materials, money, etc.

The key result areas of the job and the standards expected These may include such aspects as the degree of precision required and/or the consequences of error

With whom does the post-holder work? These may include other staff, students, etc.

Terms and conditions of the post Unsocial hours, necessity to work regular overtime, and any restrictions on periods during which annual leave can be taken, etc.

The job description provides a basis for drawing up a 'person specification', i.e. the skills and experience required to carry out the duties of the job.

The person specification

Purpose The person specification forms the basis of the recruitment process from the advertisement through to the final interview stage. It describes the skills, aptitudes and experience needed to do the job and should be based on the job description, rather than a subjective view of the sort of person you would like to see filling the job. Generally, person specifications are laid down under standardized headings.

Qualifications and Training

1. *General education* It may be more appropriate for applicants to have certain levels of literacy or numeracy rather than academic qualifications. If qualifications are stipulated, equivalent qualifications that would be considered must be included
2. *Specific training* e.g. vocational certificates, professional qualifications, apprenticeship certificates, etc.

Knowledge This is knowledge without which the job cannot be done, e.g. of computer systems. It should not include knowledge that can be imparted in an induction programme.

Experience Either directly relevant or similar experience in a different environment might be considered. The type, range and depth of experience should be qualified (e.g. staff supervision). Specifying length of experience is usually unhelpful as some people learn more in a shorter time than others will learn in a longer time.

Skills and abilities This includes such aspects as the ability to communicate effectively, numeracy, analytical skills, attention to detail, etc. However, these skills must be clearly measurable as part of the selection process.

Special requirements This should only form part of the specification where it is relevant to the job, e.g. a special type of driving licence if fork lift truck driving is to be part of the job, travelling, staying away from home, etc. The required characteristics are then entered against the appropriate heading, and subdivided into essential and desirable categories. The candidate who meets both the essential and desirable criteria will do the job particularly well, but obviously this person may be hard to find. Training and development may be needed in some areas. The person specification should be realistic. Too high an ideal will mean that potentially good candidates are excluded.

The seven-point plan This was devised by Alec Rodger who developed a systematic approach for constructing person specifications. Having defined the demands of the job and evaluated the knowledge-base, skills, personal orientations, pre-dispositions and preferred values, the recruiter identifies the ideal 'qualities' needed for the job. Using the seven headings, the aim is to determine whether the candidate satisfies the essential criteria (factors that should disqualify candidates if they do not possess them). Desirable factors are ones that could be developed through training or development activities but could help in the process of distinguishing one eligible candidate from another – Does one candidate present a better profile than another?

1. **Physical make-up**
   What does the job demand in the way of general health, physical strength, stamina, eyesight, hearing, speech, appearance, etc.? Legislation to prevent discrimination has stopped most of the specifications for 'attractive', 'young', etc. The increasing number of disabled people in the workforce has encouraged many managers to re-evaluate just what physical attributes are necessary for a post.

2. **Attainments**
   What general education, technical knowledge, specialized training and relevant experience are required? To avoid becoming too overpowered by qualifications and diplomas, it is more useful to list specific knowledge areas, e.g. a marketing research job holder needs a proven knowledge of statistical sampling techniques. Conversely, sometimes there is an unwillingness amongst employers to recognize the value of working hard to achieve formal marketing qualifications when appointing marketing professionals.

Questions need to be asked to establish the job candidate's experience. Experience indicates knowledge and skill and how these have been used together. Much personal development comes from experience.

3. **General intelligence**
   What level of reasoning and learning ability is required? This can be a difficult area to evaluate since it is subjective in nature. For some jobs, the need is for people who prefer to have clearly structured rules and procedures to follow. For other jobs, the need may be for someone who doesn't mind ambiguity where little is clear cut and each situation is different.

4. **Special aptitudes**
   Aptitudes and abilities are difficult to quantify, but they can be specified as the ability to be creative in generating solutions, to work under pressure, to think strategically, to negotiate contracts, etc. Once specified, it is possible to devise ways for assessment and evaluation.

5. **Interests**
   Are any general interests likely to be relevant to job success?

6. **Disposition**
   Does the job require people to get on with people, to be a self-starter, work on their own initiative, to accept responsibility, to work under pressure, to influence others? What attributes are needed to be able to fit into the culture of the department, section, etc. Disposition is important when individuals are going to be working as part of a team. An attempt should be made to assess how they might fit in and what contribution they might make. Characteristics such as loyalty and reliability may be more suited to the role of a product manager than to a sales person who needs to be outgoing and independent, self-motivated and confident.

7. **Candidate's circumstances**
   What domestic circumstances are relevant? – daily travel from home to work, time spent away from home on business. Is working overtime possible, if needed? However, care needs to be taken when asking such questions and the following are to be avoided – 'Are you married?', 'Do you have children?' 'Are you intending to start a family?' These are not relevant to the selection decision and could be perceived as discriminatory because they are about the person rather than the ability to do the job.

Munroe Fraser – 5 Point Plan
This focuses more upon a candidate's career to date as an indicator of future potential.

The 5 Points:

- *Impact on others* Whether a person's appearance and demeanour are important
- *Qualifications and experience* Skills and knowledge required
- *Innate abilities* How quickly and accurately a person's mind works
- *Motivation* The kind of work that appeals to a person and the amount of effort they are prepared to put into it
- *Emotional adjustment* Capability of working with others.

Activity 2.4

Using one of the sets of headings identified above, draw up a person specification for the Media Relations post below:

1. *Job Purpose*
    The Media Relations Executive will work in conjunction with the Trust's senior executives to develop and implement a comprehensive communications strategy. This will require building sound media contacts to ensure positive media coverage for the Trust's activities

2. *Tasks*
    o   Conduct a comprehensive review of media relations, and provide a diagnostic report for the Board of Directors
    o   Develop and implement a Trust media relations strategy
    o   Provide a quarterly analysis of media coverage with recommendations to improve coverage
    o   Arrange and publicize corporate events and host media representatives
    o   Anticipating and responding to events by issuing press releases, giving professional advice and guidance to other Trust managers
    o   Co-ordinate press conferences as necessary
    o   Provide in-house training on media relations and skills to Trust staff according to need
    o   Establish robust relationships with key media representatives.

Preparing for the interviews

o   Produce an interview assessment from the person specification to provide a commonality to the evaluations of yourself and any others who are involved
o   Book time for the selection procedure in the diaries of all concerned
o   Reserve special accommodation, equipment, etc. as needed.

Panel interviews

Ideally, the date and time of interviews should be agreed prior to the advertisement for a post and be included in the advertisement. Those on the panel must not be related to or have a personal interest in the appointment of the candidate. All interviewers should be made aware of the responsibilities for equal opportunities. Panel interviews can provide a better picture of a candidate than a one-on-one interview. There is more chance to think about a candidate's responses because the interviewer is more of an observer than a participant. This increases the validity of the assessment. In most one-on-one interviews, the interviewer is often thinking about what question to ask next, rather than listening to a candidate's answer.

Interviewers don't judge answers as much during the response, because others are asking for clarifying information. More in-depth responses are possible. More of the candidate's personality is revealed in a panel interview, especially if most of the questions are about how accomplishments were achieved.

Panel interviews save time. It takes only three or four people one to two hours to know a candidate, rather than a whole day. The assessment is more accurate and consistent. Because everyone is using the same information to make an assessment, consistency is achieved. If the panel interview is led by a good interviewer, the information obtained is insightful.

Source: Adler, L., 2002

The interview room

It is essential that candidates be made to feel relaxed so that a proper assessment of their suitability for the job can be made. In the case of interview panels, care should be taken to ensure that the candidate is not seated too far away from the interviewees so as to feel isolated, nor so close as to be able to read the interviewers' notes.

Planning the interview

For an interview to be successful, it should be conducted in an orderly, empathetic but efficient manner. It is recommended that interviewers should undertake the following preparation:

- o Compare the candidate's application form with the person specification and pick out the points which need investigating further, e.g. experience, qualifications, gaps in a career history and inconsistencies.
- o Once the interview panel has done this, they should then prepare a plan of how the interview is to be conducted to ensure that nothing is omitted.
- o Questions need to be planned. These should be designed to probe the selection criteria of the person specification; namely a candidate's knowledge, ability and experience. Other questions should be aimed at a more general assessment of the candidate.
- o Where a candidate is attending an interview and they have informed you of any disability that they have which may affect them during the interview process, it is a requirement of the Disability Discrimination Act to carry out 'reasonable' adjustments in order to ensure they can perform to their maximum potential, e.g. if access is a problem for a candidate, the interviews should be held in a room accessible to all.
- o Identify key questions pertinent to the job that is asked of all candidates. This ensures that they have been asked equivalent and relevant questions.
- o Allocate the subjects to be explored. Each interviewer can cover different areas, e.g. work experience and training.
- o The candidate should have an opportunity to ask questions and interviewers should be prepared for the more obvious ones, such as hours of work and annual leave.

Objectives for an interview

Interviewers should be clear on the objectives of the interview:

- o To find out whether a candidate is suitable for the job advertised
- o To find out whether the job and the department/organization are suitable for a candidate's needs (an aspect which is often overlooked)
- o To fairly select the most suitable candidate.

Conducting the interview

The interviewer should control the focus of the interview:

- o Introduce the members of the panel. Start the interview slowly, to allow the candidate to relax
- o Explain the structure of the Interview and what it is trying to achieve
- o Give an overview of the context of and brief background for advertising the job
- o Put the candidate at their ease and begin your questioning by identifying areas that are familiar, e.g. his/her present job before working through to the candidate's thoughts on the job for which he/she has applied.

Questioning

Encourage the candidate to speak freely, by asking open-ended questions such as 'tell us what you think about...?' or 'how do you deal with.....?' Closed questions do not encourage the candidate to express his/her opinions in his/her own way.

Open-ended questions start with: 'How', 'what', 'why', 'when' or 'where'.

Behavioural questions are a good way of exploring what candidates have actually done in areas relevant to the job, for example:

'Give us an example from your last job when you had to persuade others to adopt a particular course of action.'

Hypothetical questions, e.g. 'what would you do if?' should be used with care.

- o Allow the candidate time to think of his/her answers
- o Summarize if you need to clarify ambiguous answers and to keep the interview on course
- o Listen closely to what is being said and how it is expressed; as by observing keenly, an interviewer can pick up clues that will enable him/her to explore an issue in more depth
- o Be aware of your own biases for or against certain types of dress, appearance, etc. as this could impair your judgement on the candidate's ability to do the job
- o Make sure the candidate is aware of any special requirements of the job and that these are acceptable
- o Allow time for the candidate to ask questions and invite him/her to do so
- o Take brief notes which will allow you to return to a point later and to deliberate at the end.
- o To make comparative judgements of candidates, you must be able to remember the key points that each candidate made.

Finishing the interview

Once the interviewers have obtained all they need from the interview, they should check that the candidate has no further questions and then signify the end of the interview. They should then:

- o Tell the candidate when he/she can expect to know the outcome
- o Check the candidate's expenses are covered, if appropriate
- o Thank the candidate for attending the interview and see him/her out.

Key points

- o Remove as much stress from the interview as possible
- o Ask open-ended questions
- o Ascertain all relevant facts, and probe ambiguous or vague answers
- o Listen to what the candidate has to say
- o Provide information relevant to the job
- o Provide opportunities for the candidate to ask questions
- o Tell the candidate when to expect to know the outcome of the interview.

The interview assessment

When a succession of candidates are seen over a period, it is essential to record accurate views on each immediately after each part of the process. Never allow interviewers to rely on memory.

The interview assessment allows each of your defined categories to be rated and a justification noted. This greatly facilitates the discussions that must take place at the end of the session as the short-list is constructed or the successful applicant is identified. Do not allow any sharing of views about candidates until after individual assessments have been recorded in writing.

Debriefing

Arrange a debriefing to:

- o Short-list or reject candidates
- o Make improvements to the recruitment and selection procedures
- o If possible, provide advice to the unsuccessful candidates – this is good for public relations and is used routinely in the public sector

The following Case Study introduces another type of team – the Self Directed Work Team where everyone can be a leader some of the time for some activities. This type of arrangement could be suitable for some contexts but is unlikely to work in all contexts. Sometimes it is important to have clear responsibilities and a clear chain of command, particularly if health and safety is a major concern.

Case Study

Team formation at Honeywell Scarborough Manufacturing Operations, Canada

The implementation of an empowered workforce, particularly within a team concept, is anything but quick. The empowered Self-Directed Work Team (SDWT) concept at Honeywell is a major contributor in helping Honeywell to achieve national recognition for quality. In some types of teams, such as task or project teams, team leaders are likely to be required. However, in a SDWT mode, leaders may simply replace the supervisor and, thus, continue the hierarchical structure. SDWT members would probably wait for the leader's guidance, deferring the development of empowering skills. Team leaders are not imposed at Honeywell but individual team members can exercise 'leadership' in particular developed skills and help others with deficiencies.

Source: Department of Indian Affairs, 2001

Summary

Teams differ in many ways, including size, purpose, type of work performed, structure, leadership, influence and decision-making ability. It is important to recognize that teamworking is not the best solution in every situation, and teams are not always more effective and efficient than individuals working to solve a problem. However, in many business situations, the ability to work in teams is valuable and teams can accomplish more than individuals who plough their own furrow. Criteria for an effective team were identified. An effective team has cohesion and a common purpose. Recruitment and selection guided by a personnel specification and proper preparation for interviews is of key importance.

Working with diversity is an important skill for managers and team members, and they need to have good cultural and interpersonal awareness. The differences amongst individuals and groups should be acknowledged, accepted and valued. Working with people in different countries raises particular issues of cultural awareness.

Further study

Read Boddy, D. (2002). *Management: An introduction*, Chapter 4, 'The international context of management' and Chapter 15 'Teams'.

Hints and Tips

It is always good to demonstrate your broader knowledge of marketing. So try to include examples from the marketing press, textbooks, journals and the Internet to support your answers. This is one way to demonstrate your knowledge and understanding to the senior examiner. Marketing is a highly practical activity and using examples to illustrate theory in practice is important. However, do make sure that your examples are relevant to the question in hand. Many questions do not explicitly ask for examples, but, where it is appropriate, do use them.

Bibliography

Ashton, C. (1998). Strategic considerations in facilitative evaluation approaches. [Internet] The Action Evaluation Project. Available from www.aepro.org/inprint/conference/ashton.html [23 April 2000].

Hamel, G., Doz, W.L. and Prahalad, C.K. (1991). Collaborate with your competitors and win. *Harvard Business Review* **67**(1), 133–139.

Pettigrew, A. and Whipp, R. (1991). *Managing change for competitive success*. Oxford: Basil Blackwell.

Wertheim, E.G. (2000). Surviving the group project: A note on working in teams [Internet] http://www.cba.neu.edu/~ewertheim/teams/ovrvw2.htm [20 April 2000].

Wilcox, D. (1994). The guide to effective participation. Brighton, UK, Partnership. (Available at www.partnerships.org.uk/guide/index.htm).

Reference

Achrol, R. and Kotler, P. (1999). Marketing in the Network Economy, *Journal of Marketing*, **62**, pp 146–163.

Adler, L. (2002). *Hire with Your Head*, New York: John Wiley and Sons.

Bartlett, C.A. and Ghoshal, S. (1989). *Managing Across Borders*, Cambridge, Mass: Harvard Business School.

Department of Indian and Northern Affairs, Canada, (2003). http://www.ainc-inac.gc.ca. These ideas are adapted from the Department of Indian and Northern Affairs website.

Department of Indian Affairs, (2001). www.nqi.ca/english/ex8_spring_2001_empowerment.htm.

Dobson, D. and Dobson, M. (2000). *Enlightened Office Politics*, AMACOM.

Earley, P.C. (1993). East Meets West Meets Mid East: Further Explorations of Collectivist and Individualist Work Groups. *Academy of Management*, **36**(2), pp 319–348.

Katzenbach, J.R. and Smith, D.K. (1993). *The Wisdom of Teams*, Harvard Business School.

Kotler, P. (2003). *Marketing Management*, Prentice Hall. 11th Edition.

Lester, Don H. (1998). Critical Success Factors for New Product Development, *Research Technology Management*, Jan–Feb, pp 36–43.

Maclaurin, I. (1999). Strategic Direction, *Human Resource Management International Digest*, July/August.

Robbins, H.A. and Finley, M. (2001). *The New Why Teams Don't Work: What Goes Wrong and How to Put it Right*, San Francisco: Berrett Kohler.

Trompenaars, F. and Hampden Turner, C. (2001). *21 Leaders for the 21st Century: How Innovative Leaders Manage in the Digital Age*, London: Wiley and Sons. This is the latest book from the authors. Their best known book is *Riding the Waves of Culture* (1997), Nicholas Brealey Publishing.

Wynter, Leon E. (1997). Business and Race: Hispanic Buying Habits Become More Diverse. *Wall Street Journal*, January 8, pp B1.

Sample exam questions and answers for the Marketing Management in Practice module as a whole can be found in Appendix 3 at the back of the book.

unit 3
developing the team

○ Explain how you would use the techniques available for selecting, building, developing and motivating marketing teams to improve performance. This objective was partially covered in the previous unit

○ Allocate and lead the work of marketing teams, agreeing objectives and work plans with teams and individuals

○ Evaluate individual and team performance against objectives or targets, and provide constructive feedback on their performance.

Study Guide

Teams – Differ in many ways, including size, purpose and type of work performed, structure, leadership, influence and decision-making ability.

Types of teams include:

1. natural work group
2. management
3. project improvement
4. process redesign or re-engineering
5. cross-functional, i.e. design and production include people of various skill levels from throughout the organization
6. new product and service design teams.

Stages of team development

In the 1970s, Psychologist, B.W. Tuckman developed this model and suggested that there are four team development stages that teams have to go through in order to be productive (Tuckman, B.W., 1965).

Some teams may go through the four stages fairly rapidly and move from forming through to performing in a relatively short space of time. A lot depends on the composition of the team, the capabilities of the individuals, the tasks at hand, and the team management and leadership.

Forming

Polite but not yet trusting. Formalities are maintained and members are treated as strangers. This can be a stressful phase when new teams come together. Everyone is a bit wary of each other, particularly if they do not know anyone and particularly if the manager is new. At this stage, each individual tends to want to establish his or her personal identity within the group.

Storming

Testing others. Members start to communicate their feelings but probably do not yet view themselves as part of the team. Most groups go through a conflict stage when initial consensus on purposes, leadership, norms of behaviour and work, is challenged and re-established. No matter how clear the team was in relation to the goals, roles and rules during the forming stage, it is often the case that individual interpretations of these are somewhat different in reality. At this stage, personal agendas are revealed and a certain amount of interpersonal hostility is generated. If successfully handled, this period of storming leads to a new and more realistic setting of objectives, procedures and norms. This stage can be important for testing the norms of trust in the group.

Norming

Valuing other types. People feel part of the team and realize that they can achieve work if they accept other viewpoints. Norming is characterized by acceptance. The group needs to establish norms and practices. When and how it should work, how it should take decisions, what type of behaviour, what level of work, and what degree of openness, trust and confidence is appropriate. Whereas in the storming stage, people were apt to rebel very quickly; this is not the case now and if someone has a grievance, complaint or suggestion then the proper processes are used. Goals are understood and roles are clarified. The rules and regulations are being adhered to and people are working together positively. Relationships become stronger as people are more aware of each other.

Performing

Flexibility from trust. The team works in an open and trusting atmosphere where flexibility is the key, and hierarchy is of little importance. Not every team makes it to this stage. Many get stuck at Norming and although everything appears normal, there is a lack of momentum and motivation towards achieving all the important team goals. At the performing stage, team members are focused on team goals and are aware of the strengths and weaknesses of the team. Only when the three previous stages have been successfully completed, will the group be at full maturity and be able to be fully and sensibly productive. Some kind of performance will be achieved at all stages of the development but it is likely to be impeded by the other processes of growth and by individual agendas.

Roles in a team

Based on research with over 200 teams conducting management business games at the Administrative Staff College, Henley, in the UK, Belbin (Belbin, R Meredith, 1996) identified nine team types. People usually have a mix of roles and will have dominant and sub-dominant roles.

Co-ordinator

The co-ordinator is a person-oriented leader. This person is trusting, accepting, dominant, and is committed to team goals and objectives. The co-ordinator is someone tolerant enough to always listen to others, but strong enough to reject their advice. This is a person who calls meetings, keeps people on track and pays attention to group processes. For example, the facilitator makes sure that everyone is involved and notices when someone is upset. Some of the things that successful facilitators try to do are:

o focus team on task
o engage participation from all members
o protect individuals from personal attack
o suggest alternative procedures when the team is stalled
o summarize and clarify the team's decisions.

Shaper

The shaper is a task-focused leader who has a high motivation to achieve and for whom winning is the name of the game. The shaper is committed to achieving ends and will 'shape' others into achieving the aims of the team. He or she will challenge, argue or disagree and will display aggression in the pursuit of goal achievement. According to Belbin, two or three shapers in a group can lead to conflict and in-fighting.

Plant

The plant is a specialist idea maker characterized by high IQ and introversion, while also being dominant and original. The plant tends to take radical approaches to team functioning and problems. Plants are more concerned with major issues than with details.

Weaknesses are a tendency to disregard practical details and argumentativeness.

Resource investigator

The resource investigator is the executive who is never in his room, and if he is, he is on the telephone. The resource investigator is someone who explores opportunities and develops contacts. Resource investigators are good negotiators who probe others for information, and support and pick up other's ideas and develop them. They are characterized by sociability and enthusiasm, and are good at liaison work and exploring resources outside the group.

Weaknesses are a tendency to lose interest after initial fascination with an idea, and they are not usually the source of original ideas.

Company worker/implementer

Implementers are aware of external obligations, and are disciplined, conscientious and have a good self-image. They tend to be tough-minded and practical, trusting and tolerant, respecting established traditions. They are characterized by low anxiety and tend to work for the team in a practical, realistic way. Implementers figure prominently in positions of responsibility in larger organizations. They tend to do the jobs that others do not want to do, and do them well: for example, disciplining employees. Implementers are conservative, inflexible and slow to respond to new possibilities.

Monitor evaluator

According to the model, this is a judicious, prudent, intelligent person with a low need to achieve. Monitor evaluators contribute particularly at times of crucial decision-making because they are capable of evaluating competing proposals. The monitor evaluator is not deflected by emotional arguments, is serious minded, tends to be slow in coming to a decision because of a need to think things over and takes pride in never being wrong.

Weaknesses are that they may appear dry and boring or even over-critical. They are not good at inspiring others. Those in high-level appointments are often monitor evaluators.

Team worker

Team workers make helpful interventions to avert potential friction and enable difficult characters within the team to use their skills to positive ends. They tend to keep team spirit up and allow other members to contribute effectively. Their diplomatic skills together with their sense of humour are assets to a team. They tend to have skills in listening, coping with awkward people and to be sociable, sensitive and people oriented.

They can be indecisive in moments of crisis and reluctant to do things that might hurt others.

Completer/finishers

The completer/finisher dots the i's and crosses the t's. He or she gives attention to detail, aims to complete and to do so thoroughly. They make steady effort and are consistent in their work. They are not so interested in the glamour of spectacular success.

Weaknesses, according to Belbin, are that they tend to be over-anxious, and have difficulty letting go and delegating work.

Specialist

The specialist provides knowledge and technical skills within the team. They may be introverted and anxious but tend to be self-starting, dedicated and committed.

Significance of Belbin team roles

Where there is an uneven spread of roles in a group there may be problems in addressing the task allocated. Team members need to be aware of their main team role, know their second-best role and see if these can complement the other group members' roles. In this way, an effective team can be constructed. There is a tendency in top teams for too many 'Shapers' and 'Plants' with few if any 'Completer–Finishers'. This means that everyone likes to talk, wants their own ideas to be accepted by all and relies on others to take the follow-through actions. Another role that often is lacking in top teams is that of 'Monitor–Evaluator' – this person may be perceived as trying to prevent things from happening by introducing balance and reality into the discussions.

Specific teams

Knowing the predominant Belbin roles of your team may provide an explanation as to why a particular team does not work well. Where there is a role that is not fulfilled at all in the team, then either the leader will need to ask someone to take on the role, or it needs to be covered by the team members.

Leadership and management of teams

Not all leaders are managers and not all managers are leaders. However, managers can be leaders and vice versa. Leadership is derived from an Anglo-Saxon word meaning the road or path ahead. Managing comes from a Latin word 'manus', meaning hand, and is more associated with handling a system or machine of some kind. There have been many descriptions of how the two differ, for example, consider the following list:

Managers

- Administer and copy
- Maintain
- Focus on systems & structure
- Rely on control
- Short-range view – bottom line
- Ask how and when
- Accept the status quo
- Classic good soldier
- Do things right.

Leaders

- Innovation and originality
- Develop
- Focus on people
- Inspire trust
- Long-range view – the horizon
- Ask what and why
- Challenge the status quo
- Own person
- Do the right things.

(Bennis, Warren, G., 1994)

As indicated above, some managers will do some of the same things that leaders do and vice versa. It is more a question of the balance of activities that comprise a job, and the expectation is that leaders would spend more time focusing on the strategic direction of the organization. However, there are many different theories about leadership and, in the 1980s a new paradigm emerged called transformational leadership as opposed to transactional leadership. The relative instability and unpredictability of the environment has given rise to this new conception of leadership, and there is a premium on leadership to ensure that an organization can adapt to and be successful in a world of constant change. The transformational leader motivates and inspires staff, and ensures that staff understand the vision for the future of the organization.

Five characteristics of leadership

o Challenging the process – Encouraging others to develop new ideas and judicious risk taking
o Inspiring a shared vision about the future
o Enabling others to act – Encouraging collaboration, co-operation, building teams and empowering others
o Modelling the way – Planning and reviewing progress and taking corrective action in a way that gains the respect of others. Clear about values and act in a manner consistent with them
o Recognizing and celebrating others' achievements.

(Kouzes, J.M. and Posner, B.Z., 2002)

Transactional marketing

Whilst transformational leadership does appear to chime in with contemporary developments in organizations, there is also a need for transactional leadership. In marketing, the term transactional marketing is often contrasted with relationship marketing.

Transactional marketing emphasizes the exchange of product for money. It focuses on the individual sale, promotes product features and places relatively little emphasis on customer service. Relationship marketing, on the other hand, focuses on product benefits and is geared toward long-term retention of customers.

Transactional marketing is a relatively low cost way to go to market because there is no need to invest a great deal of time or money in sales people and support personnel. Its main disadvantage is that it generates little customer loyalty. If customers have a bad experience or perceive a marginally better deal elsewhere, they are quick to leave. Because customers are heavily influenced by price, profit margins tend to be slim. Relationship marketing requires a greater investment in sales and service resources, and is more complicated to implement. The pay-off is that customers are more loyal and less likely to jump to a competitor on a whim.

Relationship marketing

1. Make it easy for customers to reach you. For example, automated answering services can be confusing by offering endless choices which, in effect, tell customers that its their responsibility to figure out who can help them

2. Don't wait for customers to contact you. The conversation you have today may include information that you can use in the future
3. Anticipate customer needs. This is a natural outgrowth of keeping in touch with customers and listening to what they say
4. Be the expert in your field. In transactional marketing, customers figure out what they need; in relationship marketing, you help them make the right choice
5. Sell benefits, not features. A feature describes a product but a benefit describes what a product does for the customer
6. Make it right if you make a mistake. Dissatisfied customers who make a complete break with a supplier rarely come back
7. Empower sales and service personnel to make decisions. If customers hear 'I'm not authorized to do that', it tells them that they aren't important enough to talk to someone who can make a simple decision
8. One size doesn't fit all. You may need to work with key customers to modify your offering to meet their needs
9. Don't let the salesperson become the company. Make sure that at least one other person is versed in the needs of key customers.

Relationship Marketing by Daniel J. Ott, Director of Sales & Marketing, Tramont Corporation, (Ott, Daniel, J, 1999)

While it is difficult to identify precise types of businesses in which relationship marketing is most appropriate, there are some companies that by their very nature are likely to practice purely transactional marketing. A self-service fuel station is a good example. A customer fills up his fuel tank, pays for it and leaves. There is no further interaction between the buyer and the seller until the next purchase, if there is one. The station offers its products, posts the price and takes the next person in line. There is no serious attempt to develop a long-term relationship with a customer. Transactional marketing makes sense with a product like petrol. Customers tend to purchase commodities based almost entirely on price and convenience, provided the product meets some basic quality and performance standards (see Table 3.1).

Table 3.1 A comparison of transactional and relationship marketing

	Transactional Marketing	**Relationship Marketing**
Purpose	Make a sale (close a deal)	Create a customer
Status of sale	Sale as end result	Sale as beginning of relationship
Business defined by	Products	Customer relationship
Status of price	Price as input	Price as outcome of negotiations and joint decision-making
Communication	Aimed at aggregates of customers	Targeted and tailored
Marketer valued for	Products and prices	Present and future problem-solving capability

Table 3.1 continued

	Transactional Marketing	Relationship Marketing	
Objective	Increase number of customers and sales	Satisfying existing customers and retaining them	
	Buying orientation	Procurement orientation	Supply management orientation
Process	Discrete transactions	Repeat transactions	Long-term relationship
Relationship	Arm's-length, often adversarial relationship; Distributive negotiations, focus on price	Management of external resources	Integration and co-ordination of purchasing with other functions within the organization as well as other firms in the value network
Buyer influence	Little, if any, input concerning to what, when and what quantity to acquire	draw upon resources of suppliers to gain quality improvements and cost reductions (TQM, JIT)	Measures like co-developing
Focus	Minimizing price paid	Reduce total costs associated with use of product/service	Obtain maximum benefits relative to costs and price from an offering
Central objective	Obtain best deal in terms of price, quality, availability	Improve productivity by:	Focus all of the firm's efforts on delivering value to end-users
		Improving quality	
	Maximize power over suppliers	Reducing total costs	Concentrate the firm's own resources on a set of core competencies
	Avoid risk wherever possible	Co-operating with suppliers	
			Build a supply network that efficiently completes required business processes
			Sustain highly collaborative relationships with select supplier firms

Team leadership

John Adair's (Adair, J., 1988) Action-Centred Leadership model is based on three parts:

1. defining the task
2. managing the team or group
3. managing individuals.

People need to be briefed properly about the objectives that need to be achieved, what needs to be done, why, how and when. The extent to which all of this needs to be spelled out by the leader or manager will depend on the people involved, the work context and the nature of any particular tasks. In a situation where there is an expectation that tasks will be delegated, there is no need to go into great detail about how something should be done because this will be the responsibility of the person carrying out the task. The purpose of the business is to deliver something of value to people. The leader is responsible for ensuring that the marketing task determines what that value is, and then organizes work in the most effective and efficient way to deliver it (see Figure 3.1).

Marketing tasks

These could include:

o Identifying market conditions
o Identifying segments to target and buyer behaviour
o Identifying competitive responses to customer needs and their competitive position
o Designing products/services that match customer needs
o Designing integrated marketing communication activities that educate and motivate internally, and that generate awareness and stimulate interest and action externally
o Building, maintaining and protecting the brand and competitive position
o Co-ordinating the delivery of value to customers
o Measuring the effectiveness of marketing activities.

Figure 3.1 Team Leadership: John Adair, *What a Leader has to do?* (1988)

Responsibilities as a manager for achieving the task

o making the plan
o allocating work and resources
o controlling quality and rate of work
o checking performance
o adjusting the plan – setting standards.

Responsibilities as a manager for the team

- o maintaining discipline
- o building team spirit
- o encouraging, motivating, giving a sense of purpose
- o ensuring communication within group
- o training the group

If teams are to perform, a manager needs to:

- o communicate his or her expectations
- o set clear objectives
- o assign tasks and responsibilities
- o establish performance standards and targets
- o measure effectiveness.

Responsibilities as a manager for each individual

- o attending to personal problems
- o recognizing and using abilities
- o developing and training.

While teamwork is important, teams comprise individuals, each of whom has strengths and weaknesses, aspirations and ambitions. Ensuring that the individual gains job satisfaction and is able to develop in their role is a shared responsibility between the manager/leader and the team member. The rotation and delegation of tasks, reward and recognition all play a part in helping to keep the individual motivated to give their best.

The 12-minute interview

A regular meeting with an employee to talk one-on-one about issues, problems, and progress in work and the workplace.

Why should it be used? – To make sure that employees have direct contact with the team leader. Talking to staff regularly encourages each employee to contribute to the team effort. If time is invested, it will help to avoid losing touch with people when it is a busy time.

How can this tool help? – One of the concerns of front-line staff is a lack of direct contact with their supervisor or manager. This tool helps to build meeting time into the daily routine.

How does it work? – Create a rotating schedule so that, for example, every day at a particular time the team leader meets with a different member of staff.

Doing – Ensure that 12 minutes at the set hour. Don't try to control the session; what is important will come up.

Follow up – Once the 12-minute interview becomes part of workplace culture, it will enable better and more planned use of time. Staff will keep note of questions, problems and issues that can be addressed during their regular interview and only ask for special meetings for more urgent or complex matters.

National UK management standards

The national management standards include an element on leading the work of teams and individuals to achieve their objectives. A competent manager must show, amongst other things, that he or she manages the performance of teams and individuals. It covers allocating work, agreeing objectives, and setting out plans and methods of working. It also involves monitoring and evaluating the work of the team and its members, and providing feedback to them on their performance.

Allocating responsibilities

In order to allocate work to teams and individuals, the manager needs to decide with the team how to distribute tasks and responsibilities. This means ensuring that the allocation makes best use of team members' abilities, and provides opportunities for them to learn and develop in their roles. The manager needs to make it clear what is expected of team members. Where resources are limited, a manager may have to prioritize objectives or reallocate resources while minimizing the disruption this may cause.

Objectives and work plans

In order to agree objectives and work plans with teams and individuals, they need to be SMART, that is, specific, measurable, realistic, time-bound and consistent with the organization's overall objectives and policies. Ways of working need to be explained, and there is a need to update objectives and work plans in the light of progress and changes. In order to assess the performance of teams and individuals, the manager needs to make it clear why performance is monitored and assessed. Individuals and teams need to be encouraged to evaluate their own performance wherever possible.

Feedback

Regular feedback based on objective assessments of performance needs to be given. This should acknowledge achievements and provide constructive suggestions and encouragement. Individuals and teams should have the chance to respond to feedback and suggest how they could improve their performance.

Core functions of leadership

Adair sets out the core functions of leadership that are central to the Action Centred Leadership model (see Figure 3.2):

- o *Planning* – Seeking information, defining tasks, setting aims, initiating – briefing, task allocation, setting standards
- o *Controlling* – Maintaining standards, ensuring progress, ongoing decision-making
- o *Supporting* – Individuals' contributions, encouraging, team spirit, reconciling, morale
- o *Informing* – Clarifying tasks and plans, updating, receiving feedback and interpreting
- o *Evaluating* –Feasibility of ideas, performance, enabling self assessment.

The Action Centred Leadership model therefore does not stand alone, it must be part of an integrated approach to managing and leading. There should be a strong emphasis on applying these principles through training.

Adair's Leadership Checklist

Key Functions		Task	Team	Individual
Define objectives	C o m m u n i c a t i o n	❑ Clarify task ❑ Obtain information ❑ Identify resources and constraints	❑ Assemble team ❑ Give reasons why ❑ Define accountability	❑ Involve each person ❑ Gain acceptance
Plan & Decide		❑ Consider options ❑ Establish priorities ❑ Plan time	❑ Consult ❑ Encourage ideas ❑ Agree standards	❑ Listen ❑ Assess abilities ❑ Delegate ❑ Agree targets
Organize		❑ Establish control ❑ Brief plan ❑ Obtain feedback	❑ Structure ❑ Answer questions ❑ Prepare and train	❑ Check under-standing ❑ Counsel ❑ Enthuse
Control & Support		❑ Maintain standards ❑ Report progress ❑ Adjust plan if necessary ❑ Set personal example	❑ Co-ordinate ❑ Maintain external co-operation ❑ Relieve tension	❑ Guide and encourage ❑ Recognize effort ❑ Discipline
Review		❑ Evaluate results against objectives ❑ Consider action	❑ Recognize team's success ❑ Learn from setbacks	❑ Appraise performance ❑ Identify further training needs ❑ Aid personal growth

Figure 3.2 Adair's leadership checklist

Generic role definition for Team Leaders (Armstrong, M., 1996)

Purpose of role To lead teams in order to attain team goals and further the achievement of the organization's objectives.

Key result areas:

- o agree targets and standards with team members which support the achievement of the organization's objectives
- o plan with team members work schedules and resource requirements which will ensure that team targets will be reached, indeed exceeded
- o agree performance measures and quality assurance processes with team members
- o co-ordinate the work of the team to ensure that team goals are achieved
- o ensure that the team members collectively monitor the team's performance in terms of achieving output, speed of response, and quality targets and standards
- o agree with team members any corrective action required to ensure that team goals are achieved
- o conduct team reviews of performance to agree improvement plans
- o conduct individual reviews of performance to agree areas for improvement and personal development plans
- o recommend appropriate team performance rewards and individual rewards related to the acquisition and effective use of skills and capabilities.

Capabilities:

- o builds effective team relationships, ensuring that team members are committed to the common purpose
- o encourages self-direction amongst team members but provides guidance and clear direction as required
- o shares information with team members
- o trusts team members to get on with things – not continually checking
- o treats team members fairly and consistently
- o supports and guides team members to make the best use of their capabilities
- o encourages self-development by example
- o actively offers constructive feedback to team members, and positively seeks and is open to constructive feedback from them
- o contributes to the development of team members, encouraging the acquisition of additional skills and providing opportunities for them to be used effectively.

Motivation

One of the best known theories is McClelland's motivational theory (McClelland, D. et al, 1953) which is based on three types of motivational need that are found to varying degrees in all workers and managers.

Achievement motivation – The 'achievement motivated' person seeks attainment of realistic but challenging goals, and advancement in the job. There is a strong need for feedback about achievement and progress, and a need for a sense of accomplishment.

Authority/power motivation – The 'authority motivated' person needs to be influential and effective to make an impact. There is a strong need to lead and for their ideas to prevail. There is also motivation and need towards increasing personal status and prestige.

Affiliation motivation – The 'affiliation motivated' person has a need for friendly relationships and is motivated towards interaction with other people. The affiliation driver produces motivation, and need to be liked and held in popular regard. These people are team players.

Most people possess and exhibit a combination of these characteristics. Some people exhibit a strong bias to a particular motivational need, and this affects their behaviour and working/ managing style. McClelland felt that people with a strong 'achievement motivation' made the best leaders although there was a tendency to demand too much of their staff in the belief that they too are highly achievement-focused and results-driven.

McClelland suggested that for achievement-motivated people:

- o achievement is more important than material or financial reward.
- o achieving the aim or task gives greater personal satisfaction than receiving praise or recognition
- o financial reward is regarded as a measurement of success, not an end in itself
- o security is not the prime motivator, nor is status
- o feedback is essential, because it enables measurement of success, not for reasons of praise or recognition (the implication here is that feedback must be reliable, quantifiable and factual)
- o achievement-motivated people constantly seek improvements and ways of doing things better
- o achievement-motivated people will logically favour jobs and responsibilities that naturally satisfy their needs, i.e. offer flexibility and opportunity to set and achieve goals, for example sales and business management, and entrepreneurial roles.

McGregor XY Theory (McGregor, D., 1960)

Achievement-motivated people tend towards X-Theory style, due to their high task focus.

1. *Theory X Assumptions:*

   - People inherently dislike work
   - People must be coerced or controlled to do work to achieve objectives
   - People prefer to be directed.

2. *Theory Y Assumptions:*

   - People view work as being a natural activity
   - People will exercise self-direction and control towards achieving objectives to which they are committed
   - People learn to accept and seek responsibility.

Hertzberg motivators and hygiene factors (Hertzberg, F. et al., 1959)

Hertzberg (1959) constructed a two-dimensional paradigm of factors affecting people's attitudes about work. He concluded that such factors as company policy, supervision, interpersonal relations, working conditions and salary are hygiene factors rather than motivators. According to the theory, the absence of hygiene factors can create job dissatisfaction, but their presence does not motivate or create satisfaction. In contrast, motivators are elements that enriched a person's job; he found five factors in particular that were strong determiners of job satisfaction: achievement, recognition, the work itself, responsibility and advancement. These motivators (satisfiers) were associated with long-term positive effects in job performance while the hygiene factors (dissatisfiers) consistently produced only short-term changes in job attitudes and performance, which quickly fell back to its previous level.

Satisfiers describe a person's relationship with what she or he does, many related to the tasks being performed. Dissatisfiers, on the other hand, have to do with a person's relationship to the context or environment in which she or he performs the job. The satisfiers relate to what a person does while the dissatisfiers relate to the situation in which the person does what he or she does. A manager may not be able to easily influence all the hygiene factors of a person's job but he or she can have a big influence on many of the motivators.

1. *Motivator factors that increase job satisfaction:*

   - Achievement
   - Recognition
   - Work itself
   - Responsibility
   - Advancement
   - Growth.

2. *Hygiene factors – absence of 'good' factors can create job dissatisfaction:*

   - Company policy
   - Working conditions
   - Salary
   - Peer relationships
   - Security.

(Frederick Hertzberg, *Work and the Nature of Man*, 1966)

Equity theory

Adams' Equity Theory is based on the principle that individuals want a fair balance between the inputs, or what they give to their job, and the outputs, or what they get from it. Employees develop a view of what is fair by comparing their own situation with other people who they regard as 'referents'. Typical inputs might be effort, loyalty, hard work, commitment, skill. Typical outputs are obvious ones such as pay and expenses but also more intangible ones such as recognition, praise, responsibility, sense of achievement, etc.

If people feel that their inputs outweigh the outputs then they may become demotivated. In this situation, some people switch off and do the minimum that they can, or even become disruptive. Others aim to seek to improve the outputs by making pay claims or looking for other work. The key aspect of the theory is that extrinsic rewards such as level of pay are neither motivating nor demotivating in themselves. Rather it is how fair we perceive them to be when we compare ourselves with significant others, i.e. people who we feel should be paid less than or about the same as ourselves, or people whom we expect to be paid more than us.

If we feel that inputs are fairly and adequately rewarded by outputs (the fairness benchmark being subjectively perceived from market norms and other comparable references) then we are happy in our work and motivated to continue inputting at the same level.

Creating a culture of teamwork

To make teamwork happen, these actions need to occur:

o   Leaders need to communicate the clear expectation that teamwork and collaboration are expected. No one completely owns a work area or process all by himself. People who own work processes and positions are open and receptive to ideas and input from others.

o   Leaders and managers model teamwork in their interaction with each other and the rest of the organization. They maintain teamwork even when things are going wrong and the temptation is to slip back into former behaviour.

o   Teamwork is rewarded and recognized. The lone ranger, even if he or she is an excellent producer, is valued less than the person who achieves results with others. Compensation, bonuses and rewards depend on collaborative practices as much as individual contribution and achievement.

o   The performance management system needs to emphasize and value teamwork. Often 360 degree feedback is integrated within the system; this feedback from colleagues, direct reports and managers can have a powerful impact on work behaviours.

o   Teams need to be formed to solve real work issues and to improve real work processes. Provide training in systematic methods so that the team expends its energy on the project, not on how to work together to approach it.

o   Hold department meetings to review projects and progress, to obtain broad input, and to co-ordinate shared work processes. If group members are not getting along, examine the work processes they mutually own. The problem may not be the personalities of the people. Rather it may be the fact that they often haven't agreed on how they will deliver a product or a service or the steps required to get something done.

o   Celebrate group successes publicly.

o   A team leader should be focused on achieving the task, building and maintaining the team and developing the individual.

Managing team behaviour

Behaviour to avoid is self-serving behaviour that has nothing to do with the team performing. For example:

o   Attention getting – nobody seems interested in what I have to say
o   Aggression – don't care what you say, you're wrong
o   Withdrawal – we're getting nowhere, why don't we each work on the problem by ourselves.

Managing team behaviour requires skill and a clear understanding of what is required. Again good communication skills can significantly improve team behaviour. Communications skills that help encourage team members to focus on the task include:

o   Initiating – where shall we start?
o   Clarifying – Isn't Jo suggesting that...?
o   Direction –Don't you think we should be moving the discussion along?
o   Information seeking –Don't you have some sales figures on...?
o   Information giving – The latest marketing research report shows...

Building and maintaining the team

Most teams are created to increase productivity, maximize co-operation and communication, and minimize conflict. Work teams, which are part of larger systems like managerial or production systems, perform a wide array of activities within the organization. Teams usually have well-defined physical and task boundaries, matching technical systems, and norms or rules governing interaction and behaviour. The internal leader may be a full-time team member. Management may appoint an external leader, who serves as co-ordinator, facilitator, mentor, encourager, cheerleader, or consultant. The leadership role may also be shared by several people, or the leader may perform several functions.

Characteristics of good team building

o   High level of interdependence among team members
o   Team leader has good people skills and is committed to team approach
o   Each team member is willing to contribute
o   Team develops a relaxed climate for communication
o   Team members develop a mutual trust
o   Team and individuals are prepared to take risks
o   Team is clear about goals and establishes targets
o   Team member roles are defined
o   Team members know how to examine team and individual errors without personal attacks
o   The team has capacity to create new ideas.

There are two critical elements to effective team building: a connection between all members of the team, and a shared understanding between the leadership and each team member.

Team-building

The Six Deadly Sins of Team-Building – (Bacal, R., 2002)

If the need for team development is recognized, there are some pitfalls to avoid.

1. **Lack of a model** It is not uncommon for people leading a team-building process to focus on a single aspect of team functioning. Often the emphasis will be on communication practices, to the exclusion of other elements that are critical to team success and effectiveness. A one-dimensional team-building process may increase frustration, and destroy the credibility of the process.

2. **Lack of diagnosis** Each team is different. Each team has distinct strengths and weaknesses, and team-building must build on these specific strengths and address weaknesses. Without knowing these strengths and weaknesses, the team-building leader runs the risk of using a process that will be irrelevant.

3. **Short-term intervention** It is not uncommon for a manager to arrange for a team-building day, without developing a longer term strategy for team development. At best, a single day on its own will result in a brief motivational surge that quickly fades. At worst, the day will bring to light issues that cannot be solved during that day, and are left to fester.

4. **No evaluation of progress** It is common for team-building efforts to take for granted that things are improving without putting in place a mechanism for regular evaluation of team functioning. The team-building leader must be able to identify barriers so that the team can work to eliminate them.

5. **Leadership detachment** Management sometimes enters into team-building in a somewhat detached way. The detached manager treats it as something that will help others change, so that the team will function more effectively. However, team effectiveness cannot be improved unless the manager is willing to look at his/her contributions to the team. Management usually has to change too.

6. **Doing it all internally** Team-building generally will not succeed unless conflicts and problems can be brought into the open and dealt with properly. The problem is that poorly functioning teams are characterized by a climate of blame, defensiveness and a lack of ability to deal with conflict. Poor teams lack the ability to improve themselves.

Conclusion – Whether you are leading team-building activities, or hiring someone, it is important that you stay away from the six deadly sins.

The Stand-up

A tool to help create a group identity and a sense of shared purpose.

A regular, standing-up, 15-minute team session.

To make sure that everyone is aware of all the important things in your workplace that affect you and your work.

How can it help?

It helps to address the 'Why am I never told?' syndrome. The Stand-up is an easy way to make sure that everyone is up-to-date. There is no time for long descriptions of the progress of each person's work.

How does it work?

It requires a shared understanding among the members of your group about what this 'anti-meeting' should accomplish and how it works.

Planning

There is no chairperson and no agenda but only raise those items that concern the whole group. Meet regularly in a central location where everyone has room to stand.

Doing

Keep it simple, optimistic, focused and fun. It is better to say nothing than to talk about something of no concern to the group. Talkers learn to listen and listeners have an opportunity to talk.

Conflict in organizations

Workplace conflict can lower morale and productivity, increase turnover and employee burn-out, and add greatly to sick pay costs. Some conflicts are good and some not so good. Conflict occurs naturally when people interact, and teams, organizations and even individuals can grow as a result of the new ideas and the new ways of thinking that can emerge through conflict. However, conflict can also be destructive for individuals and for organizations. Organizational change can require members of an organization to work together in new ways and under new rules. Competition can exacerbate personality conflicts and the complexities of communication can make it more difficult for culturally, economically, and socially diverse workers to resolve the issues and problems they encounter on the job.

Source: Lankard Brown, Bettina, 1998.

Some strategies for dealing with conflict

1. Non-verbal alert   Non-verbal behaviour can be an early warning sign of conflict. Ask people to verbalize their feelings wherever possible.

2. Team development phase   See the Tuckman forming, storming, norming, performing model above. Sometimes conflict is predictable because that is what happens at one particular phase of group development.

3. Resort to authority   This means bringing in someone using a legitimate power base (and perhaps other power bases) to lay down the law. This may be necessary if team members are playing destructive roles.

4. Planning   Planning techniques, such as task scheduling, timelines and project diaries and meetings may provide an authoritative and neutral way of sequencing tasks to be performed by different individuals or sub-groups, thus reducing potential for conflict.

5. Use communication skills more effectively   Sometimes it is best to utilize what you know about good communication skills. Try to control destructive role-playing. Acknowledge individuals by praising their input.

6. Conflict management techniques

  i. *Collaborating*: win/win
  ii. *Compromising*: win some/lose some
  iii. *Accommodating*: lose/win
  iv. *Competing*: win/lose
  v. *Avoiding*: no winners/no losers.

Collaborating

I win, you win

Fundamental premise Teamwork and co-operation help everyone achieve their goals while also maintaining relationships

Strategic philosophy Working through differences will lead to creative solutions that will satisfy both the parties' concerns.

When to use:

- When there is a high level of trust
- When you don't want to have full responsibility
- When you want others to also have 'ownership' of solutions
- When the people involved are willing to change their thinking as more information is found and new options are suggested
- When you need to work through animosity and hard feelings.

Drawbacks:

- Takes lots of time and energy
- Some may take advantage of other people's trust and openness.

Compromising

You bend, I bend

Fundamental premise Winning something while losing a little is OK

Strategic philosophy Both ends are placed against the middle in an attempt to serve the 'common good' while ensuring each person can maintain something of their original position.

When to use:

- When people of equal status are equally committed to goals
- When time can be saved by reaching intermediate settlements on individual parts of complex issues
- When goals are moderately important.

Drawbacks:

- o Important values and long-term objectives can be derailed in the process
- o May not work if initial demands are too great
- o Can create cynicism, especially if there's no commitment to honour the compromise solutions.

Accommodating

I lose, you win

Fundamental premise Working toward a common purpose is more important than any of the peripheral issues

Strategic philosophy Appease others by downplaying conflict, thus protecting the relationship.

When to use:

- o When the issue is not as important to you as it is to the other person
- o When you know you can't win
- o When its not the right time
- o When harmony is extremely important
- o When what the parties have in common is a good deal more important than their differences.

Drawbacks:

- o One's own ideas don't get attention
- o Credibility and influence can be lost

Competing

I win, you lose

Fundamental premise Associates 'winning' a conflict with competition

Strategic philosophy When goals are extremely important, one must sometimes use power to win.

When to use:

- o When you know you are right
- o When you need a quick decision
- o When a strong personality is trying to steamroller you
- o When you need to stand-up for your rights.

Drawbacks:

- o Can escalate conflict
- o Losers may retaliate.

Avoiding

No winners, no losers

Fundamental premise This isn't the right time or place to address this issue

Strategic philosophy Avoids conflict by withdrawing, sidestepping or postponing.

When to use:

o   When the conflict is small and relationships are at stake
o   When more important issues are pressing and you don't have time to deal with this one
o   When you see no chance of getting your concerns met
o   When you are too emotionally involved and others around you can solve the conflict more successfully
o   When more information is needed.

Drawbacks:

o   Important decisions may be made by default
o   Postponing sometimes makes matters worse.

Source: Culbert, H., 2002.

Groupthink

Groupthink is a concept that was identified by Irving Janis, referring to faulty decision-making in a group. Groups experiencing groupthink do not consider all alternatives, and they desire unanimity at the expense of quality decisions. Janis listed seven symptoms that show that consensus seeking has led the group astray. The first two stem from overconfidence in the group's prowess. The next pair reflect the tunnel vision members use to view the problem. The final three are signs of strong conformity pressure within the group.

o   Incomplete survey of alternatives
o   Incomplete survey of objectives
o   Failure to examine risks of preferred choice
o   Failure to reappraise initially rejected alternatives
o   Poor information search
o   Selective bias in processing information at hand
o   Failure to work out contingency plans (Janis, 1982, p 175).

An illustration of groupthink

Report of the presidential commission on the space shuttle Challenger disaster

1. **Illusion of invulnerability** Despite the launchpad fire that killed three astronauts in 1967 and the close call of Apollo 13, the American space programme had never experienced an in-flight fatality. When engineers raised the possibility of catastrophic O-ring blow-by, NASA manager George Hardy nonchalantly pointed out that this risk was 'true of every other flight we have had'. Janis summarizes this attitude as 'everything is going to work out all right because we are a special group'.

2. **Belief in inherent morality of the group** Under the sway of groupthink, members automatically assume the rightness of their cause. At the hearing, engineer Brian Russell noted that NASA managers had shifted the moral rules under which they operated: 'I had the distinct feeling that we were in the position of having to prove that it was unsafe instead of the other way around'.

3. **Collective rationalization** Despite the written policy that the O-ring seal was a critical failure point without back-up, NASA manager George Hardy testified that 'we were counting on the secondary O-ring to be the sealing O-ring under the worst case conditions'. Apparently, this was a shared misconception. NASA manager Lawrence Mulloy confirmed that 'no one in the meeting questioned the fact that the secondary seal was capable and in position to seal during the early part of the ignition transient'.

4. **Out-group stereotypes** Although there is no direct evidence that NASA officials looked down on Thiokol engineers, Mulloy was caustic about their recommendation to postpone the launch until the temperature rose to 53 degrees. He reportedly asked whether they expected NASA to wait until April to launch the shuttle.

5. **Self-censorship** We now know that Thiokol engineer George McDonald wanted to postpone the flight. But instead of clearly stating 'I recommend we don't launch below 53 degrees', he offered an equivocal opinion. He suggested that 'lower temperatures are in the direction of badness for both O-rings. . . .' What did he think they should do? From his tempered words, it's hard to tell.

6. **Illusion of unanimity** NASA managers perpetuated the fiction that everyone was fully in accord on the launch recommendation. They admitted to the presidential commission that they didn't report Thiokol's on-again/off-again hesitancy with their superiors. As often happens in such cases, the flight readiness review team interpreted silence as agreement.

7. **Direct pressure on dissenters** Thiokol engineers felt pressure from two directions to reverse their 'no-go' recommendation. NASA managers had already postponed the launch three times and were fearful the American public would regard the agency as inept. Similarly, the company's management was fearful of losing future NASA contracts. When they went off-line for their caucus, Thiokol's senior vice president urged Roger Lund, vice president of engineering, to 'take off his engineering hat and put on his management hat'.

8. **Self-appointed mindguards** 'Mindguards' protect a leader from assault by troublesome ideas. NASA managers insulated Jesse Moore from the debate over the integrity of the rocket booster seals. Even though Roger Boisjoly was Thiokol's expert on O-rings, he later bemoaned that he 'was not even asked to participate in giving input to the final decision charts'.

Conflict within groups or teams can often lead to bad decision-making and problem-solving, rash decisions, inadequate consideration of alternative solutions and poor perception of what is happening in a given situation.

Source: Griffin, Em, 1999.

Developing the team

 Activity 3.1

Evaluate Your Team Development

Rating Team Development

How do you feel about your team's progress? (Circle rating).

1. Team's purpose
   I'm uncertain   1 2 3 4 5   I'm clear

2. Team membership
   I'm out   1 2 3 4 5   I'm in

3. Communications
   Very guarded   1 2 3 4 5   Very open

4. Team goals
   Set from above   1 2 3 4 5   Emerged through team interaction

5. Use of team member's skills
   Poor use   1 2 3 4 5   Good use

6. Support
   Little help for individuals   1 2 3 4 5   High level of support for individuals

7. Conflict
   Difficult issues are avoided   1 2 3 4 5   Problems are discussed openly and directly

8. Influence on decisions
   By few members   1 2 3 4 5   By all members

9. Risk taking
   Not encouraged   1 2 3 4 5   Encouraged and supported

10. Working on relationships with others
    Little effort   1 2 3 4 5   High level of effort

11. Distribution of leadership
    Limited   1 2 3 4 5   Shared

12. Useful feedback
    Very little   1 2 3 4 5   Considerable

Learning in teams

Team learning is essential for organizational learning. Learning between teams, and the structures for this shared learning, is how organizational learning builds. Different people learn in different ways and therefore a training programme that suits one type of person might not suit another. Training should contain a variety of activities so that everyone finds something that is suitable for them. One of the best known approaches to learning styles is the work of David Kolb through his 'Learning Styles Inventory'. Peter Honey and Alan Mumford published *The Learning Styles Questionnaire* (1982) which extended Kolb's work.

Learning Styles
Activist

- o Learns best from short here-and-now tasks
- o Tries anything once and is enthusiastic about new activities
- o Throws him/herself into action-based courses, games and exercises.

Reflector

- o Learns best from standing back and observing what's happening
- o Prefers to collect and analyse data before coming to a conclusion
- o Enjoys watching people in action
- o May not enjoy interacting with a computer screen.

Theorist

- o Learns best when reviewing content in terms of a system, model or theory
- o Tends to be detached and analytical
- o Emphasizes rationality and logic.

Pragmatist

- o Learns when there is an obvious link between the subject matter and a problem, or opportunity on the job
- o Searches for new ideas and the chance to apply them to a relevant situation
- o Likes to get on with things, rather than having long, open-ended discussions.

Training and development

In the last 12 months prior to the survey:

88 per cent of employers had provided any job-related training.

55 per cent of employers had provided off-the-job training. The average amount is 2.3 days per employee. The average per trainee is 8.2 days.

78 per cent of employers had provided on-the-job training for their employees.

30 per cent of employers helped employees learn things not directly connected to their job.

NVQs/SVQs are the initiatives with the highest level of awareness.

Source: Learning and Training at work, 2001, DfES David Spilsbury IFF Research Ltd.

Induction training

All new employees need some form of introduction to the organization and the job. A well-planned system of induction provides regular training and/or development sessions. For example, large department stores have a continuing programme of induction with a new course starting every week and special provision for part-time workers. This leaves individual managers in the comfortable position of receiving staff who have at least received training that is specific to their job. Some training, such as health and safety awareness, should be given to all employees.

In larger organizations line managers may take responsibility for monitoring and encouraging each individual at their place of work and for off-the-job training. However, there may be a specialist training and development section that is usually part of the Human Resources Department.

The benefits of training and development

- *Improved motivation* Individuals see their skills base extending and their promotion prospects being enhanced
- *Lower turnover* Opportunities for self-improvement, leads to people staying longer in one employment
- *Higher levels of performance* Trained and motivated staff are more likely to give of their best, which, in the end, justifies the training budget.

'The most successful teams are those who have demonstrated the greatest commitment to their people. They are the ones who have created the greatest sense of belonging. They have done most in-house to develop their people.' – Bill Walsh, Head coach San Francisco 49ers, Quoted in the *Harvard Business Review*.

On-the-Job Training (OJT)

Although people's learning styles differ, learning theory suggests that most people learn and retain more through doing and practising activities. OJT is the most common form of training in organizations. To be effective it needs to:

- be properly planned and specified in advance
- take place at trainees' normal work positions
- be accepted that there will be 'downtime' when little is being produced by the people carrying out the training.

It is often carried out with a line manager or other experienced staff but often they will not have received any training in this role so the quality can be variable. OJT is not always the best approach to developing broader transferable skills but it is good for job-specific skills. Training that takes place at or near the job can be more easily tailored to meet specific needs and arranged at convenient times. The involvement of colleagues, supervisors or managers in OJT can also help to build a strong team spirit. OJT is often associated with the development of new employees, but it can also be used to update and widen the skills of existing employees.

Off-the-Job Training and development

A key issue is making sure that the event matches up to the values the organization is trying to promote and the expectations of the staff who are taking part in the training. One aspect of this is the venue and, for example, if the intention is to focus on customer care it is important that the participants are treated well as customers. Everything about the training needs to model the behaviour it is trying to promote.

McDonald's puts great emphasis on OJT as a Training handbook. Staff are given a training card on which to record their achievements. They are expected to check with their managers to ensure progress is properly recorded and that they gain experience in all work areas. New employees are teamed up with a 'buddy', a member of the Training team. Job rotation is practised and there are 19 work areas to which staff can be assigned.

Observation and questioning are used to assess staff and two observations must be passed before someone is regarded as 'competent'. Restaurant managers spend a lot of time on a one-to-one basis with new recruits. Managers have training responsibilities and can spend 60 per cent of their time on the floor with the crew. Their own training involves learning everything a crew member needs to know and further classroom training.

Online training and education

Online training can be used as a supplement to face-to-face encounters. In some instances, instructors can supplement their material by placing related material on the web. Some uses include:

- Aspects of induction training which are routine and technical such as health and safety procedures
- Business training on procedures used to protect information within the company
- Teaching the use of common business applications, such as Microsoft Office.

Managers need to understand their own Learning Style preferences and those of the people they manage. Responses to e-learning may be according to Learning Style preference. E-learning is more likely to deliver knowledge-type learning, rather than skills development. It may not be the most suitable answer to a particular individual's learning needs.

Evaluation of training

Most management and employee training is only assessed by the individuals involved in the process and much of the feedback is taken from questionnaires. Although many organizations have developed strategies for developing managers, the evaluation of their training and development is often ineffective. Over a decade ago, research undertaken in the UK entitled 'Training in Britain: A Study of Funding, Activity and Attitudes' revealed that 85 per cent of UK employers made no attempt to assess the benefits gained from undertaking training. The reasons for this are:

- difficulty in quantifying the effects
- difficulty in disentangling the effect of a number of variables which might affect performance
- cost of evaluation that could outweigh the value of the benefit achieved
- sensitivity of the trainers who are keen to ensure that their training is shown to have had a positive affect.

The ultimate goal of training and development is to effect change in an individual's knowledge, understanding, skills and behaviours. However, for practical reasons of time and resources, often it only focuses on knowledge and to a lesser extent on understanding.

A model of effective evaluation: Joyce and Showers model

The first of five components of this model is the presentation of theory or the description of a new skill or behaviour deemed useful or desirable.

The second component of the Joyce and Showers model is demonstration or modelling of the new strategy or skill. This could be achieved by observing someone.

The third component is initial practice in a protected or simulated setting – most often in a workshop session. The individual or the group participates, trying out the new skill.

The fourth component is providing structured and open-ended feedback about performance.

The fifth component is coaching. As the new idea or skill is being applied and tried in a real setting, follow-up help with implementation is given to the participant.

When participants were given only the first component, a description of the new skill, 10 per cent of the persons could transfer or use the skill in the workplace. When the second component, demonstration of the skill, was included, 2–3 per cent more persons could perform the skill in the classroom. When practice, the third component, was added, 2–3 per cent more transfer occurred; similarly, when the fourth component, feedback, was included, another 2–3 per cent transfer occurred. Thus, four components resulted in 16–19 persons out of 100 able to perform the new skill in the classroom. However, when coaching, the fifth component, was part of the staff development process, up to 95 per cent of the participants transferred the skill into their actual practice. The coaching component was a critical one in effecting a change in the skills of an exceedingly large number of persons.

Source: Joyce and Showers (1980)

Coaching

Coaching is a learning opportunity and individual learning preferences need to be considered as part of this. To be an effective coach, the team leader needs to build trusting relationships. Focused listening is one of the most important skills for establishing such a relationship.

There are three levels of understanding and skill required for effective coaching:

- o   recognizing managerial situations as opportunities
- o   creating an effective learning process
- o   establishing an acceptable helping relationship.

Organizational benefits of coaching

- o   To improve individual performance – to expand an individual's range of skills, knowledge and insight in order to help them do the job better
- o   To provide a supportive working environment
- o   To value people
- o   To improve communication
- o   To promote effective teams
- o   To ensure appropriate allocation of tasks and projects
- o   To develop managerial skills, e.g. to improve the skills of team leaders
- o   To expand the range of skills, knowledge and insight of someone in order to enhance their prospects for a different job
- o   To develop people for more senior jobs
- o   To increase organizational effectiveness and efficiency
- o   To enable best use of resources.

Benefits of coaching to the individual

- o Support for individual learning needs – tackling the tasks and the issues that concern people in their day-to-day job
- o On-the-job development for both coach and individual – it can be a learning experience for both participants in the opportunity to reflect on skills, knowledge and behaviour
- o Increased motivation
- o Improved capability at work
- o Potential to support career development.

Some of the skills needed for coaching

- o communication: listening skills, e.g. active listening, reflective listening, open listening
- o appropriate questioning strategies
- o giving feedback
- o negotiating and agreeing objectives
- o analytical skills, evaluative skills – ability to reflect and learn from experiences and encourage others to do this.

Activity 3.2

Tick any items where you feel you have a need for coaching. Put them in order of priority for you. Next to your priorities, write the names of people in your organization who might help you with these activities. Work out a strategy for approaching the people concerned.

Coaching checklist

1. Providing guidance and support _____ _____
2. Helping to get the 'big picture' in the organization _____ _____
3. Helping with networking/making contacts _____ _____
4. Interpreting organizational politics _____ _____
5. Translating organizational jargon _____ _____
6. Being a sounding-board for action plans _____ _____
7. Appraising/reviewing performance _____ _____
8. Providing day-to-day advice on problems _____ _____
9. Listening and questioning _____ _____
10. Being a resource person – able to point to opportunities/learning resources
11. Evaluating progress.

Mentoring

Mentoring can be provided in various ways but its aim is to develop people and organizational effectiveness.

Management development

Torrington and Hall (1998) show that management training and management development can be differentiated in four important ways:

1. Management development is a broader concept. It is more concerned with developing the whole person rather than emphasizing the learning of narrowly defined skills.
2. Management development emphasizes the contribution of both formal and informal work experiences.
3. The concept of management development places a greater responsibility on managers to develop themselves than is placed on most employees to train themselves.
4. Although in training generally there is always a need to be concerned with the future, this is especially emphasized in management development. Managers are developed as much for jobs they will be doing as for jobs that they are doing. Both the managers and the organization benefit from this approach.

K Shoes first implemented teams in 1990, and 45 per cent of the employees are in teams of 5–8 people. Their responsibilities include: managing team resources based on marketplace demand for styles of shoes, understanding the business and marketplace issues and their impact on demand, and the handling of materials and equipment budgeting. Other responsibilities are controlling team profit and loss, identifying team training needs, and conducting cross-training and problem-solving during non production time. Also described in the case study are the training and compensation of teams, member selection, performance evaluation and the impact of teams on the organization.

The primary benefits of undertaking a management development programme for the individual is the modification of their management style, technical or professional skills, while the primary benefits for the organization of such a programme focus on its ability to act as a catalyst in transforming the organization by providing the skills and knowledge to manage innovation and change (Doyle, 2000). These benefits are complementary in developing both the individual and the organization.

A significant trend in management development in the 1990s has been the move away from case-based programmes to problem-solving, focusing on real life issues.

1. the individual participating must see the issue involved as important
2. it must involve some analysis
3. it must involve some aspect of creativity
4. there must be practical application of the suggested improvement.

Goals of management development

Given that there is some uncertainty about what successful managers actually do, it is difficult to establish clear goals for management development. In general, however:

o Management development will focus on the abilities to do, rather than on pure knowledge
o Management development will focus on the needs of individuals and tailor 'developmental opportunities for each'
o Individuals will be expected as a matter of course to take the initiative in their own self-development.

Performance management

A systematic approach to improving individual and team performance in order to achieve organizational goals. It encompasses processes that aim to improve the performance of both the individual and the organization, by, for example, coaching and encouraging the individual, by ensuring that the organization learns from the process and by providing a means of aligning the interests of the individual with those of the organization. It is concerned with creating a shared vision of the purpose and aims of the organization, helping each employee to understand and recognize their part in contributing to them.

Team reward

Team reward aims to reinforce behaviour which leads to effective teamwork. It encourages group endeavour rather than just individual performance. Most team reward systems emphasize team pay rather than non-financial rewards. However, teams may respond to all types of reward from pay, bonuses and public recognition. An advantage is that team pay can encourage co-operative work and behaviour, and develop self-managed and directed teams.

In 2001, the Chartered Institute of Personnel and Development (CIPD) conducted research into reward management in 970 organizations in the United Kingdom – the findings included information on team reward. Team bonuses were present in only 18 per cent of organizations and performance related increases were present in less than 57 per cent of organizations.

Team pay works best if teams stand alone with agreed targets and are composed of people whose work is interdependent. For it to work well, everybody must understand and accept the targets and the reward must be linked clearly to effort and achievement.

Teams may be able to plan and implement their own improvement programmes if they receive feedback and meet regularly to discuss performance. Team reward is a way for organizations to demonstrate that they value teams and individuals who perform well, and that high levels of performance are important. The quality of teamwork depends on:

- culture
- structure and operating processes
- values
- performance management
- management style
- employee development programmes.

Constructive feedback

Feedback is a way of learning more about ourselves and the effect our behaviour has on others. Constructive feedback increases self-awareness, offers options and encourages development.

Start with the positive

Most people need encouragement to be told when they are doing something well. If the positive is identified at the beginning, negative points are more likely to be acted upon.

Be specific

Generalized comments are not very helpful. Try to be specific about particular examples of behaviour that is not acceptable. Try to identify what a person did well or behaviour that can be praised.

Refer to behaviour that can be changed

Give feedback about something that the person can change.

Offer alternatives
If you give negative feedback suggest what the person could have done differently. Turn the negative into a positive suggestion.

Be descriptive rather than evaluative
Tell the person what you saw or heard and the effect it had on you rather than merely saying that something was good, bad, etc. Explain fully.

Own the feedback
All that anyone is entitled to give is our own experience, of that person, at a particular time. Comments such as 'you always. . . .' or 'you are . . . .' as if they are agreed statements about what a person is like are not productive. It is important that we take responsibility for the feedback that we offer.

Leave the receiver with a choice
Feedback which demands change may meet with resistance. Skilled feedback offers people information about themselves in a way which leaves them with the choice about whether to act on it or not. It can help to examine the consequences of any decision to change or not to change.

Discipline
A disciplinary interview can be thought of as having three stages:

Establishing the gap – Future performance is the main concern so any discussion about present behaviour should be focused on changes that are needed for the future and how to achieve them. It is important to be specific about concerns and to provide evidence or examples of how there is a gap between present behaviour and what is required.

Exploring the reasons for a gap – It is important to allow the person subject to a disciplinary interview to explain the circumstances and to put forward their point of view about the gap. This may uncover problems or issues that the manager is unaware of but will need to be dealt with in some way, e.g. suggesting that they seek advice and guidance or specialist help.

Eliminating the gap – There will need to be agreement to a plan of action that may involve training. Arrangements for keeping the situation under review will need to be agreed, and the person should be aware of how and when their performance is going to be monitored. The aim is to help facilitate an improvement in performance.

Summary

Members of a team can contribute to it in two distinct roles: their professional or technical role (production, sales, etc.) and their team role. The effectiveness of the team will depend on the extent to which its members correctly recognize and adjust themselves to the relative strengths within the team. Each team needs a balance of team roles and the optimum balance will depend on the tasks that the team needs to perform and its objectives. Personal attributes fit some roles well but limit the ability to succeed in other roles.

Further study

Read Boddy, D. (2002). *Management: An Introduction*, Chapter 13 'Motivation' and Chapter 15 'Teams'.

Hints and Tips

If you are asked to interpret some information, it usually means that you need to explain the meaning of it, making it clear that you understand the data provided. This is a likely scenario if undertaking Marketing in Practice. This exam will contain data that needs interpreting.

Bibliography

Adair, J., (1988). *Effective Leadership*, London: Pan.

Armstrong, M., (1996). *A Handbook of Personnel Management Practice*, London: Kogan Page.

Bacal, R., (2002). http://www.work911.com/articles/teambuidingsins.htm. The Six Deadly Sins of Team Building

Belbin, R. Meredith, (1996). *Management Teams: Why they Succeed or Fail,* London: Butterworth- Heinemann.

Belbin, R. Meredith, (1996). *Team Roles at Work* , London: Butterworth. Heinemann.

Bennis, Warren, G., (1994). *On Becoming a Leader*, New York: Perseus. 2nd Edition

Culbert, H., (2002). http://home.snu.edu/.
Conflict Management Strategies and Styles: Improving Group Dynamics

Griffin, Em, (1999). www.firstlook.com. Report of the Presidential Commission on the Space Shuttle Challenger Disaster. From the 3rd Edition of *A first Look at Communication Theory*, McGraw Hill

Herzberg, F. et al., (1959). *The Motivation to Work*, New York: John Wiley.

Kouzes, J.M. and Posner, B.Z., (2002). *The Leadership Challenge*, New York: Jossey Bass. 3rd Edition.

Lankard Brown, Bettina, (1998). http://ericave.org/docs/conflict.htm. Conflict Management

McClelland, D. et al., (1953). *The Achievement Motive*, New York: Appleton Century Crofts.

McGregor, D., (1960). *The Human Side of Enterprise*, New York: McGraw Hill.

Ott, Daniel, J., (1999). http://www.egsa.org/powerline/past/MA99relmktg.htm.

Tuckman, B.W. (1965). Developmental Sequences in small groups, *Psychological Bulletin*, **63**, pp 384–399.

Tuckman later revised his model to include a fifth stage but this is not as well known as his 4 stage model. See Tuckman, B.W. and Jensen, M.A.C., Stages of small group development revisited in *Groups and Organization Studies*, number 2, 419–427

Sample exam questions and answers for the Marketing Management in Practice module as a whole can be found in Appendix 3 at the back of the book.

unit 4 market research

Managing and delivering marketing research projects

o   Design a research project aimed at providing information as part of a marketing audit or for marketing and business decisions

o   Manage a marketing research project by gathering relevant information on time and within the agreed budget

o   Make arrangements to record, store and, if appropriate, update information in the MkIS, a database created for the purpose or another system

o   Analyse and interpret information and present, as a written report or oral presentation, appropriate conclusions or recommendations that inform the marketing and business decisions for which the research was undertaken.

Study Guide

In order for organizations to make informed decisions about the future, information is needed about a wide range of issues. This unit looks at information and knowledge management and market research. Marketing research provides a useful link between the supplier and the customer by keeping up to date with customer needs and wants. The unit also looks at the range of issues that needs to be taken into account when conducting a market research project, and in using the results of such projects.

Market Intelligence Systems (MkIS)

A Market Intelligence System (MkIS) gathers and processes critical business information, transforming it into intelligence to support marketing decisions. A good MkIS should encourage people throughout the organization to focus externally and provide quick, efficient and cost-effective information that is easily accessible. It can serve a number of purposes – it can help sales and service personnel in the field who want pricing information; marketers and planners who want to know about market and product trends so as to be able to develop marketing plans and adjust the marketing mix and directors and senior managers who are interested in market developments that affect investment and other strategic decisions.

Information management processes

Many people having external information delivered to their desktops, from online services such as Reuters and from the Internet. However, this is raw information and, to be useful, it needs transforming into intelligence.

Intelligence development processes

An intelligence system should link the needs of decision makers to the processes of turning the information into actionable intelligence. This requires interpretation, communication and sharing of information between internal and external sources of information. Interaction across departmental boundaries needs to be encouraged.

Knowledge management

Knowledge management is concerned principally with how people are managed to collaborate and share their experiences in exchanging knowledge. Managing knowledge is concerned with developing a culture where people within the organization are willing to share knowledge so that the organization can be successful. This may involve changing the culture of the organization and putting processes in place to enable knowledge creation and transfer.

Differences between data, information and knowledge

Data is unorganized words, numbers and images. It has no meaning and context. Information is data that has been organized or categorized and has meaning or value added to data. Knowledge refers to the use of information. Organizations, therefore, can gather/capture information about their customers and competitors but they can only become knowledge-driven if they have the systems in place to use the information. Whether the organization becomes a knowledge-driven organization depends on leadership, culture and trust. Organizations such as management consultancies and R&D centres rely almost completely on their employees' skills and know-how for their success. Knowledge-intensive firms need employees who are able to spread knowledge across organizational boundaries. However, the following case study provides an indication of some of the barriers to sharing knowledge across organizations.

Why ideas don't travel well

There are a number of reasons why good ideas that emerge in one part of an organization don't get picked up elsewhere. These include:

o *'What's in it for me?'* To get people to transfer or take on a good idea there must be something in it for them, which could be recognition, thanks, career progression or learning
o The *'not invented here'* syndrome: Why should I learn from people I don't know much about? How do I know that what worked there will work here?
o *Lack of leadership:* Many leaders do not spend any time promoting idea-sharing or rewarding those who contribute to it
o *Lack of time:* This is often a way of saying 'not enough of a priority'
o *Failure to apply learning design expertise:* Good ideas or business practices are turned into long documents that capture facts but are not designed to help people learn
o *Lack of context sensitivity:* Many organizations believe that what works well in one part of the organization (often the biggest part, such as the home country) can be applied without any modification in very different business environments
o *Underinvestment in facilitating knowledge transfer:* Leaders may say that 'sharing best practice' is a business priority but fail to give anyone the accountability or resources to make it happen.

Market research

A market research project can include a marketing audit, that is, a comprehensive appraisal of an organization's marketing activities. It involves a systematic assessment of marketing plans, objectives, strategies, programmes, activities, organizational structure and personnel. There are a number of models that can be used for a marketing audit, for example, a SWOT analysis or a PESTLE can each yield useful data that can inform a marketing audit. The Marketing Audit and the models that contribute to it are discussed in Unit 8.

Objectives

Are the marketing objectives of your department consistent with the overall company objectives?

Should these objectives be altered to fit changing environmental variables?

Are objectives consistent with one another?

How do objectives relate to marketing strengths and market opportunities?

Strategy

What is the relationship between objectives and strategies?

Are resources sufficient to implement the strategies?

What are the company's weaknesses?

How do you compare your strategies with those of competitors'?

Product decisions

How are new products developed within your business unit?

How are existing products evaluated?

How are products phased out of the line?

Pricing decisions

How are pricing decisions made?

How do pricing decisions reflect the influences of competitors and the concerns of channel members?

Distribution decisions

How are channel members selected, evaluated and dropped, if necessary?

How are channel members motivated?

How are decisions to modify channel structures reached?

Promotion decisions

How are promotion mix decisions made?

How are salespeople selected, monitored and evaluated?

How are pay-offs associated with promotional efforts estimated?

Market information

How is marketing research information transmitted to, and used within, the business unit?

Is a global information system in place?

Activities and tasks

How are tasks scheduled, described and planned? How are the responsibilities of individuals determined?

What spans of supervision, reporting relationships and communication patterns exist? How are they evaluated?

Personnel

What level of competence has been attained by personnel in each position?

Are remedies to problems, if necessary, being planned? What are they?

What is the state of morale? motivation? What are the present plans in these areas?

Describe career development paths. Have potential replacements for personnel in key positions been identified?

Benchmarking

Another complementary approach to an audit would be to use a benchmarking approach that compares one organization with another that is regarded as being very successful. Obviously, in some organizations, this can be difficult because of commercial sensitivities and the need to retain competitive advantage. However, a table could be constructed that could compare the organization along the dimensions that are felt to be important for marketing. The precise details will vary for each organization but, for example, it might look something like the following table:

Table 4.1 Comparing the organization with high and low performing organizations

Poor	Good	Excellent
Product driven	Market driven	Market driving
Mass-market oriented	Segment oriented	Niche oriented and customer oriented
Product Offer	Augmented product offer	Legendary

The EFQM Excellence Model

Another way of contributing to an audit is to use a recognized quality model. Usually, these kind of models are very comprehensive and too detailed for a marketing audit because they cover the whole of an organization's activities. One of the most widely used models in the private and public sectors is the The EFQM Excellence Model. It was introduced at the beginning of 1992 as the framework for assessing applications for The European Quality Award. It is a non-prescriptive framework that recognizes many approaches to achieving sustainable excellence. Increasingly, organizations use the outputs from self-assessment as part of their business planning process and as a basis for reviewing the organization.

Within this non-prescriptive approach, there are some Fundamental Concepts which underpin the Model. It is a non-prescriptive framework based on nine criteria. Five of these are 'Enablers' and four are 'Results'. The 'Enabler' criteria cover what an organization does. The 'Results' criteria cover what an organization achieves. 'Results' are caused by 'Enablers', and feedback from 'Results' helps to improve 'Enablers'. The model is based on the premise that:

Excellent results with respect to Performance, Customers, People and Society are achieved through the enablers of Leadership driving Policy and Strategy, that is delivered through People Partnerships, Resources, and Processes.

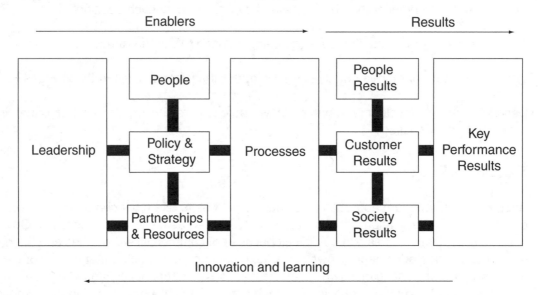

Figure 4.1
Source: http//www.efqm.org

Results orientation – Achieving results that delight all the organization's stakeholders.

Customer focus – Creating sustainable customer value.

Leadership and constancy of purpose – Visionary and inspirational leadership, coupled with constancy of purpose.

Management by processes and facts – Managing the organization through a set of interdependent and interrelated systems, processes and facts.

People development and involvement – Maximizing the contribution of employees through their development and involvement.

Continuous learning, innovation and improvement – Challenging the status quo and effecting change by using learning to create innovation and improvement opportunities.

Partnership development – Developing and maintaining value-adding partnerships.

Corporate social responsibility – Exceeding the minimum regulatory framework in which the organization operates and strives to understand and respond to the expectations of their stakeholders in society.

An example – Partnerships and Resources Element of the EFQM Model

How is information and knowledge managed in the organization?

Areas to address

This could include:

- o How information and knowledge is collected, structured and managed in support of policy and strategy?
- o How unique intellectual property is cultivated, developed and protected in order to maximize value?
- o How appropriate access to relevant information and knowledge for both internal and external users is provided?
- o How the organization seeks to acquire and use information and knowledge effectively?
- o How the organization assures and improves the validity, integrity and security of its information?
- o How the organization generates innovative and creative thinking within the organization through the use of relevant information and knowledge resources?

RADAR

The method of assessment is based on the RADAR model which looks at the evidence of what the organization achieves. This is based on documenting what it sets out to do, what evidence there is that its aims and objectives are actually translated into practice; whether it assesses the appropriateness of its approach and how successful its reviews have been. In this way, the self-assessment goes beyond what an organization claims it is doing to look for evidence that it is actually being implemented in practice.

Results What an organization achieves.

Approach What is it we are trying to do in order to address the issue?

Deployment How widely is the approach used across the organization?

Assessment Do we ever think about how appropriate the approach is?

Review Can we/do we measure success of the approach?

An example of the kind of format in which information could be collected is as follows:

Table 4.2 Recording the outcomes of the process

Review your descriptions of the approaches as a whole, then record your views on where things have been successful, where improvements could be made and actions to be taken based on this analysis

Strengths (+)	Areas for improvement (−)

Activity 4.1

Use the 'How' questions above to find out how your organization acquires and uses information. What are the strengths and weaknesses of its approach and how could it be improved?

Introduction to marketing research

Market research is a cost-effective way of finding out what people believe, want, need or do. It is information that cannot usually be obtained from any other source. Until recently, limited budgets kept most types of market research out of reach of small organizations, but through the Internet there are more research options. The most important role of market research is to minimize risk by researching a product or service before it reaches the market. Thus, market research is a fundamental part of the marketing planning process. Market and social research is used, amongst other things, to:

o test new products (everything from foods, to magazines, to cars) during their development stages
o assess customer needs and reaction to a company's and its competitors' products
o learn about and monitor customer satisfaction, for example, shops, holiday destinations, arts centres, products, local authority services, etc.
o learn about and monitor staff satisfaction and morale, and develop and evaluate communications and methodology.

Marketing research

This links the consumer, customer and public to the marketer through information used to:

o identify and define marketing opportunities and problems
o generate, refine, identify and evaluate marketing actions
o monitor marketing performance
o improve understanding of marketing as a process.

Market research

    o   specifies the information required to address these issues
    o   designs the method for collecting information
    o   manages and implements the data collection process
    o   analyses the results
    o   communicates the findings and their implications.

Source: American Marketing Association

The term marketing research covers market research, marketing research, product research and research to support pricing, distribution and promotional activity. Market research is used to supply information about the market for particular products and services. Therefore, market research has a narrower focus compared to marketing research.

Characteristics of good marketing research

Scientific method The principles are careful observation, formulation of hypotheses, prediction and testing.

Research creativity Research should develop innovative ways to solve a problem.

Multiple methods The research should use more than one method to increase confidence in the results.

Interdependence of models and data A recognition that data are interpreted from underlying models that guide the type of information sought.

Value and cost of information A concern for estimating the value of the research against its cost. Costs are easy to determine but the value of the research is harder to ascertain.

Ethical marketing Marketing research should be conducted according to a recognized code of practice that respects informants.

The most important distinguishing characteristics of marketing research are that:

    o   its primary objective is to apply research methods to the collection of information that will help in describing and understanding markets, planning strategies and monitoring outcomes
    o   in most cases, it achieves this by studying relatively small, and usually representative, samples of the relevant populations
    o   it is primarily, but not exclusively, concerned with analysing and reporting on aggregated groupings of those interviewed: it does not report information which can be linked to identifiable individuals
    o   it guarantees the confidentiality of the information provided by respondents. Such information can be disclosed only with the respondent's consent, and then only for research purposes and to research organizations involved in the project.

Marketing research is concerned with a one-way channel of communication, from respondents to the client via the confidential filter of the researcher. It does not provide a facility for any form of commercial or similar communication in the opposite direction, from client to individual respondent, nor does it seek to influence the respondent's views or behaviour as a result of the research.

The characteristics of direct marketing are different from those of marketing research

o The primary objective of direct marketing is to conduct promotional and selling activities directed at specific individuals and organizations. Marketing analysis provides aggregated and cross-analysed information of various kinds – but this is normally a secondary rather than the primary objective of collecting the data, and does not affect the other characteristics of direct marketing referred to here.

o It normally involves the collection and use of personal data from very large numbers of the general population or from as many as possible of a specific group (e.g. customers) The emphasis is on maximizing the total number of the target audience covered rather than on the representativeness of the final data.

o The data collected are purposely stored and made use of on an individually-identified, disaggregated basis since they would not otherwise be fully exploitable in direct marketing.

o Since the personal data collected are permanently linked to the individuals who have supplied the data, there can normally be no guarantee of anonymity. In many cases the personal data will be made available to a variety of users, most often for non-research purposes such as promotion and direct selling.

o Unlike marketing research, direct marketing is usually a two-way process whereby the individual who provides the data receives promotional and/or sales approaches based on the use of that data. Direct marketing is a form of 'commercial communication'.

Stages in the marketing research process

Stage 1 – Defining the marketing problem to be addressed and research objectives

This includes specifying the objectives of the specific research project or projects, to formulate the problem precisely. The art is to strike a balance between too broad and too narrow a definition of a problem. Too broad a definition can lead to a lot of information that is superfluous, whilst too narrow a definition means that some necessary information about issues that impact on the subject is not collected. It depends on how much is known about the problem. If relatively little is known, exploratory research may be used, for example, qualitative research as well as secondary research. Some research is causal – its purpose is to test a cause and effect relationship. A marketing problem needs to be formulated as a marketing research problem. So, for example, a marketing problem might be that sales are too low but the marketing research problem could be to assess customer perception of the price of the product in terms of its perceived value relative to the competition.

Sometimes, a researcher will be designing a research programme according to a research brief. However, the brief may not exist in a definitive form, and the researcher may need to work with the client to refine it and make sure that it can be operationalized.

Research briefs
When drafting a research brief for an agency to respond, as much detail as possible should be given. This helps to refine and clarify thinking about the project, including the target audience, the kinds of questions and issues that ought to be addressed, and why. Specify the deliverables expected. Below is a checklist of questions which could be used by the researcher to draw out the background to design a research programme.

Checklist to guide a researcher when taking a brief

History

- o How long has the company been established?
- o How long has it concentrated on its present product/service range?
- o Has the company always been sited in its present location?
- o What factors have influenced its location?

Company background

- o What is the principal business of the company? What are its subsidiary activities?
- o What is its total turnover?
- o Describe any holding companies/subsidiary companies
- o How many employees are there at the establishment?

Product details

- o What are the important products (or services) in the range (by size, capacity, shape, material, etc.)?
- o What proportion of the total turnover does each of the above groups account for?
- o To what extent are the products standard/custom built?
- o What proportion of an assembled product is made in-house or bought out?
- o How important are spares in terms of revenue versus profit?
- o Are any of the products built under licence?

Pricing

- o What are the prices for each of the important products or services?
- o How do prices compare with those of the competition?
- o Is there a published price list?
- o What is the discount policy?
- o What power does the sales representative have to alter prices?
- o How price-sensitive is the product?

Sales force

- o Number of representatives
- o Are they a general or a specialized sales force – in what way are they specialized?
- o How many calls a day do they make?
- o Does the salesforce bring back orders, or are they sent in independently?

Markets

- o What are the major user markets for the products?
- o What proportion of total sales are to each of these markets?
- o Are any markets known for the product, where the company currently does not/cannot sell?
- o Which markets are believed to offer the greatest scope for expansion of sales?

Decision makers

- o Who are the key decision makers who specify and buy this type of product? What roles do they play?
- o What do decision makers look for from suppliers? PROBE price, quality, delivery, sales service?

Competition

- o Who are the most important competitors? Where are they based?
- o What is their rank order/market share?
- o What is each company's (including the client's) perceived strengths and weaknesses?
- o To what extent do competitors rely upon this market for their turnover and profit?

Quality

- o Where does the product fit against the competition in its quality?
- o What are the special features of its quality?
- o Where is it weak on quality?
- o How long will the product last?
- o When it finally fails, why will it do so?

Deliveries

- o What is the current delivery period?
- o What is the competition's delivery?
- o What is the ideal delivery?

Distribution

- o How is the product distributed?
- o What proportion goes direct/indirect? What is the policy which leads to this split (e.g. size of account – OEM versus replacement, etc.)?
- o What are distributors' margins?
- o What other products do distributors sell?
- o Do distributors actively sell, or just take orders?
- o Who are the major distributors
    - a. used by the company?
    - b. not used by the company?
- o What is the average size of a direct account and a distributor account?

Promotion

- o How big is the promotional budget?
- o How does this break down between: (a) media (b) exhibitions (c) PR (d) print (e) direct mail (f) websites?
- o Which media are used? Which are most successful?
- o What proportion of sales leads come from promotion? How many? What is their quality?
- o Which exhibitions are attended? What is their perceived value?
- o What opportunities exist for e-commerce?

Other data

- o Full details of names (initials as well) of persons present at briefing; date of briefing; address of company; address to which proposals should be sent; how many copies of the proposal are required to be sent?

Preparing a research proposal

Having received the brief, the researcher, whether in-house or from an agency, must submit a written proposal to the sponsor which states an appreciation of the problem, the objectives, the research method and the timing. If an agency is preparing the proposal, a statement of cost must be given. An in-house job may omit this but many managers still like to see an estimate as a benchmark to compare with other surveys and as a perspective that they can use to relate to the size of any decision which may be taken. If the proposal is accepted, it becomes the contract between the researcher and the sponsor.

The following Case Study is an extract from one of the many produced by the U.S. Department of Commerce. Note what it says about the importance of language even though English is spoken in both countries. When conducting market research that has an international focus, all the cultural factors that were mentioned in previous units need to be taken into account.

Entering the U.K. market

The British still tend to buy package tours put together and advertised in catalogues and brochures by tour operators. Travel agents use these catalogues and brochures to help clients choose where to go and to decide virtually every detail of their vacation.

Tour operators and travel agents therefore are pivotal in the U.K. travel industry. Consumer marketing should be the last, never the first, step.

It can be a costly error to assume that, because English is a shared language, materials developed for the U.S. market are automatically suitable for use in the U.K.

Many words have subtly or radically different meanings in U.K. and American English, which can lead to confusion or misunderstanding. For example, 'cheap' in American parlance is often used to mean 'inexpensive'. To a Briton, however, 'cheap' means 'shoddy'. 'Homely' to an American means 'ugly'; to a Briton it has the very positive meaning of 'homelike'. 'Mean' to an American means 'unkind', while to a Briton it means 'tight with money'.

Source: STAT-USA on the Internet, US Department of Commerce, http://strategis.ic.gc.ca/

Stage 2 – Develop the research plan and determine research design

This involves developing an efficient plan for gathering the necessary information. A marketing manager needs to know the cost of the research before agreeing it can go ahead. One of the issues to be considered is what is the need for primary and/or secondary research. If primary research is needed, then what type? Research design specifies the type of research required. Secondary research usually precedes primary research to see whether the problem that needs to be investigated can be addressed without having to spend resources on acquiring primary data.

Exploratory research

The goal of exploratory market research is discovery. The underlying questions are, 'What is new?' and 'What are we missing?' The goal of confirmatory techniques is resolution: 'Is this the right choice?' 'What results can we expect?' Exploratory market research is used to broaden a vision, whilst confirmatory research is used to narrow options and concentrate efforts (McQuarrie, 1996).

Exploratory and confirmatory market research techniques are used at different stages in a research project's decision cycle (Table 4.3). The decision cycle calls for sequential market research activities and questions, as the research design and strategy are developed and implemented. Each activity requires different market research techniques as the researcher's informational needs change from initial exploratory information to final confirmatory information.

The four decision cycle activities in Table 4.3 are further described in relation to each activity's objectives and suggested market research techniques.

Research design

Table 4.3 Four Decision Cycle Activities

Activity/Questions	Objectives	Techniques
Scan the Environment How are we doing? What's going on?	Identify, describe, monitor	Main: Secondary research, user visits Supporting: Focus groups, surveys
Generate Options What are the possibilities?	Generate, define, explore	Main: User visits, focus groups Supporting: Secondary research
Select an Option What is the explanation? Which option is best?	Evaluate, test, select, prioritize	Main: Experiments, surveys, choice models, usability tests Supporting: Secondary research
Evaluate Success What will we achieve? How are we doing?	Measure, track, assess	Main: Surveys, secondary research Supporting: user visits

Source: Adapted from McQuarrie, 1996, p 24.

A survey of the literature will usually precede all research designs.
This is to:

o   learn from previous research in the area
o   prevent expensive primary research being undertaken when research results are available.

Surveys of people with particular experience, or knowledge of the subject under investigation should be undertaken. For example, interviews of commercial directors to find out about trends in football merchandising. Examine the best and the worst examples to see if any conclusions may be made. For instance, a detailed investigation of top and bottom sales people to try and understand the factors that contribute to success or failure.

o   Repeated investigations over time; for example, monthly opinion surveys of consumers.
o   Single investigation; for example, a single survey of 100 business leaders to find out their attitudes to the training of their employees. Field experiments are carried out in the normal context, such as in a store, while a laboratory experiment is undertaken in an artificial environment.
o   A field experiment is where, for example, the store changes the price of products in store and assesses changes in the quantity and value purchased. In this context, the experiment is in a normal environment and the consumer is unaware that it is taking place.

Sampling

Organizations will target specified customer groups for their marketing activity. These customer groups, or segments, will be the basis on which any marketing research is undertaken. They will be the focus of any sampling activity. The potential population in this context could be any target group, ranging from large populations, such as the potential purchasers of television sets, to relatively small markets, such as widescreen plasma T.V. sets. Sampling allows conclusions to be drawn about the wider market, without needing to talk to everyone in the market place. Sampling estimates the numbers, attributes and beliefs of a population. The key to a good sample is to define the population of customers that are of interest and to select enough random members of that population. If the attitudes of buyers to a new type of hand-held computer were needed before planning a marketing campaign, the target population will be those who are affluent. This target population could be found, for example, by buying a mailing list from a computer magazine and specifying post codes in a 30 mile radius of the store with the highest incomes.

However, what you really need to know is who has the highest disposable income with an interest in electronic gadgets. This may not coincide with the most affluent. A young person in a well paid job, living at home with his parents may have more disposable income than an older person with twice the annual income. Therefore, you might want to cross-refer salary data with other data relating to marital status and age. However, marital status is not much of a guide to anything because many people are unmarried but living with partners. These latter points serve to illustrate the complexity of some of the factors when drawing up a relevant valid and reliable sample. The main decisions to be made when selecting a sample are:

1. The process by which the sample is to be selected is known as the sample design. The quality of all statistical analyses and procedures is governed by the quality of the sample data. If the sample data is not representative of the population, analysing the data and drawing conclusions from it will be unproductive and invalid. A representative sample will require the introduction of randomness in the sampling procedure.
2. From which list to draw a sample? This involves selecting a sample frame (i.e. a list of all members of the population) – unless people are just being interviewed randomly in the street.
3. How large a sample to select?

Sample design

The main approaches to sample design:

○ non-probability sample design
○ probability sample design.

A key issue is the cost of sampling versus the benefits. The main difference between probability and non-probability sampling is that, with the former the result of a sample can be projected to the whole population whereas this cannot be done with non-probability samples.

Probability samples

Probability sampling requires the researcher to know the size of the population, and for each individual in the population to have a known and equal chance of being selected (using a sampling frame). The most commonly used sampling frames are telephone numbers and postcodes. There are four major ways to contact those being surveyed:

○ telephone
○ personal (e.g. door-to-door)
○ mail
○ Internet.

Telephone, mail and e-mail provide the most control over the characteristics of those who are surveyed. The Internet and e-mail are the cheapest, and the respondents may not be representative of your target population.

Random sample – Everyone has the same chance. The advantage of the random sample is that it is the best representation of the population that can be obtained. The disadvantage is the difficulty of obtaining an entire population list. It works better with a small population because it is easier to get hold of that list.

What does it mean to be random?

Stratified random sample – The population is divided into groups/levels of interest, e.g. socio-economic status. This is a more representative type of sample.

Cluster sampling – This is based on sub-sets of the population, for example, geographic regions.

Non-probability samples

These are samples in which you do not know what is the chance of being selected. The precise size of a population or even who is in the population is not known. Examples of non-probability samples include:

Convenience sample – Samples are selected for interviews based on the ease of finding a sample from the researchers' point of view, i.e. from their convenience. They are not random and they use readily available subjects, for example, students.

Quota sample – Respondents are recruited because they possess particular characteristics – perhaps they may be selected on the basis of age or gender if these are believed to be important influencing factors in purchase decisions. Different individuals with different characteristics are sampled to meet the quota – e.g. gender: 50 male, 50 female. This type of sample design attempts to reflect key attributes of the general population in the selection of the sample to be researched. It is a common sampling technique used by commercial marketing research companies.

Judgement sampling – In this approach, the researcher believes that the results of the research will be improved if some judgement is exercised in selecting a sample, maybe by asking 'experts'.

Stage 3 – Data collection methods

Market research works because, by talking to a relatively small number of people, it is possible to find out about a far larger number, but it only works if the people who are interviewed (the sample) are a representative subgroup of the total group of interest (the universe), and if the right questions are asked. The universe might be the population as a whole, or parents, car drivers, elderly, shoppers, voters, IT managers, etc.

There are four basic data collection methods employed for surveys: 1) personal interviews, 2) telephone interviews, 3) mail surveys and 4) web-based surveys. The choice of the data collection method will depend on the objectives of the survey, and the relative importance of factors such as level of accuracy required, the amount of data to be collected, the sample bias acceptable, the budget required, speed and any administrative issues.

Primary data is information collected for a specific purpose

An example is the research required to identify the market for an innovative new product. It is unlikely that such research has previously been undertaken. Therefore, it is specially commissioned and, generally, the results belong to the organization commissioning the work. However, some research firms will conduct limited and less expensive primary research with the requirement that they can make the results available to other companies. More affordable primary research methods – both qualitative and quantitative – are available online as well. Inexpensive ways to conduct qualitative research via the Internet are through do-it-yourself online focus groups.

Compared with primary research, secondary research is generally:

o   quicker
o   cheaper
o   less relevant to the topic under investigation
o   out of date if it refers to fast changing contexts or issues.

As someone else has conducted the secondary research, users of this material must look carefully at how the data was derived and how valid and reliable are the conclusions.

The following Case Study is an example of primary research with a difference. Does this count as market research?

Case Study

What women want

Leslie Blodgett uses QVC to sell cosmetics, and to reach out to customers who tell her what sells and what doesn't. Using on air calls to cosmetic groupies in private homes, Blodgett asks viewers what they like and don't like, what new products might work, what old ones should come back. Blodgett claims that the ivory tower marketing research ruins brands because they are so far away from the customer.

Source: Forbes, 12 November 2001, p 124.

Activity 4.2

What do you see as the advantages and disadvantages of this kind of research? What kind of factors would you need to guard against before deciding to invest in developing new products?

Secondary research is the study of existing information

It includes research surveys carried out by other people, for other purposes, which make it unnecessary to carry out a completely new survey. It is sometimes called desk or library research.

Secondary research can use internal company sources (for example, purchasing information by customers – How much? What? When? What combinations?). There are many external sources of secondary information. Governments produce substantial amounts of national and regional information. Transnational/ international organizations (for example, Organization for Economic Co-operation and Development, European Union, ASEAN, World Bank) produce comparative international statistics as well as detailed sector and national studies. The most detailed information is available from the private sector. These range from organizations which specialize in the publication of reports on products and markets (such as Mintel, *The Economist* Intelligence Unit) to periodicals and newspapers (such as *Financial Times*, BBC, CNN, *Newsweek*, *Agra Europe*, etc.) which produce paper and/or electronic versions for access via the Internet.

Activity 4.3

Identify secondary research sources for your organization's products, services and markets. List specific reports that would be useful for marketing.

Evaluating secondary information

1. **What was the purpose of the study?** Was it undertaken by an impartial source or by a pressure group that is attempting to put across a particular point?

2. **Who collected the information?** In the UK, it is possible to obtain statistics on the number of vegetarians from the Vegetarian Society, or from the meat industry. These two sources of information do not provide the same estimate for the number of vegetarians!

3. **What information was collected?** Figures from two sources may differ because of the use of different sources of information, or because different timescales are used. However, sometimes it can be because each wants to prove a point.

4. **When was the information collected?** If there has been a recent food scare, for example mad cow disease, consumption levels of beef will be low and consumption of substitutes will be high.

5. **Is the information consistent with other information?** Most secondary information tends to be quantitative rather than qualitative.

Quantitative data

- Tends to be on large numbers of people
- Findings are expressed numerically
- Concerned with 'how many', 'how often' and 'what' rather than 'why'?
- Quantitative research problem: How many consumers buy the company's shampoo?

Qualitative

- Fewer people
- Deals with data difficult to quantify – concerned with 'why' rather than 'how many', or 'how often'?
- Concerned with attitudes and motivations
- Qualitative research problem: What shape of bottle do consumers find appropriate for the brand values we are trying to communicate?

Primary research

There are four main types of primary research:

- surveys
- observation
- experimentation
- simulation.

Personal interviews

Benefits

- Interviewer can select a good quality sample
- Interviewer can interpret strange answers and ask for clarification
- The interviewer can classify interviewees to save time
- Longer questionnaires can be asked with this method
- Can use visual images.

Problems

- Costly
- Possible interviewer bias
- Possibility of fake interviews.

Focus groups

This is one of the most frequently used techniques in marketing research. Successful research requires a skilled moderator (i.e. the person who directs the topics of discussion and creates a balanced environment to encourage the contribution of all members of the group). Members of the focus group should be selected from the target population for the firm's products and services.

Benefits

- A wide range of ideas can be obtained
- In-depth understanding of consumer attitudes and purchase motivations may be obtained
- Ideal when managers are looking for ideas or need to clarify some details
- A certain synergy can be obtained from a group discussion that allows a deeper probing of issues
- Can use visual images
- Relatively easy to record (video and audio tape) for future analysis.

Problems

- Costly
- Success is highly dependent on the skill of the interviewer and on the selection of the sample to attend the focus group
- Possible problem of domination of the group by a strong and forceful individual, which will result in group conflict or only the views of the forceful individual being obtained.

Telephone surveys

Benefits

- Quick and easy to do
- Reach geographically dispersed sample
- Ease of sampling, for example, random digit dialling
- Complex routing through questionnaire is automated
- Low cost
- Possibility of recording to confirm that interview took place.

Problems

- ○ Method can only handle very short, simple questionnaires
- ○ Sample obtained can be biased, depending on the type of people who are willing to complete a telephone interview
- ○ Lack of access to households without telephones.

Skills survey

It is billed as the largest fact-finding mission of its type, the mother of all surveys – so big that it will take not one but a trio of polling organizations to pull it off. Squads of questioners will be bashing the phones of 70,000 employers of all sizes across England asking whether or not they train their workforces, how and why. No doubt it will yield an unprecedented cornucopia of data. But is it all necessary? There seems to be a rough consensus that, despite all the quizzing of industry and the results this throws up such as the Labour Force surveys produced by the Office of National Statistics, there are things we still need to know; the sorts of data which are reputedly easily available in the Netherlands and Germany. The CBI director applauds the new survey, 'I think its good that they are drilling down in more depth. ' However, there are some sceptics who feel that we need to know the fine detail of the sorts of training that people are getting, how well it fits their needs and how likely it is to raise their skills levels. However, they feel that this is the sort of information that won't be gleaned from a telephone survey. The researchers who conducted a survey of mathematical skills in the workplace said 'What we found out, we found out by talking to people on the shopfloor. There's absolutely no way we would have got that depth of information from a telephone survey. They concluded that it was vital to ask open-ended questions rather than the typical questionnaire enquiries which ask the respondent to select one of a range of ready made answers.

Adapted from Questions Remain, Peter Kingston, *Guardian* newspaper, 18 March 2003.

 Activity 4.4

What do you think of the advantages and disadvantages of using a telephone survey for this kind of work? Do you think the sceptics are being unrealistic in expecting in-depth interviews in the workplace, or do they have a point?

Postal surveys

Benefits

- ○ Low cost
- ○ Ease of contacting geographically dispersed sample
- ○ More complex questions can be asked.

Problems

- ○ Usually quite a low response rate
- ○ The interviewee can misinterpret the questions
- ○ It can take a long time to get back replies
- ○ Minimal chance of interpreting the extent to which the respondent is answering truthfully.

Internet surveys

Benefits

- o Very fast: instant analysis may be undertaken
- o Very low cost
- o Highly targeted
- o Ease of contacting the sample.

Problems

- o Method can only handle very short, simple questionnaires
- o Very limited potential for 'open' questions
- o People with access to the Internet are not representative of the total population for all markets. They tend to be higher income and higher socio-economic groups. This is less of a problem for business-Internet surveys.

Qualitative approaches

- o Fewer people
- o Deals with data difficult to quantify – concerned with 'why' rather than 'how many', or 'how often'?
- o Concerned with attitudes and motivations.

Some of the more important criteria, when selecting research method include:

- o Cost
- o Speed
- o Access to target population (including ability to sample the target population)
- o Type of questions that can be asked
- o Quantity of data
- o Response rate.

Observation

This is literally where the individual's behaviour is monitored and recorded. One of the most popular applications of this technique recently is in researching in-store shopping. Consumer movement through the store is observed and recorded. Researchers have been able to classify individuals in supermarkets according to their speed of movement through the store, their willingness to scan the shelves for products and to divert from a pre-planned shopping list, where one exists.

Experimentation

This is where the researcher attempts to establish causality between two factors by varying one factor and holding all other factors constant.

Laboratory experiments

Laboratory experiments take place in an artificial environment created by the researcher, which allows one factor to be varied. For example, an advert can be placed within a magazine that has been created specially for research purposes. Consumers can be given the magazine to look through, and are then asked to comment on the advertising. If unfavourable comments are made, then the advert is changed and consumers are asked to repeat the procedure. In this way researchers are able to assess changes in advertising on consumer response.

Field experiments

Field experiments take place in a more natural environment. Researchers often change a factor in order to observe the influence on purchase quantity/sales revenue. Examples of experimentation in a retail environment include changing:

- shelf location
- price
- pack design
- sales promotion activity.

As each of these factors is varied, the researcher observes the effect on sales volume and on revenue.

Simulation

Simulation is where researchers build a model (usually a computer model) of an environment and use this as the basis for experimentation. Simulation is employed when a problem is judged to be too complex for ease of mathematical formulation. In building a simulation, the researcher sets the framework (parameters) of the model and within that framework, the researcher or business manager may experiment.

The power of images

Pictures selected by tongue-tied shoppers can help companies learn what consumers really want. When words fail, the images consumers choose can serve as a window into their thoughts. These images can be used to tap non-verbal reactions and to probe below the surface for deeper feelings. The insights gleaned can be incorporated into marketing campaigns that resonate with consumers on an emotional level.

Source: American Demographics, November 2001, p 32.

Cross-section versus longitudinal research

Researchers need to be clear about the type of data they require. Cross-sectional data is where a 'snapshot' picture of the current situation is obtained. A survey undertaken this month reports on the situation *as it is* for this month. For various reasons, the results may not be relevant at any other time. Longitudinal data is obtained over a period of time, often over many years.

Tracking studies

A tracking study may involve conducting a survey every month, or even every week, to establish and track consumer reaction. In such studies, advertising managers want to assess the peak level of response, such as awareness, and the rate at which this decays between advertising activity. As longitudinal research is very expensive for individual companies to buy, groups of companies join together to purchase the same data using 'syndicated research'.

Syndicated research

Only companies within the syndicate have access to the data. A relatively low-cost method of collecting 'cross-sectional data usually' is the omnibus survey. A company will run a regular survey (say, every month) with a specified target population. Often a theme is specified, such as financial services or children. Any company is then able to pay to add their own questions.

Stage 4 – Data collection

The most common approach to collecting information is the questionnaire. There are two main types of questions used in questionnaires: open questions and closed questions.

Open questions are used when the researcher wants to explore some ideas. They may be used when trying to design a new product or explore consumer opinion about the company brand, for example, what features would you like in a robot vacuum cleaner?

Closed questions are most frequently used to count the number of people who exhibit a particular trait.

Closed question, example:

Do you buy products made by the firm?

- o   never?
- o   once per year?
- o   once per month?
- o   more frequently than once per month.

There are many types of closed and open questions. Some closed questions are able to achieve more than simply a count of people or attributes. They may be used to investigate attitudes held by consumers, in particular the intensity of attitude.

Closed questions
Closed questions may include two (dichotomous) or more (multichotomous) options from which the respondent selects an answer.

Semantic differential scale
Semantic differential scale respondents are presented with a set of bipolar adjectives and asked to indicate the point on the scale which best describes the intensity of their feelings.

Open questions
Open questions gather ideas and attitudes but they are time-consuming to analyse and require knowledgeable analysts.

Open questions invite facts and opinions, whereas closed questions seek either the answer 'yes' or 'no'.

The danger of using too many closed questions is that they:

- o   prevent people from expressing views
- o   restrict the flow of information.

Simple open questions
These leave the respondent free to answer as they wish.

Leading questions
These are phrased in such a way that makes it clear that you only expect one answer: 'I'm sure we all agree that . . .'?

'Isn't it true that ...?' – 'Don't you think that ...?' They are to be avoided because they can cause resentment at trying to put words into their mouths or trying to persuade them, against their own judgement, to agree with you. Ultimately, the data gathered is flawed because it may not represent what the respondent really thinks or believes.

Multiple questions

People can only answer one question at a time, so do not fall into the trap of issuing a stream of questions, such as:

'What's the situation with ... and how will we ... and when by?'

Listening

Questioning skills will not bring results unless equally effective listening skills are being practised. There are three levels of listening:

- o hearing the words – you must be able to actually hear and understand the words that are being spoken
- o understanding the meaning – you must understand the overall meaning
- o perceiving the inference – you must be able to perceive the inferences that lie behind the words.

Signals

When listening, and when you are being listened to, you should be aware of the stream of signals which are given off by somebody who is speaking. These verbal and non-verbal signals can transmit a significantly different message to other members of the meeting than the literal meaning of the spoken words.

Facial expression – if the speaker's expression does not match the words, it is the expression which carries more weight.

Body language – shrugged shoulders or dismissive hand gestures have the same impact as facial expression.

Tone of voice – Listeners can perceive strong signals through tone of voice and emphasis on certain words. The tone of voice, consciously or sub-consciously, can significantly influence the way in which the question is perceived. For example the question: 'Do you think this is achievable?' is apparently a neutral, closed question which seeks without expectation the answer 'yes' or 'no'. However, in a different tone, it could also imply that there is the slightest chance that the results can be achieved. Conversely, the same question spoken in an enthusiastic voice would convey the impression that you were looking for a 'Yes!' If you want the honest opinion of other members, you should take care to keep any expectation – either positive or negative – out of your voice.

Stage 5 – Present the findings

The market research report should present findings that are relevant to the major marketing decisions facing management.

Online research

Online research covers all Digital Interactive Media, including Digital TV, WAP and new entertainment technologies. Online research can be appropriate if the target market is visitors to a specific website or Internet-users in general – but it is still not a medium for general public surveys. This may change eventually as penetration grows among women and older groups. Internet research has an advantage for surveys among staff, employees and customers or subscribers to online services in any situation where the universe is known, and the e-mail addresses are available and up-to-date. Business e-mail addresses tend to be less volatile compared to consumers. The barriers to conducting online research are very low. The most important issue for research is declining respondent co-operation rates. Approaches like showing interactive stimuli material such as clips from ads, all work well on the Internet. But while it is feasible to show TV clips, they can slow down load times. With interactive digital TV, there is a lot more potential.

CAI
Computer Assisted Interviewing (CAI) involves the use of a computer to collect, store, manipulate and transmit data relating to interviews conducted between the interviewer and the respondent(s).

CAPI
Computer Assisted Personal Interviewing (CAPI) (personal interview by an interviewer using a portable computer at the home or business of the respondent) is one component of CAI. Other components include Computer Assisted Telephone Interviewing (CATI) and Computer Assisted Self Interviewing (CASI). The three chief theoretical benefits of CAPI are: better quality, improved timeliness and lower cost after the initial investment. CAPI has the potential to provide improvements in the areas of data quality, survey timeliness and cost effectiveness but cost savings directly attributable to CAPI are less well documented than the other benefits. On large-scale continuous surveys and on other operations where the hardware can be efficiently utilized and the costs spread over time, net savings might be expected but otherwise the costs might well be greater for CAPI. CAPI also provides the opportunity to apply experimental design principles to survey testing, and the flexibility to enable collection of important policy related data for difficult topics.

Online focus groups
An online focus group is essentially a formal chat session. A trained moderator leads a group of participants through a pre-determined discussion over the Internet. Participants are often recruited through a research firm's own panel and are paid a fee for participating. A focus group could be set up inexpensively by using a chat room and recruiting your own participants. If a panel is used, the following checklist is useful to note.

Online panel users

A good online panel can offer real advantages over other approaches. But how do you know it's a good panel?

Here's a checklist of questions to ask a panel supplier.

Recruitment sources How are the panel members found? What biases does this recruitment approach build in?

Screening Are prospective panel members screened (off-line) to confirm age, residence, etc.? Many panel members belong to several different panels, to the point where some have become almost professional respondents.

Representative membership How well does the profile of panel members match an independently derived profile of net users as a whole? Is there a bias toward the heavier or more experienced users?

Maintenance of representativeness What steps has the panel supplier taken to ensure that the membership profile remains up-to-date? Drop-out and the changing profile of net users can lead to biases in the panel membership, if it is not regularly monitored.

Sampling methods How are samples drawn from the panel membership? Is it a random sample from the whole database? Are quotas or over-sampling used to allow for differential response rates?

Differential response rates What monitoring has the agency done on differential response rates? Some people respond every time, some rarely, so that the achieved sample for any survey may be biased, even if the panel as a whole is representative.

Survey frequency How often are panel members asked to complete surveys? Professional respondents are not representative.

Lifestyle profiling Are panel members profiled according to lifestyle criteria? If not the panel could be less cost-effective if you are only interested in, for example, people who have booked travel online, or people who regularly work from home.

Source: http://www.mori.com/pubinfo/nep-onlineresearch.shtml Online Research – ESOMAR Research World Interview.

Feedback forms

A simple way to conduct ongoing qualitative research is through a feedback form. You can gain valuable insight by asking website visitors for suggestions, and/or asking them their opinions. You can do this through a form directly on your site and/or via e-mail to those on your opt-in list.

Primary quantitative market research

Quantitative research is used when you are looking for hard numbers and precision. To produce a top-quality primary quantitative research study, you must generally work through a research agency. For a small-budget business, this type of research is expensive. The Internet has made more inexpensive means of data collection and analysis possible. With the help of software or web-based tools, you can perform research through customer surveys and collect visitor-use patterns through web logs.

Customer surveys

The Internet has made conducting surveys quicker and less expensive. Options range from do-it-yourself programmes to research services with screened panels. You can use surveys in a variety of ways – segmenting your customers, improving/developing your product or site and gauging brand awareness, for example.

Use patterns

Another approach to quantitative research on the web is to look for visitor-use patterns such as, routes taken through your site, pages viewed, or ordering behaviour. By studying web logs, you can know which pages are most popular, how visitors navigate through your site, common entry pages, and where visitors often leave the site. You can also determine the number of different visitors to your site as well as the percentage of visitors converted to customers. By using a traffic-analysis service or software (often available through your hosting service), you can streamline the process. An alternative to conducting primary research is to find secondary research, or research that originated elsewhere. You can obtain secondary research either by purchasing the information or finding it through free resources.

Further points about secondary market research

As a small-budget business, much of your research will be limited to secondary research. Potentially, secondary research can be identified from numerous sources. Press releases and news articles often quote studies. Industry leaders and suppliers publish white papers or other studies. Annual reports are also good places to look for industry information. Research firms' sites are another source of secondary research. Their main business is conducting primary research for clients or compiling and selling detailed syndicated reports. Secondary data is data originally collected for a more general purpose, usually by a third party. The process of collection is usually termed secondary research or desk research. Research is either quantitative (it deals mostly with numerical information) or qualitative (dealing with less tangible data such as interview responses, individual opinions and the outcome of group discussions).

Competitive analysis of French children's clothing market

New products should be aggressively marketed to appeal to French children's tastes and to influence their fashion preferences. The media has a tremendous impact on French children. Music and television are influential at an early age, and are thus excellent means for promoting products that are specifically directed towards children. According to analysts, children spend an average of 2 hours per day watching television. Additionally, 25 per cent of French children have their own television sets. U.S. imports are expected to grow, given the fact that French children are greatly influenced by American trends and television. The easy-to-wear clothing of American colleges and the street wear of large cities appear especially attractive to French children. As a result, U.S. products such as T-shirts, polos and jackets with names of football teams or American colleges are in high demand. Proof of the success of American brands in France can be seen in the opening of a Gap store for children in Paris. There appears to be numerous opportunities for U.S. companies to successfully penetrate the French children's wear market.

Further points about qualitative methods

Qualitative research tends to be exploratory and directional in nature. It is designed to bring out issues associated with the subject matter as well as the best general direction to proceed. Qualitative methods can be useful in all stages of development and are very tangible to marketers and developers. There are two basic qualitative data collection methods:

1. Depth interviews
2. Focus/discussion groups.

Further points about focus groups

Focus groups can be used to cover a variety of topics, but they are best used to understand 'why' a particular group feels or acts in a particular way. If an interviewee says something of particular interest during a focus group, the interviewer can probe deeper into the topic, uncovering information. Topics often covered in focus groups include reactions to product ideas and product prototypes, messaging tests, ad testing and customer-needs identification. The groups are taped (video and audio) for later analysis and can be observed during the focus group – either at a specially designed facility, or via a videoconference or web-based hook-up when the session proceedings can be viewed remotely. Sometimes hard-to-reach people will not come to a focus group but they may be reached by depth interviews which are one-on-one discussions with a researcher. While qualitative data is very accessible, it can fall short on reliability.

Further points about depth interviews

Depth interviews involve one-to-one contact with respondents and are usually conducted face-to-face, although telephone interviews are sometimes used. The depth interview is different from the tightly structured interview used in quantitative surveys or opinion polls: it is not only longer (45–60 minutes), but also more discursive and open-ended. The interviewer also has a greater level of flexibility since they are not constrained by the order or wording of questions; she/he is able to cover the issues specified in the topic guide in a more context-sensitive way, as they 'naturally' emerge, and to probe responses to gain a full understanding of their meaning and/or implications.

Quantitative research

Quantitative research produces results that are more statistically accurate than qualitative research results. Often, companies first conduct qualitative research when developing a concept or looking for ideas, and later complete quantitative research to fine-tune and optimize. It is usually conducted via surveys or behavioural tracking. It's based on the principle that the characteristics of a randomly selected group of people will closely reflect the characteristics of the entire group from which the sample was taken. So, when marketers and site developers need to know, with relative certainty, the answers to specific questions, quantitative methods are used.

Quantitative research focuses on the left brain – objective, comfortable with logic, numbers and detailed, convergent reasoning rather than divergent reasoning. Qualitative research deals with the right brain – the hemisphere accountable for processing data such as words, emotions, feelings, colour and music. Traditional survey questionnaires are weak at eliciting follow-up data from respondents, as they usually require responses pre-categorized by the researcher. Often managers greeted the receipt of such surveys with the response 'So what?'. They answer questions related to such issues as market share, predicted revenue, statistical trends and past behaviour of customers well, but statistics are not good for answering questions about human behaviour, perceptions, future behaviour and involvement with a product. As a result of the need for companies to obtain richer data about their customers, prospective customers and the market as a whole, qualitative research became more in demand. While data collection techniques are now better developed, data analysis methodologies have not kept up. The new 'So what?' reaction from management is in response to the often confused summaries of the pages upon pages of focus group or interview transcripts. Running quantitative research alongside qualitative research offers a synergy whereby objective data can provide a structure to the analysis of subjective qualitative data. Generally, quantitative and qualitative research are presented as two separate entities. Yet, the smart market researcher knows how to combine both kinds of data.

Source: Adapted from: http://www.asiamarketresearch.com/columns/market5.htm

The market research industry

The market research industry consists of hundreds of firms and consultancies. Each of these will have their own areas of specialization. The leading agencies, and many of the smaller ones, have directors and executives who are members of the Market Research Society. The Society has a Professional Code of Conduct which lays down rules and good practice with respect to their responsibilities to clients (confidentiality), respondents (anonymity), the public as a whole and to each other.

Agency selection

It is possible to buy research and a reputable agency should give advice on the most cost-effective, way of researching a target audience. It will discuss the advantages and disadvantages of different research options, and help to design and write questions. It will endeavour to achieve a representative sample and report the main findings in whatever form is preferred. The agency should also be willing to discuss the implications of any findings for the business.

Qualitative and quantitative market research: where the twain meet...

Why can't advertising agencies and market researchers just get on?

Advertising agencies attract creative people, often innovators and independent thinkers who also often lack pragmatic and rational thinking. On the other hand, market research agencies attract a different sort of person – methodical and objective, often more introvert, detail-minded and conservative in outlook. Advertising agencies think they can do the research better than the market research agencies, and market research agencies think they can do the advertising better than the advertising agencies. Research departments within advertising agencies often lack power and crumble under the pressure of their more extravert advertising colleagues at meetings. The reverse is true with research-based organizations that venture into advertising. It may be difficult for the extrovert, creative people who make up advertising agencies to listen to market researchers whose research suggests that a wonderfully original and unique ad may cause a negative reaction, and similarly it is difficult for researchers to get excited by new and paradigm-challenging ideas.

Source: http://www.asiamarketresearch.com/columns/market1.htm

Rod Davies, Orient Pacific Century, 12 February 2000.

Rod Davies, Orient Pacific Century, October 2000.

The British Market Research Association (BMRA) website lists its member agencies with their specialisms. Smaller agencies are good for niche areas but larger agencies will tend to have specialists who focus on particular sectors, such as the voluntary sector, financial services, telecommunications, education, etc.

Summary

There are many different approaches to market research but the most important aspect is to choose an approach that is fit for the purpose and will deliver the kind of data that will be useful. Sophisticated market research is costly so it is important to conduct a cost benefit analysis of any proposal. No approach is perfect and the main choice is between knowing a lot about a little, or a little about a lot.

Further study

Boddy, D. (2002). *Management: An Introduction*, Chapter 7 'Managing Marketing'.

123

Hints and Tips

You need to be able to show that you know the issue that needs to be decided when designing a research project aimed at providing information as part of a marketing audit or for marketing and business decisions. On a practical level, you will need to be able to analyse and interpret information and present, as a written report or oral presentation, appropriate conclusions or recommendations that inform the marketing and business decisions for which the research was undertaken.

Sample exam questions and answers for the Marketing Management in Practice module as a whole can be found in Appendix 3 at the back of the book.

unit 5
project management

Learning objectives

- Describe the main stages of a project and the roles of people involved at each stage

- Describe the main characteristics of successful and less successful projects and identify the main reasons for success or failure

- Explain the importance of, and techniques for, establishing the project's scope, definition and goals

- Use the main techniques available for planning, scheduling, resourcing and controlling activities on a project

- Explain the importance of preparing budgets and techniques for controlling progress throughout a project to ensure it is completed on time and within budget

- Explain the main techniques for evaluating the effectiveness of a project on its completion.

Key definitions

Business case – This is used to define the information that justifies the setting up, continuation or termination of the project. It answers the question 'Why should this project be undertaken?' It can be updated at key points throughout the project.

Critical path – The series of tasks that must be completed on time for a project to finish on schedule. Each task on the critical path is a critical task; any delay to it would delay the project's schedule. Often displayed as:

Critical path analysis – A method for scheduling when tasks will happen. Comprising of a forward pass and a backward pass, it determines how quickly and how slowly the tasks can be accomplished.

Customer – Customer is used to represent the person or group who has commissioned the work and will be benefiting from the end results.

Gantt chart – A graphical representation of the project's current schedule. It will often contain bars for normal tasks, summary tasks, milestone tasks, and slack values. Gantt charts are also referred to as Bar Charts as they depict task bars against a timescale.

PERT analysis – Is a simple form of quantitative risk analysis and can be applied to a schedule to help estimate the duration of a task. After the entry of optimistic, pessimistic and expected durations for each of the tasks, Microsoft Project will calculate a weighted average of the three durations, and determine a single duration estimate for each task. Gantt charts can display the results of critical path analysis taking all tasks at their optimistic, pessimistic and expected values. A button on the analysis toolbar provides access to PERT commands.

Product, deliverable or outcome – Terms used to describe everything that the project has to create or change, however physical or otherwise these may be. Results of projects can vary from physical items such as buildings to intangible things such as culture change.

Programme – This is a collection of projects that together achieve a beneficial change for an organization.

Project objectives – Three basic objectives that a project must meet to ensure its successful conclusion:

- Time Objective
- Cost Objective
- Quality Objective

Project objectives are often a contractual agreement between the project manager, the project's sponsor and the project's stakeholders.

Project definition – What a project will deliver and how it will be judged.

Project resources – Work, time and cost are resources of the project that are consumed in its execution. For example, doing some work will take some time and incur some cost, as its accomplishment adds to meeting the project's overall objectives.

Supplier – This refers to the group that is providing specialist resources and skills to the project, or goods and services, to create the project outcome required by the Customer and User(s).

User – A user is the person or group who will use or operate the final product. In some situations, the customer and the user may be the same group of people.

Introduction

When studying the Marketing Management in Practice module, CIM recommends that two thirds of the sessions should be allocated to a significant practical project involving the formulation and implementation of an operational marketing plan. This should cover the management of information, communications and human resources. The emphasis should be the application of this theory within a marketing team. A typical project will consist of:

- Planning the project to be undertaken to meet the brief given
- Undertaking the task. This will involve collecting and analysing information and developing a marketing plan

   o   Planning, scheduling and resourcing marketing activities within the plan, identifying and overcoming problems during implementation
   o   Measuring and evaluating the outcomes
   o   Reflecting on the performance of the team and the individuals in it.

Some of the underpinning knowledge for this is covered in other modules and units, and a key part is contained in the final unit – Developing marketing plans.

What is a project?

In recent years, project teams and a project management approach have become common in many organizations. The basic approach to project management should be the same regardless of the type of project or sector in which the project is carried out. Services marketing professionals, in particular, are facing greater complexity in managing programmes and projects. Typical marketing programmes within large IT services organizations involve teamwork with different functional areas such as research and development, training, manufacturing, communication, as well as with business partners. Global marketing organizations require managing collaboration across numerous cultures and time zones.

Project management may not always come easy to marketers, who may want to focus more on the 'creative' side of the work. Without a project management method, those who commission a project, those who manage it and those who work on it will have different ideas about how things should be organized and when the different aspects of the project will be completed. Those involved will not be clear about how much responsibility, authority and accountability they have and, as a result, there will often be confusion surrounding the project.

A project should possess identifiable goals, and a definite starting and finishing point. Project goals should be defined clearly. The major constraints on the completion of projects are time, resource availability and the need to achieve the required standard of performance for the project.

While marketing projects are getting more complex, marketing managers need to demonstrate a clear and strong return on marketing investment (ROI). One response to these pressures is the establishment of a 'project management office' – a team of people that uses management methodologies and tools. Although such a structured approach might not be necessary or appropriate for every organization, many marketing professionals need to understand project planning and implementation.

Feasibility studies

Before a project is given the go ahead, a feasibility study might be conducted before the launch of a project. Support for a project could be important, so the aim of a feasibility study is to carry out a preliminary investigation to help determine whether a project should proceed further and how it should proceed.

The questions asked and the focus of a study will depend upon, for example, such things as the nature of the project that is being contemplated, the risk factors involved and its cost. The cost of carrying out a feasibility study needs to be weighed against the cost of a project not delivering what is expected of it. There is no point in carrying out an actual feasibility study if the cost of it would exceed the actual cost of the project. In this situation, the feasibility of a project would need to be determined in other ways on the basis of information that is already available.

127

However, a feasibility study will need to consider the following:

Cost Is it within the budget set by the organization or within the capabilities of the organization to finance it?

Timing Are there any time constraints and will it be possible to complete the project within these constraints?

Performance Will the project deliver the benefits that are claimed for it?

Effect on the organization Is it feasible in the context of the organization and the effect which it will have upon it? – Does it fit the culture of the organization? – Will it draw resources away from other important activities?

Resourcing: Are the necessary skills, technology and physical infrastructure available? Or, if not can they be easily recruited?

Stages of a project

Project definition

Once the project has received formal approval to proceed, the objectives of the project and how the work will be undertaken can be determined. The project manager will carry out this work, in consultation with the client, and any sub-project manager if there are sub-projects. Large projects may be divided into sub-projects, with each sub-project requiring its own sub-project definition. The aim is to identify all prerequisites are in place. Before a definition can begin, there should be a project brief or terms of reference signed off by all parties involved in the project and giving the authority to proceed.

This is the stage where objectives, assumptions and constraints need to be identified so that everyone can be clear about the basis on which the project will proceed. As the project gets underway, there are likely to be changes to it because it is very difficult to know everything at the outset. Some of the assumptions made may need to change in the light of experience or, for example, the availability of resources or key personnel, and the original scheduling may need to be revised. All this is easier if the objectives, assumptions and constraints have been identified in the first place.

A project covers interrelated activities or tasks with definite start and finish times, identifiable objectives and an integrated system of complex but interdependent relationships. An activity or task is a unit of work whose scheduling is overseen by a project manager.

Projects have three elements:

- o Budget
- o Schedule
- o Deliverables.

The aim of project management is to ensure the effective scheduling of tasks and use of resources to deliver the objectives of a project on time, within cost constraints and with outcomes that meet the needs of the end-users.

Determine project scope

Determining the scope of the project helps to clarify objectives and set the boundaries of the project. It is often useful to state limitations, i.e. what the project will not cover.

Project brief

A project brief should take the objectives and translate them into targets and goals. Any key constraints should also be identified and stated at this stage. This brief should be agreed by the client and communicated to the project manager. Success criteria should be established for the project, preferably criteria that are tangible and measurable. The success criteria should be provided in response to the conditions adhering to the project.

Contents of a project brief

A project brief will identify:

o **Objectives** – Why you are doing it, as listed in the client requirements definition, the business benefits that the project will provide when it is completed – often broken down to three basic project objectives: Time, Cost, and Quality
o **Scope** – Project boundaries
o **Deliverables** – What it will provide
o **Accountability** – Success criteria

How you will be performing it – major milestones, change control procedures.

o **Constraints** – Question of how would you know if your project had been successful
o **Assumptions** – Listed unknowns about the project
o **Resources**

Key personnel – Who is responsible for what? Who are the stakeholders?

Objectives – Three basic objectives that a project must meet to ensure its successful conclusion:

o Time
o Cost
o Quality.

The objectives form the basis of the project's strategic information. They also relate to one another; for example, a reduction in time may incur additional cost or may reduce overall quality. Project objectives are often a contractual agreement between the project manager, the project's client and the project's stakeholders.

The client is one of the project's stakeholders who will receive the benefits that the project will provide. He usually provides or authorizes the terms of reference and communicates strategic information to and from the project manager. Stakeholders are individuals or organizations with a vested interest in a project. The most obvious stakeholder is the sponsor.

Assumptions

Project assumptions can be checked with stakeholders who can critique them and, if necessary, a revised set of assumptions agreed when there are changes. A schedule can be revised when new information becomes available.

Areas where assumptions may need to be made include:

o The materials, resources, people and equipment that will be available
o How long particular tasks will take to complete – Are the assumptions based on realistic information or are they the result of inspired guesses?
o How important is cost to the project – What are the arrangements if a budget needs to be increased?
o Will all the project tasks be completed in the timescale available and to an acceptable quality level?
o Are the project aims deliverable in line with what the key stakeholders are expecting?
o What are the management arrangements for overseeing the project – Will there be a steering group to whom the project director or manager will report?
o What kinds of reports will be needed, by when?

Constraints

There can be constraints on the completion of projects, arising from the different objectives of:

o Time scale
o Resource availability
o Quality factors
o Human factors.
o **Performance specifications** These may be set out in terms of the ability to deal with certain demands. For example, this could be number of patients or transactions processed, or the number of enquiries dealt with.
o **Specific quality standards** This could relate to technical standards and tolerance, or may be the achievement of a favourable report from an outside inspection agency.
o **Meeting deadlines** For example, a new system may need to be implemented, ready for the start of the financial year, or a new development may have to meet time requirements as laid down in contract specifications.

Calculate resource requirements

Calculate requirements for each time period. Identify needs for each resource type (e.g. systems analyst, user staff) and identify needs for special skills or scarce resources.

Calculate costs

Calculate costs for the sub-project. This should include 'hardening up' items such as cabling, training, etc. for which an order of costs had been produced previously.

Determine overall costs of the project

The cost/benefit justification should have already been stated in the feasibility study. This stage provides the opportunity to review the case in the light of more detailed information. An important criterion may be to complete the project within a cost limit or budget which has been determined. Additionally, there may be requirements in terms of the ongoing cost of the completed project. For example, a new system may be required to make savings for the organization on a continuing basis.

Deliverables

A deliverable is a tangible verifiable outcome of work done to produce a product or service. To be verifiable, the deliverable must meet pre-determined standards for its completion, such as design specifications for a product or a checklist of steps that is completed as part of a service. Deliverables have external stakeholders who receive the finished product or service such as customers and internal stakeholders like a project manager and team members who work directly on the deliverable. A project may have only one or many deliverables.

Define key project tasks

To help in breaking a project down into smaller and more manageable pieces of work, the project's objectives and scope are broken down into more detail in terms of duration, work and links. The most common approach is to plan from the overall objective and then to break this down into sub-objectives (or phases). Sub-objectives may relate to products, functions, disciplines and cost areas. The sub-objectives need to be broken down further into lower levels of detail until quantifiable tasks are at the bottom of the structure. The smaller the task, the more accurately it can be estimated. Tasks should be allocated to a named person, group or organization for implementation.

Once a project's tasks have been defined, the next stage is to determine how the tasks relate to one another. This creates sequences of tasks within the project and identifies when each of the tasks can occur.

In determining the sequence of tasks – the tasks that must be accomplished before a particular task can take place – its predecessor(s) needs to be identified. This technique is known as precedence analysis and is the common way of determining how tasks relate.

These relationships are referred to as dependencies or precedencies, and when planning a project it is important to establish the order of precedence of dependent activities, and to establish those activities which can be performed in parallel with other activities.

Not all tasks within a project start at the same time. There will always be some form of sequence. The simplest relationship is where the commencement of one task depends upon the completion of just one task that precedes it. This is a dependent relationship.

Building a project plan

The complexity of the project plan will depend on the size of the project, as larger projects demand greater planning and structure than smaller ones. Software such as Microsoft® Project can be used to build project plans and will help with listing the project tasks, organize them into phases, schedule tasks, set dependencies, deadlines and constraints, and specify and assign the resources to tasks.

If the timeline indicates that the project will run over its deadline, a check should be made to ensure that resources aren't under- or over-allocated. Resolving this is called Resource Levelling and it may assist in sorting out the timeline. If it doesn't work, more resources may be needed. However, adding another person to a task doesn't necessarily mean that the task will necessarily be completed more quickly if the person needs to be trained and familiarized with the specific project. It may also slow down an existing member of the team if they need to brief and coach the newcomer. The timeline might be shortened through working overtime, though excessive overtime reduces productivity. If this does not work and the deadline really is unmovable, the

131

project requirements may need to be scaled back to meet the date. When the project plan is agreed, it becomes a baseline that can be used to compare with the progress of the project.

Determine work structure

Large projects are more likely to be successful if they can be divided into smaller units of work (sub-projects). Identify tasks which can be arranged into logical groups to form sub-projects. Grouping could be on the basis of, for example:

- o   tasks relating to one functional area
- o   tasks to be performed by staff in one geographic location
- o   tasks relating to a particular deliverable
- o   tasks to be performed by team members belonging to the same division or department.

Ensure project structure and responsibilities are established.

Determine management systems

These will vary according to the size and nature of the project but should always include:

- o   a progress control system for recording planned and actual times. This could be an automated system or a manual one
- o   agreed procedures for formal review and agreement of each project deliverable
- o   scheduled management checkpoints.

If the project is divided into sub-projects, it is important that consistent management systems are used across them all.

Assign sub-project managers where appropriate. Clarify composition and responsibilities of the project steering group, and responsibilities of the project sponsor and the project manager.

Produce a project organization structure to show reporting lines.

Assemble and organize the project team

Projects are sometimes carried out by a team of people assembled for that specific purpose. The activities of this team may be co-ordinated by a project manager. Project teams may consist of people from different parts of the organization, and in some cases, people from different organizations. The selection of the team will be dependent upon the skill requirements of the project, and upon the matching of those to individual members of the team. Within a project, roles and responsibilities define the relationships between the project team and the work that has to be done. Project work is often multifaceted, requiring a combination of skills and activities for planning, execution and completion. Every key project activity should be clearly defined in terms of roles and responsibilities. Some team members will have dual responsibilities of involvement in the project, in addition to a commitment to other projects or management of a functional area on a day-to-day basis. It is at this stage that a project manager should be appointed and responsibilities made explicit for all members of the team.

Project scheduling

Scheduling the project
The aim is to ensure that resources are available when they are needed. This needs to be checked before building a project plan.

Creating a cost schedule

This phase is primarily concerned with attaching a timescale and sequence to the activities to be conducted within the project. Materials and people needed at each stage of the project are determined, and the time each is to take will be set. When resources are assigned to tasks, they create measurable work. This work in turn can incur cost. One common occurrence when working with resource assignments is that demand will invariably exceed supply. Some key people will be overworked and others will have time to spare. This inefficiency can be overcome by firstly looking at how people are utilized, and then by looking at the tasks within the project and determining how much free time (slack) they possess. Once these factors are understood, actions can be taken and decisions can be reached regarding who does what (most efficiently), when.

Resource conflicts

If resource demand exceeds supply, this is known as a resource conflict and needs to be resolved. An assignment is the relationship between a task and a resource. This relationship creates work – somebody doing something to achieve the objective of the task. Work, time and cost are resources of the project that are consumed in its execution. Doing some work will take some time and incur some cost.

Milestones

Milestones – measurable objectives that signal the completion of a major deliverable and indicate that you have reached a significant point in the project. Milestones can be established quickly if the project is on schedule, and can be useful when reporting on progress to management and clients.

Milestones are used to signify that something significant has been completed or something significant is ready to occur; for example, the start or beginning of a phase or the achievement of a key deliverable. The milestones and the information that need to be received and provided for different parts of the project need to be agreed with the project stakeholders. The information can be strategic and tactical.

Strategic

Strategic information would normally be provided for and by key stakeholders and would include:

- o Timing reports for the start and finish of major project phases
- o Start and finish dates for discrete tasks within a project phase
- o Cost schedules summarized by phase
- o Start and finish dates for tasks assigned to a particular skill or resource
- o Milestone date schedules a task's sub-deliverables, or a To-Do List.

Tactical

Tactical information would normally be shared between the project manager and members of their workgroup. This should include:

- o Start and finish dates for discrete tasks within a project phase
- o Cost schedules summarized by phase
- o Start and finish dates for tasks assigned to a particular skill or resource.

Gantt charts

Gantt charts are particularly helpful when scheduling and controlling a project which has a number of repetitive activities within it. The graphic display afforded by the Gantt chart not only helps the operations management of the project but also helps to co-ordinate the various activities in an efficient way.

The Gantt chart takes its name from Henry Gantt, the American engineer who created it. It is a technique that can be used for sequencing project activities. The chart is the most common report in all project management systems. It is a form of bar chart with horizontal bars drawn against a time scale for each project activity. The length of each bar represents the time taken to complete an activity.

To construct a Gantt chart, the various activities are listed on a vertical axis, and the horizontal axis is used to represent time. Activity precedences are taken into account by starting a horizontal bar to represent the next activity at an appropriate point after its preceding activities, i.e. those activities which must take place before the next activity can start, have taken place. Normally, this would be at the earliest time that it could start after its preceding activities had finished.

The timescale should cover the duration of the project – from the start to the project finish date. In between these dates, it should be divided into equal increments. Gantt charts are sometimes known as milestone plans and they provide a useful way of monitoring the progress of a project. The advantage of using them are:

- all activities are planned for
- the sequence of activities is accounted for
- the activity time estimates are recorded
- the overall project time is recorded.

Task Name	1 2 3 4 5 6 7 8 9 10 11 12 13 14 15 16 17 18 19 20 21 22 23 24 25 26 27 28 29 30

Figure 5.1 A Gantt timescale of 30 days

Once the chart's timescale has been created, tasks can be added. These tasks should be the complete list of sub-tasks as described within the network diagram, or from the lowest level of the outline (Work Breakdown Structure). The chart's timescale can be in days, weeks, months and so on. It must be linear and in equal increments, for Figure 5.2 increment per day or one increment per week.

Task Name	1	2	3	4	5	6	7	8	9	10	11	12	13	14	15	16	17	18	19	20	21	22	23	24	25	26	27	28	29	30
Design structure	■	■	■	■	■																									
Write body text								■	■	■	■	■	■	■	■	■	■	■	■	■										
Set page layouts																														
Create exercises								■	■	■	■	■	■	■	■	■	■													
Test exercises																														
Create contents & index																														

Figure 5.2 Example of a schedule for developing an online course

MONTH	APR	MAY	JUNE	JULY	AUG	SEPT
Marketing						
Broad sheet advertisements			▓			
Face-to-face meetings with clients			▓			
Direct mailing inserts into Marketing Success			▓			
Arrange corporate ID		▓				
Arrange printing of business cards		▓				

	APR	MAY	JUNE	JULY	AUG	SEPT
		▓				
Recruitment						
Recruitment Period				▓	▓	▓
London Recruitment fair			▓			
Programme Starts						
Administration						
Administration Support recruited			▓			
Partnership Agreement signed		▓				
Arrange professional indemnity insurance		▓				
Purchase Domain Name	▓					
Register with Data Protection Act	▓					
Finance						
Arrange online credit card payment system	▓					
Arrange bank loan	▓					
Website						
Design website	▓					
Design activities for website		▓	▓			
Write web guide			▓	▓		

Figure 5.3 Six month activity schedule

Displaying link lines between tasks

When a Gantt chart has a lot of links between tasks (especially cross-project links), the chart can become very busy with detail. When producing a Gantt chart for a client or a sponsor, decide if it is appropriate to tell them how tasks relate. They probably only need to know when tasks are scheduled to occur.

Once the project's schedule has been calculated (with critical path analysis) and a Gantt chart created, the next step in the planning process is to create some resource assignments. These assignments add the people dimension – someone doing something. What is important is a general understanding of the relationship between the task (something that needs to be achieved) and the resource (the individual that performs the work to achieve the task's objective). Gantt charts also provide a summary of the project as a whole, and can be used as a rough and ready means of assessing progress at the project control phase. At any date, the project manager can draw a dateline through the Gantt chart and see which activities are on time, which are behind schedule and generally record project status against plans.

Activity 5.1

Choose a project that you will be involved with at work and construct a Gantt chart which will provide an overview of the planned project.

When do you anticipate that you will start?

How soon could the project be completed?

Which activities need to be completed on time in order to ensure that the project is completed as soon as possible?

Show the shortest time it will take to complete the project.

Network analysis

The first step in network analysis is to divide the project into discrete 'activities' and 'events'. An event marks a point in time equating to the start or finish of an activity. An activity is a task or combination of small tasks that occurs between two events. Any activity that can be disaggregated and described by activities and events may be analysed within a network. The two most common and widely used project management techniques that can be classified under the title of Network Analysis are Programme Evaluation and Review Technique (PERT) and Critical Path Method (CPM).

PERT/CPM

There are six stages common to both PERT and CPM:

1. Define the project and specify all activities or tasks
2. Develop the relationships amongst activities. Decide upon precedences
3. Draw network to connect all activities
4. Assign time and/or costs to each activity
5. Calculate the longest time path through the network: this is the 'critical path'
6. Use network to plan, monitor and control the project. A network diagram is used to express how all the tasks in a project relate to each other. It helps to show how all the project tasks interrelate. A network diagram is also good for showing cross-project links.

Both models can help to answer the following questions for projects with thousands of activities and events, both at the beginning of the project and once it is underway:

1. When will the project be completed?
2. What are the critical activities (i.e. the tasks which, if delayed, will affect time for overall completion)?
3. Which activities are non-critical and can run late without delaying project completion time?
4. What is the probability of the project being completed by a specific date?
5. At any particular time, is the project on schedule?
6. At any particular time, is the money spent equal to, less than or more than the budgeted amount?
7. Are there enough resources left to complete the project on time?

Probability analysis

Once the expected completion time and variance have been determined, the probability that a project will be completed by a specific date can be assessed. The assumption is usually made that the distribution of completion dates follows that of a normal distribution curve. If the project is to be completed in a shorter time, what is the least cost means to accomplish this and what are the cost consequences?

Critical path analysis

This is a method for scheduling when tasks will happen. A critical task is one that must be completed on schedule for the project to finish on time. If a critical task is delayed, the project finish date might also be delayed. A series of critical tasks make up a project's critical path.

As the tasks within a project have links between them, they cannot all happen at the same time. Critical path analysis (CPA) can be used to determine what can happen when. It calculates how quickly and how slowly the tasks can be performed, taking into account the sequence of tasks and the interrelationships between them. Gantt charts are created as a result of CPA.

Critical path analysis is a procedure that calculates a project's schedule. Taking each task in turn, it first calculates how quickly the task can be accomplished – its early start and early finish dates. Once all these dates have been calculated, the project finish date can also be determined. With this finish date known, CPA can then calculate how slowly each task can be accomplished (late start and late finish dates). Once all this information is known for each task, CPA will also calculate the slack that the task possesses.

The objective of CPA is to determine times for:

ES = Earliest Start Time. This is the earliest time an activity can be started, allowing for the fact that all preceding activities have been completed.

LS = Latest Start Time. This is the latest time an activity can be started without delaying the start of following activities which would put the entire project behind schedule.

EF = Earliest Finish Time. The earliest time an activity can be finished.

LF = Latest Finish Time. The latest time that an activity can finish for the project to remain on schedule.

S = Activity Slack Time. The amount of slippage in activity start or duration time which can be tolerated without delaying the project as a whole.

Once these values are known, the overall project can be analysed. The critical path is the group of activities in the project that have a slack time of zero. This path of activities is critical because a delay in any activity along it would delay the project as a whole. Finding the critical path is a major activity in controlling a project. Managers can derive flexibility by identifying the non-critical activities and replanning, rescheduling and re-allocating resources such as manpower and finances within identified boundaries.

PERT

The major difference between CPM and PERT is that the latter employs three time estimates for each activity. Probabilities are attached to each of these times which, in turn, is used for computing expected values and potential variations for activity times. CPM assumes that activity times are known and fixed, so only one time estimate is given and used for each activity. The three time estimates specified for each activity in PERT are:

- the optimistic time
- the most probable time
- the pessimistic time.

The optimistic, most likely, and pessimistic time estimates are used to calculate an expected activity completion time which, because of the skewed nature of the beta distribution, is marginally greater than the most likely time estimate. In addition, the three time estimates can be used to calculate the variance for each activity. The formulae used are as follows:

When using PERT, the expected times are calculated first from the three values of activity time estimates, and it is these values that are then used exactly as in CPM. The variance values are calculated for the various activity times and the variance of the total project completion time is the sum of the variances of the activities lying on that critical path.

Reviewing progress

It is the job of the project manager to make sure that the project stays on track and the deliverables meet the specifications detailed in the project definition document, as well as managing client expectations by keeping all relevant parties informed about the project's status. The project has a greater chance of success if the client is actively involved. The broad aims of reviewing are to:

Compare – Find variances between the baseline schedule and actual progress – cost variances and work variances.

Evaluate – Are the project's objectives still able to be met? Do the variances indicate the development of a trend?

Decide – Perform a 'what-if' analysis to overcome the variances and get the project back on track. This is a method of experimentation to determine the optimum schedule of tasks or utilization of resources. A 'what-if' analysis may need to be carried out more than once.

Inform – Inform all project team members of revisions to the project's schedule, individual schedules and deliverables met. If certain tasks or resources are constantly going over budget or always taking longer than planned, could a trend be developing?

Managing communication

Effective communication with the relevant parties is the key to a successful project. The project manager should develop a communications plan in order to gather progress information from the team, supply timely reports and gather feedback from the management and the client.

Collecting information from team members

Regular contact is needed with individual team members to evaluate the status of their work and to deal with any questions they have or issues that need to be resolved. There is no need to waste time by insisting on written reports when information can be gathered easily in other ways from face-to-face meetings, e-mail or telephone calls.

Information should be gathered at regular intervals and any issues that are raised by the project team should be dealt with promptly.

Project meetings

Project meetings give the team, including management and the client representative, an opportunity to evaluate the project's status as a whole and to highlight issues that the team as a whole need to deal with. These meetings provide an opportunity to raise issues that concern the big picture even if they are only noted to be dealt with at a later time.

Reports to management and the client

Depending on the size of the project, status reports should be submitted to the management and the client to keep those who do not attend the project status meetings up to date. These may not be necessary for small projects, but for medium and large projects bi-monthly or monthly reports would be appropriate.

Managing client expectations

Managing client expectations is one of the tasks of the project manager and the project definition document is a tool that is useful in this process. By identifying clear project deliverables and constraints, the client should know what to expect from the outset of the project.

Once the project is underway, you then need to carefully manage scope change. Any changes to scope, whether suggested by the client or a member of the team, should be carefully discussed with the client. Pros and cons of the change should be weighed up, and if it is decided to go ahead, a formal scope change document should be presented to and signed by the client.

Managing the project plan

The progress of the project can be tracked by noting the status of each task at regular intervals. Sofware such as Microsoft Project offers three methods for tracking progress:

- o **percentage of work complete** – This is the least accurate but fastest way to track. Asking team members to report their progress according to this method can result in misleading reports due to the human tendency to at times be 'almost done' for prolonged periods
- o **actual work completed** – This is more accurate, but also more time consuming
- o **hours of work completed per time period** – This is the most accurate but most time consuming, as people need to specify the exact hours they have worked in particular time periods.

Adding tasks

Sometimes the project will demand the addition of tasks that had not been previously identified, or the scope of the project may have changed. The project plan will need to be adjusted to create a new baseline.

Take note of when milestones are met and review the plan to ensure that it will meet the delivery date. If not, remedial action will be needed. Problems with the budget need to be resolved quickly, so it needs to be reviewed on a regular basis and reports submitted to the relevant parties.

Managing the scope of the project

The project manager is in charge of managing the scope of the project, so that only what was agreed is delivered unless changes have been formally agreed. The project manager needs to ensure that everybody involved remembers the project objective.

Mission creep occurs when the client or team members lose sight of the agreed project objectives. This can be avoided by creating a clear and unambiguous project and scope definition at the outset, and by constantly referring to this definition during the course of the project. The project's scope may also change upon request. Changing the scope of a project often means that a client has asked for extra work.

Budgeting

A budget is an expression of an organization's planned activities and serves a number of purposes. It is a forecast of the resources likely to be available to the organization and a plan for utilizing these resources to achieve the organization's objectives. It is also a framework for authorizing the expenditure of resources and for maintaining control over that expenditure.

Budgeting is the most common control mechanism of any planning process. Control is based on comparing actual against planned expenditure and investigating any variances calculated. It is important that sales and production targets are met and budgeting provides a standard against which the performance of the organization as a whole and the performance of individuals may be judged.

Budgeting systems also need to be flexible in enabling resources to be deployed quickly in response to changing demands from the environment and also motivate staff to use resources effectively and efficiently.

Managing quality

The project manager should ensure that the project's quality standard is understood by everyone concerned and that deliverables meet that standard. Check-lists and regular reviews focussing on the subject can assist in this process.

Post project reviews

Some issues to consider:

- Were the main objectives met?
- Was enough time allocated to each task?
- Were there any warning signs that were ignored?
- Did everyone understand the project definition and their roles?
- Was the project on time and to budget and why?
- Was the relationship with the client satisfactory, or did unforeseen problems arise?
- Was the quality control process sufficient?

Successful project management

The effectiveness of project management is critical in assuring the success of any substantial undertaking. Areas of responsibility for the project manager include planning, control and implementation.

Knowledge, skills, goals and personalities are all factors that need to be considered within project management. The project manager and his/her team should possess the necessary interpersonal and technical skills to control the project activities.

The stages of implementation must be identified at the project planning phase. In addition to planning, the control of the project is also a necessary condition of success. This means adequate monitoring and feedback mechanisms to facilitate comparisons of progress against projections. Monitoring and feedback also enables minor problems to be anticipated and addressed before they become major ones. Consulting with end-users is important for ensuring the success of a project.

Activity 5.2

Can you think of any examples where your organization needs to respond to change and a project management approach may be valid?

The reasons for project failure

Common reasons are as follows:

- Project goals are not clearly defined
- The assumptions that are made at the outset of the project are incorrect but remain unchallenged
- The project team is not sure of the project objectives or the deliverables
- The planned schedule overruns
- The budget is exceeded
- Lack of co-ordination of resources and activities
- Lack of communication with interested parties, leading to products being delivered that are not what the customer wanted
- Poor estimation of duration and costs, leading to projects taking more time and costing more money than expected
- Inadequate planning of resources, activities and scheduling
- Lack of control over progress, so that projects do not reveal their exact status until too late
- Lack of quality control, resulting in the delivery of products that are unacceptable or unusable.

Problems with project goals

- The project sponsor or client has an inadequate idea of what the project is about at the start
- Failure of communication between the client and the project manager. This may be due to a lack of technical knowledge on the part of the client or an overuse of jargon by the project manager
- Specifications may be subject to constant change. This may be due to problems with individual clients, decision-making processes at the client's end, or environmental changes. For example the government may change the basic 'rules of the game' before the completion of the project
- The project goals may be unrealistic and unachievable, and it may be that this is only realized once the project is under way
- Projects may be complex and objectives may contradict each other.

There are perhaps two stages which can help in ensuring that goals are properly defined and achievable:

Ensuring that the client specification is clear and understandable. To do this the following objectives of the project must be established:

- What is it that the organization is setting out to achieve or is being asked to achieve?
- Will the suggested project fulfil these objectives?
- Have all the alternatives been considered, and is the chosen option the best one available?
- Have the full effects of the project, both inside and outside the organization, been considered?

Constraints on the completion of projects
Time
The definition of a project stated that it was an activity which had a defined beginning and ending point. Most projects will be close-ended in terms of there being a requirement for completion by a certain point of time. This point may be the result of an external factor such as new legislation, or may be derived from organizational requirements. It may also be partly determined by other constraints. There is likely to be some relationship between the time taken for a project and its cost. A trade-off between the two constraining factors may then be necessary.

Resource availability
There is likely to be a budget for the project and this will clearly be a major constraint. Cost constraints may be set in a number of ways, for example as an overall cash limit or as a detailed budget broken down over a number of expenditure headings. Labour resources in particular may be a limiting factor on the completion of the project. Whilst the overall resource available may be, in theory, sufficient to complete the project, there may be difficulties arising out of the way in which the project has been scheduled. That is, there may be a number of activities scheduled to take place at the same time and this may not be possible, given the amount of resources available.

Quality factors
Whether the project delivers the goods to the right quality. There are techniques which can be used to overcome the problems referred to above. These include:

- budgeting and the corresponding control of the project budget through budgetary control
- procedures
- project planning and control techniques such as Gantt charts and network analysis.

The various constraints on project completion are likely to be interlinked with each other. For example, problems with time constraints or resource constraints may be overcome by spending more through working overtime, employing more people or purchasing better machines. Budget problems may have a knock-on effect on the achievement of deadlines.

Provided the project is not too complex in its activity relationships or simply too big to be mapped on reasonably sized graph paper, Gantt charts can be very useful tools for the project manager and are graphically superior to the network analysis methods of CPM and PERT.

They allow the critical activities to be found, i.e. those activities which must be performed on time if the project duration is not to increase, and any 'slack' or 'float' in the sequence of activities can easily be shown.

By timetabling the activities by horizontal bars whose lengths represent the activity times, the earliest completion date for the entire project can be mapped out by the Gantt chart, and then used as indicated above by the operations manager to check on progress as the project proceeds.

Management of projects

Gantt charts, PERT, CPM and other scheduling techniques have proven to be valuable tools in the management of large and complex projects. A wide variety of software packages are available for project managers, for use on micro or larger computers, to assist in the handling of complex network problems. PERT and CPM, however, cannot ever purport to be able to solve all project scheduling and management problems in service or manufacturing industries. Good management practices, clear responsibilities for tasks, and accurate and timely reporting systems are the most essential qualities for successful project completion. As useful as these techniques are, they are only tools to assist the manager in making better, more calculated decisions in the process of conducting large scale projects.

The role of the project manager falls into three areas:

- o   Management of stakeholders
- o   Management of the project life cycle
- o   Management of performance.

Management of stakeholders

Stakeholders' interests must be monitored to ensure that their:

- o   Interest and support is maintained
- o   Views and ideas are being adequately reflected in the project development
- o   Personal success criteria are being pursued and achieved.

Management of the project life cycle

Feedback systems need to be set up to monitor key areas.

Management of performance

This is the least tangible but possibly the most important of the three categories. How it is tackled will depend upon what kind of project is being carried out. It is likely that they will work apart most of the time, meeting up only occasionally and meeting only with the project manager from time to time. Issues that need to be considered are:

- o   How to get the best out of the team when they are together
- o   Ensuring people work when the team is apart
- o   Disseminating information and keeping everyone informed is important
- o   Ensuring continuing commitment by the team
- o   Communicating change to team members quickly and effectively
- o   It is important to look at the team and also for the project leader to look at his or her own performance.

Project management and network techniques such as CPM and PERT are valuable tools for showing relationships between project activities, and identifying critical activities but the management of people is a major factor in whether a project will be a success or not. The ability to motivate staff, to create the structures and conditions in which they can be motivated and work effectively, and dealing with any people problems that arise are also essential features of project management. The human factors are as important as having the right tools and techniques. Working in teams and motivation have been looked at in other chapters so they won't be repeated here, but they are very important.

143

Five rules for delivering criticism
Project managers need to create and maintain good working relationships but they also need to monitor others' performance and act if there is a problem.

1. Think it through before you say something
A problem worth solving demands concentrated attention and focus to gain desired outcomes. This may mean not saying anything at all until you have mentally rehearsed your delivery and envisioned the receiver's response.

2. Criticize in private
Public criticism offends the receivers and observers. When a problem arises during a team meeting, acknowledge it and say that this is something that needs to be addressed 'later' 'without taking up everyone's time'.

3. Respond to problems in a timely fashion
Realize your own propensity to put off discussing problem behaviours. Remember the difficulty in reconstructing problems because everyone remembers them differently. Compare that to the benefits of a timely focus on correcting one problem at a time.

4. Criticize without comparison
Broad, unfavourable comparisons mean that individuals will end up finding fault with you rather than dealing with the ambiguous criticism levied at them.

5. Criticize with specificity, not labels
Examples of specific behaviours are: Inaccuracy, lateness, absenteeism, interrupting, missed timelines, incompleteness, incorrectness , assumptions, data, etc. Criticism or feedback that cites specific examples such as these requires no interpretation of meaning. A missed commitment, is a missed commitment. These concrete descriptions focus on quantifiable problems and achievable improvements.

Source: Parie, Claudine. E., 2000

Activity 5.3

For a project that is already underway in your organization, identify the key areas requiring monitoring, and suggest the kind of information and procedures that would be involved.

Differences between a functional manager and a project manager
A functional manager is likely to be a specialist in the area being managed, such that when technical knowledge is required or a difficult issue arises in an area, he should be able to make some realistic recommendations about how to tackle it. (Meredith, J. and Mantel, S., 1995)

Responsibilities of a project manager

- o   To plan the project, soliciting the active involvement of all functional areas involved, in order to obtain and maintain a realistic plan that satisfies their commitment for performance
- o   To control the organization of human resources needed by the project
- o   To control the basic technical definition of the project, ensuring that 'technical' versus 'cost' trade-offs determine the specific areas where optimisation is necessary

- To lead the people and organizations assigned to the project at any given point of time. Strong positive leadership must be exercised in order to keep the many disparate elements moving in the same direction in a co-operative manner
- To monitor performance, costs and efficiency of all elements of the project and the project as a whole, exercising judgement and leadership in determining the causes of problems and facilitating solutions
- To complete the project on schedule and within costs, these being the overall standard by which performance of the project manager is evaluated.

The skills of a project manager

The PM is expected to integrate all aspects of the project, to ensure that the proper knowledge and resources are available when and where needed, and above all to ensure that the expected results are produced in a timely, cost-effective manner.

A project manager is more likely to be a generalist who is required to bring together a number of functional areas, each comprising specialists in their own fields. The PM's task is to bring them together to form a coherent whole. The project manager needs to be able to synthesize a wide range of information, whereas a functional manager must be more skilled in analysing a narrower area. The functional manager needs a depth of experience whilst the project manager needs breadth. The authors argue that an analytical approach breaks a system down into smaller and smaller parts, but a systems approach tries to understand the links between different elements. However, there is no doubt that an effective project manager needs the skills of analysis and synthesis.

Skill dimensions that a Project Manager needs to use at different points in the project management cycle (from Elbeik, S. and Thomas, M., 1998):

Administrator

- accomplishment of project tasks and goals
- strong management of repetitive tasks and procedures
- adhering to routines and systematic controls
- focus on stability and consistency
- able to meet deadlines and cope with workloads
- organizing skills
- a concern for detail and accuracy.

Analyst

- strong problem-solving orientation
- high level of critical thinking ability
- ability to synthesize other people's thought and actions
- a strategic outlook – able to see the 'bigger picture'
- able to balance short, medium and longer term requirements.

Negotiator

- influencing and persuasion skills
- diplomatic
- willingness to challenge and tackle others
- able to 'read' situations and identify motives and needs
- determination to achieve objectives.

Verbal communicator

o able to present arguments persuasively
o able to communicate effectively with people from different backgrounds and levels of seniority
o effective range of responses to most situations and able to think on his or her feet
o able to secure people's attention
o political sensitivity.

Written communicator

o able to keep written communications brief and to the point
o able to express complexity in a form that makes it accessible to the audience for whom it is intended
o can write persuasively
o can write with accuracy and precision
o political sensitivity.

Listener

Those who are answering questions need to be convinced that someone:

o is listening to them
o is interested in what they say
o understands what they are saying
o active listening is the skill of demonstrating to the person who is speaking that you are listening
o empathy and the ability to develop rapport.

Motivator

o commands respect
o persuasive and influential
o able to enthuse people
o highly developed interpersonal skills
o able to achieve results through others
o Different people may respond to various techniques of persuasion in different ways, and it is important to know how to approach people so that they will be motivated to take appropriate action.

Decision maker

o capable of making decisions in the face of incomplete information
o able to absorb a lot of information and identify what is significant about it
o able to keep project aims and objectives in mind and avoid becoming bogged down in detail.

Three questions face the PM at the outset of a project :

o What needs to be done?
o When must it be done?
o How are the resources needed by the project to be obtained?

Using IT
Computer software for project management
A wide variety of software packages is available to help with the scheduling and controlling of projects. Examples of the kind of software which an organization uses are:

- ABC Flowchart
- Harvard Project Manager III
- On-Target
- Microsoft Project
- Suretrak
- Project Schedular V5
- Super Project V2
- Time Line
- InstaPlan.

Managing large team projects
When managing a project it may be necessary to bring together partner firms, suppliers, subcontractors, and team members who don't sit in the same building, or even in the same state or country. This presents challenges of monitoring, managing and integrating:

- Information flow (up, down, and across the team)
- Scheduling, change control and logistics
- Work planning and staffing requirements.

All project team members need to be able to contribute their part of the project at the right time and place. This synergy of time, information and action depends on communication, collaboration and reporting. All of this is influenced by software capabilities.

Using a workgroup messaging system
The success of a project often depends on quick and effective communication between team members. Members of a team can be linked through a workgroup messaging system; for example, Microsoft Project allows for almost instant exchange of project information. A workgroup messaging system is a network that is used to send and receive information about task status and assignments. Each team member should have access to this network, and be able to receive and send workgroup messages.

PRINCE
PRINCE (Projects in Controlled Environments) is a project management method covering the organization, management and control of projects. Since its introduction, PRINCE has become widely-used in both the public and private sectors. Although PRINCE was originally developed for the needs of IT projects, the method has also been used on many non-IT projects. PRINCE2 is designed as a generic approach for the management of all types of projects. Each process is defined with its key inputs and outputs together with the specific objectives to be achieved.

Project evaluation
The main reasons for project evaluation and feedback are:

- to ensure that the project remains on track
- to confirm whether the project meets user needs
- to determine whether the project delivers value for money
- to transfer the knowledge and any lessons from one project to other projects.

One reason for carrying out evaluation as an ongoing process during the project, rather than as a single post project evaluation at the end of the project, is to ensure that important information and lessons are not forgotten.

The Post Project Review

The Post Project Review is performed by a project team at the end of the project's life cycle to gather information on what worked well and what did not, so that future projects can benefit from that learning. Participants in the Post Project Review process are members of the project team, key stakeholders and users of the project deliverables or results. Lessons learned from the Post Project Review should be archived so that it is easy for project team members, process improvement teams and managers to find useful information.

The Post Implementation Review/Post Project Review

The purpose of the Post Project Review is to find out whether the expected benefits of the project have been realized, and if lessons learned from the project will lead to recommendations for improvements.

Fitness for purpose checklist:

Are all benefits mentioned in the Project Brief and is the Business Case covered?

Does it describe each achievement in a tangible, measurable form?

Are there recommendations in any case where a benefit is not being fully met, a problem has been identified, or a potential extra benefit could be obtained?

Has this been conducted as soon as the benefits and problems can be measured?

Was this scheduled in the project/programme plan?

Project review checklist

When the project was complete, did the project outcomes meet user requirements without additional work?

How close to scheduled completion was the project actually completed?

What factors enabled the team to stay on schedule?

What factors caused delays?

Overall, what did you learn about scheduling on this project that will help you on the next project?

Budget

How close to the budget was the final project cost?

What did you learn about budgeting that will help you on the next project?

Team issues

What did you learn about staffing that will help you on the next project?

What worked or didn't work about team communications?

What was effective or ineffective about how information was distributed? Did you have the right skill mix?

Managing relationships

What lessons did you learn about managing the working relationship with your client?

What lessons did you learn about managing working relationships with other departments or divisions?

What techniques or systems did you develop for this project that could be used on other projects?

List any recommendations you have for future development.

If you could do the project again, what would you do differently?

Summary

In recent years, project teams and a project management approach have become common in many organizations. The basic approach to project management should be the same regardless of the type of project or sector in which the project is carried out. Project management is associated with a precise set of techniques, definitions and practices that can be used. These are all useful and demonstrate how a systematic approach can be used. However, skills in managing people are equally important. Many people are involved in managing projects as only part of their job and have to carry it out alongside other activities. A project should possess identifiable goals, and a definite starting and finishing point. Project goals should be defined clearly. Managing stakeholders expectations is a major part of a project manager's role. The major constraints on the completion of projects are time, resource availability and the need to achieve the required standard of performance for the project.

Further Study

Read Elbeik and Thomas – *Project Skills* Chapters 2 – 4.

Hints and Tips

It is useful to have an overview of the principles and techniques of project management. There are no surprises in the techniques that are used and they can be applied to a wide variety of situations where a systematic approach is needed.

Bibliography

Elbeik, S. and Thomas, M., (1998). *Project Skills*, Oxford: Butterworth Heinemann.

Meredith, J. and Mantel, S., (1995). *Project Management – A Managerial Approach*, New York: Wiley.

Paris, Claudine, E., (2000). http://www.4pm.com/.

> Sample exam questions and answers for the Marketing Management in Practice module as a whole can be found in Appendix 3 at the back of the book.

unit 6 managing change

Explain the sources and nature of change affecting organizations, and the techniques available for managing change.

Introduction

Organizations face change all the time, driven by internal and/or external influences. Most changes in organizations are minor and incremental. A few changes are major and involve completely new ways of operating. Managing change means taking active control of change because many problems are those of adaptation, i.e. they require of the organization only that it adjusts to an ever-changing set of circumstances. Factors from outside the business include: technological developments, changing market conditions, such as exchange rate movements, supplier price increases and demand from customers for new services, legislation, such as the working time regulations and the minimum wage. Factors from inside the business include: personnel changes, such as key employees leaving and new senior appointments. New management processes such as customer service initiatives are also a source of change, and there are constant pressures to improve efficiency in both the public and private sectors.

The macro-environment

This includes all factors that can influence an organization, but that are out of their direct control. A company does not generally influence any laws (although it is accepted that they could lobby or be part of a trade organization). It is continuously changing, and the company needs to be flexible to adapt. There may be agressive competition and rivalry in a market.

Globalization

Globalization is helping to remove restrictions on where people can go, what they can buy, where they can invest, and what they can read, hear or see. Economic integration is driven by two forces: advances in technology and decisions to liberalize trade. Globalization means that there is always the threat of substitute products and new entrants. The wider environment is also ever changing, and the marketer needs to take account of changes in culture, politics, economics and technology.

However, there are unanswered questions concerning those people who lose out economically, socially and culturally. Globalization has had a mixed press and has been violently denounced at demonstrations during World Trade Organisation meetings. The growth in availability of Fair Trade products signals greater interest in the ethics of trade. Critics argue that globalization has led to rising global inequality and exploitation of the poor by transnational companies.

Supporters of globalization argue that the number of people in extreme poverty – living on less than a dollar a day – fell from about 30 per cent of the world population in 1980 to 20 per cent in 1997, according to the World Bank. They also argue that the relatively rapid growth of China and India has led to an improved income distribution, not a deterioration.

A series of corporate scandals that began with the collapse of Enron has caused a crisis of legitimacy and the business of wealth creation has been tarnished. At Enron, this took the form of generating phony profits, whilst at WorldCom, accountants turned operating expenses into capital assets.

The micro-environment

This environment influences the organization directly. It includes suppliers, consumers and customers, and other local stakeholders. Micro describes the relationship between organizations and the driving forces that control this relationship. It may be more of a local relationship, and the organization may be able to exert its influence. Some external influences like globalization affect all organizations, directly or indirectly, whilst other influences may be more specific to particular sectors. For example, at present the Government has a 'modernization agenda' that claims to be aimed at improving public services, as the following insight demonstrates.

The public sector is faced with the challenge to improve the service it delivers to its customers. A gap has opened up between what commercial services can deliver and what we can expect from public services. For example, two-thirds of the people in this country now own mobile telephones and the cost of calls has fallen by nearly one-quarter over the past two years. We can buy cheap fresh food from around the world at any time of the day or night at a local supermarket or, if we prefer, over the phone or the PC. Meanwhile, it is still difficult to find a public library open before or after work or at any time on Sundays, and GP surgery hours are similarly limited. For increasing numbers of us today, the widening gulf between what we can buy as customers and what we get as public service users has created a credibility gap. Moreover, the public sector must serve all sections of society, not just those with money in their pockets. Change is not a simple, linear process, and improving the experience of users requires not only changes to systems and procedures in what are often huge, complex and interdependent organizations, but also changes in the attitudes and behaviour of individual members of staff. Change is painful and destructive as well as positive and creative. It challenges vested interests: personal, professional and institutional. Change is unavoidable; potentially both exciting and rewarding, but at the same time a messy and difficult enterprise, frequently confounding the intentions of managers, politicians and policymakers. There is no magic formula for change management, but there is a body of useful experience about what works and that can help build long-term capacity for the future.

Managing change can be aided by undertaking a stakeholder analysis:

Stakeholder analysis

Stakeholder analysis is the technique used to identify the key people who have to be won over. By communicating with stakeholders early and frequently, you can ensure that they fully understand what you are doing, and understand the benefits of your project – this means they can support you actively when necessary.

Identifying your stakeholders

The first step in your stakeholder analysis is to brainstorm who your stakeholders are. As part of this, think of all the people who are affected by your work, who have influence or power over it, or have an interest in its successful or unsuccessful conclusion.

- o Your line manger
- o Shareholders
- o Senior executives
- o Your coworkers
- o Suppliers
- o Your team
- o Interest groups
- o Customers
- o The public
- o Prospective customers
- o Future recruits.

Prioritize your stakeholders

You may now have a long list of people and organizations that are affected by your work. Some of these may have the power either to block or advance. Some may be interested in what you are doing, others may not care. For example, your line manager is likely to have high power and influence over your projects and high interest.

Key questions that can help you understand your stakeholders

What interest do they have in the outcome of your work? Is it positive or negative?

What information do they want from you?

How do they want to receive information from you? What is the best way of communicating your message to them?

What is their current opinion of your work? Is it based on good information?

If they are not likely to be positive, what will win them around to support your project?

If you don't think you will be able to win them around, how will you manage their opposition?

Write your responses to these questions.

Estimate attitude and confidence in a particular change

Estimate the stakeholder's attitude, from supportive to opposed

- o strongly in favour
- o weakly in favour
- o indifferent or undecided
- o weakly opposed
- o strongly opposed.

How confident you are about your estimate

- o fully confident
- o reasonably confident (some missing information, perhaps)
- o an informed guess
- o wild guess.

Your best estimate of the influence of the stakeholder

H – High; this person or group has power of veto, formally or informally

M – Medium; you could probably achieve your goals against this person's or group's opposition, but not easily

L – Low; This person can do little to influence the outcomes of your intended actions

Plan strategies

Plan your strategies for approaching and involving each person or group. It usually takes the form of obtaining more information, or of involving the stakeholder in the planning for the change. Highly influential people need to be involved in some way, or their influence needs to be neutralized. The people or groups who require the most attention are those who are influential and opposed to a change.

The internal environment of the organization

As mentioned above, factors that are internal to the organization are known as the 'internal environment'. As mentioned above these can include, for example, personnel changes or new management processes or demands to improve efficiency. They are sometimes ascertained by applying what is called the 'Five Ms' which are (Wo) Men, Money, Machinery, Materials and Markets. The internal environment is as important for managing change as the external. Change is likely to be needed when, for example, responding to newly identified markets, or taking up the cost-saving opportunities offered by new technologies. They may be sponsored by a 'champion', perhaps a new Managing Director or Marketing Director.

Implications for marketing

Some of the implications have been discussed in other units, for example, being sensitive to cultural differences when working in a multinational environment and the impact of information and communications technology on approaches to marketing. Marketing management is the process of planning and executing the conception, pricing, promotion and distribution of goods, services and ideas, to create exchanges with target groups that satisfy customer and organizational objectives. The emphasis is shifting from transaction-oriented marketing to relationship marketing, and organizations need to retain customer loyalty through continually satisfying their needs in a superior way.

Marketing teams must implement processes that co-ordinate all marketing and sales activities and achieve the level of data access, collection and sharing that is critical to consistent messaging, lead tracking, sales conversion and ongoing marketing intelligence. With the availability of websites, e-mail and mobile devices, and the introduction of high-powered packages for targeting customers, marketing should be easier than ever. However, the increase in marketing contact causes prospects to feel overloaded, reducing response rates and the value of marketing effort. Lack of co-ordination further erodes marketing effectiveness.

Marketers need to know when to:

- o cultivate large markets or niche markets
- o launch new brands or extend existing brand names
- o push or pull products through distribution
- o protect the domestic market or penetrate aggressively into foreign markets
- o add more benefits to the offer or reduce the price
- o expand or contract budgets for sales force, advertising and other marketing tools.

A product is anything that can be offered to a market for attention, acquisition, use, or consumption that might satisfy a want or need.

A CIPD survey (Whittington P.R. and Mayer M., 2002.) confirms that reorganizations are more successful when the commitment of employees is directly engaged. Yet, they continue to be a top-down, project-driven process where people often take second place to changes in structures and systems. This can have a detrimental effect. For example, fewer than half of the 800 reorganization initiatives covered by the survey delivered the required improvement in internal flexibility or increased customer responsiveness. Most businesses undergo a major reorganization at least once every three years. The increasing complexity of business and the intensity with which knowledge flows is placing organizational design high on the executive agenda. With the potential to maximize or destroy value, redesign is not a one-off episode; it is a high-stakes activity that managers must repeatedly engage with. Neither is it only about getting the structure right. One challenge emerging from the survey is how to manage three streams of integrated activity: changes in the structure, processes and human capability. Doing this successfully requires a sophisticated leadership that strikes the right balance between project discipline and employee involvement. Reorganizations are typically managed within project disciplines, with a clear statement of objectives, defined timescales and milestones. The image of the chief executive redrawing the lines of the organization chart on the back of a cigarette packet is a fading one. Adopting project disciplines pays, and is more likely to lead to successful outcomes. Redesigns that featured strong project discipline and employee involvement were more likely to deliver both direct bottom-line benefit, and improved morale and retention. But the survey found that employees had a say in the design in less than a third of all reorganizations, and in only a half were there consultations about how the final organizational design could be implemented.

The change problem

At the heart of change management lies the change problem. It might be large or small in scope and scale, and it might focus on individuals or groups, on one or more divisions or departments, the entire organization, or on one or more aspects of the organization's environment. Problems may be formulated in terms of 'how', 'what' and 'why' questions. Which formulation is used depends on where in the organization the person posing the question or formulating the problem is situated, and where the organization is situated in its own life cycle.

The approach to change management mirrors management's mindset

The emphasis placed on the three types of questions reflects the management mindset, that is, the tendency to think along certain lines depends on where one is situated in the organization. A person's placement in the organization typically defines the scope and scale of the kinds of changes with which he or she will become involved, and the nature of the changes with which he or she will be concerned. Thus, the systems people tend to be concerned with technology and technological developments, the marketing people with customer needs and competitive activity, the legal people with legislative and other regulatory actions and so on.

Classic skills for leaders

The most important things a leader can bring to a changing organization are passion, conviction and confidence in others. Too often, executives announce a plan, launch a task force, and then simply hope that people find the answers – instead of offering a dream, stretching their horizons and encouraging people to do the same. That is why we say, 'leaders go first'. However, leaders can use several techniques to take charge of change rather than simply react to it. In working with leaders for nearly 20 years, I have found the following classic skills to be equally useful to CEOs, senior executives, or middle managers who want to move an idea forward.

Tuning in to the environment

As a leader you can't possibly know enough, or be in enough places, to understand everything happening inside – and more importantly outside – your organization. But you can actively collect information that suggests new approaches. You can create a network of listening posts – a satellite office, a joint venture, a community service. Rubbermaid operates its own stores, for instance, even though it sells mostly to Wal-Mart and other big chains. These stores allow the company to listen to and learn from customers. Likewise, partnerships and alliances help you not only to accomplish particular tasks; they also provide knowledge about things happening in the world that you wouldn't see otherwise.

Challenging the prevailing organizational wisdom

Leaders need to develop kaleidoscope thinking – a way of constructing patterns from the fragments of data available, and then manipulating them to form different patterns. They must question their assumptions about how pieces of the organization, the marketplace, or the community fit together. Change leaders remember that there are many solutions to a problem and that by looking through a different lens somebody is going to invent, for instance, a new way to deliver health care. There are lots of ways to promote kaleidoscopic thinking. Send people outside the company – not just on field trips, but 'far afield trips'. Go outside your industry and return with fresh ideas. Rotate job assignments and create interdisciplinary project teams to give people fresh ideas and opportunities to test their assumptions. For instance, one innovative department of a U.S. oil company regularly invites people from many different departments to attend large brainstorming sessions. These allow interested outsiders to ask questions, make suggestions and trigger new ideas.

You cannot sell change without genuine conviction

You cannot sell change, or anything else, without genuine conviction, because there are so many sources of resistance to overcome: 'We've never done it before; we tried it before and it didn't work.' 'Things are OK now, so why should we change?' Especially when you are pursuing a true innovation as opposed to responding to a crisis, you've got to make a compelling case. Leaders talk about communicating a vision as an instrument of change, but I prefer the notion of communicating an aspiration. It's not just a picture of what could be; it is an appeal to our better selves, a call to become something more. It reminds us that the future does not just descend like a stage set; we construct the future from our own history, desires and decisions.

Building coalitions

Change leaders need the involvement of people who have the resources, the knowledge and the political clout to make things happen. You want the opinion shapers, the experts in the field, the values leaders. That sounds obvious, but coalition building is probably the most neglected step in the change process.

In the early stages of planning change, leaders must identify key supporters and sell their dream with the same passion and deliberation as the entrepreneur. You may have to reach deep into, across, and outside the organization to find key influencers, but you first must be willing to reveal an idea or proposal before it's ready. Secrecy denies you the opportunity to get feedback, and when things are sprung on people with no warning, the easiest answer is always no. Coalition building requires an understanding of the politics of change, and in any organization those politics are formidable.

When building coalitions, however, it's a mistake to try to recruit everybody at once. Think of innovation as a venture. You want the minimum number of investors necessary to launch a new venture and to champion it when you need help later.

Transferring ownership to a working team

Once a coalition is in place, you can enlist others in implementation. You must remain involved – the leader's job is to support the team, provide coaching and resources, and patrol the boundaries within which the team can freely operate. But you cannot simply ask managers to execute a fully formed change agenda; you might instead develop a broad outline, informed by your environmental scan and lots of good questions, from which people can conduct a series of small experiments. That approach not only confers team ownership, but also allows people to explore new possibilities in ways that don't bet the company or your budget.

Resist the temptation to pile responsibility on team members

It is not just the personalities or the team process that determine success; it's whether or not the team is linked appropriately to the resources they need in the organization (see 'Why Teams Don't Work', Winter 1998). In addition, leaders can allow teams to forge their own identity, build a sense of membership and enjoy the protection they need to implement changes. One of the temptations leaders must resist is to simply pile responsibility on team members. While it is fashionable to have people wear many hats, people must be given the responsibility – and the time – to focus on the tasks of change.

Learning to persevere

Everything can look like a failure in the middle. One of the mistakes leaders make in change processes is to launch them and leave them. Most people get excited about things in the beginning, and everybody loves endings, especially happy endings. It's the hard work in between that demands the attention and effort of savvy leaders.

Making everyone a hero

Remembering to recognize, reward and celebrate accomplishments is an important leadership skill and underutilized motivational tool. The following Case Study regarding the Chairman of Intel explains a particular approach to managing change.

Source: *Managing Segment Zero* (Grove, Andrew S., 1999)

Moving toward acceptance – and from there to action – usually involves two phases. First, you must experiment and let chaos reign. That's important because you are not likely to immediately restructure your organization at the first sign of trouble. Rather, you have to let the business units deal with and adapt to change – and while they do so you have to watch and learn from them. You watch the dissonance that grows in the company, and you think about how to close it – by changing both what you do and what you say you do. Most important, you use this period of experimentation to picture the shape of the new industry and how it will look at the end of these changes. As this chaotic period resolves, you enter the second phase of change, which I describe as the Valley of Death. Doing away with established practices and established people – tearing apart before you can put together something new – is not fun. Every organization needs to balance new effort against current commitments. One of the disciplines necessary in any organization with finite resources (which is every organization) is the ability to balance every new effort against current commitments. In other words, the 'yeses' have to equal the 'nos'. Nothing challenges leadership as much as managing the balance between the yeses – which everyone is happy to add to the balance sheet – and the nos, which no one ever volunteers for. Talking prematurely about changes that disrupt peoples' lives and are not truly believed can undermine your efforts before they have a chance to work. But once they are in place, it is essential for leadership to speak clearly about what the changes are about and what the organization is going to do. At this point, hopefully, the other side of the Valley of Death is clear, and you can describe the future that lies ahead.

Making change

The U.S. Mint needed an enterprise resource planning (ERP) system that would let our business units get at all the customer information hidden in our systems. And we had just 12 months to get it up and running. Three years into the process, we kept running into the wall of our systems. Even though the customer data was there, only a few people had access to it. The biggest challenge was to convince them to sacrifice some of their most talented people to the project. If I could do it all over again, I'd spend more money educating the organization on what life was going to be like after the implementation. We invested a lot in training, but we probably should have spent twice as much time and money. To other executives, I would say, the most critical thing is to start with a business requirement. What does your business lack that such a solution will provide? If the business requirement doesn't justify the pain, don't do it.

Source: Adapted from Philip Diehl, Making Change: HEADFIRST

zwww.darwinmag.com/read/060100/head_content.html

Because change causes fear, a sense of loss of the familiar, etc., it takes time for employees to understand and commit themselves to it in a meaningful way. Some writers (Bacal, R, 2000) argue that people tend to go through stages in their attempts to cope with change.

Stage 1: Denial

One way that people cope with change is to deny that it is happening, or that it will continue or last. People tend to avoid dealing with the fear and uncertainty of prospective change because they are hoping they won't have to adapt. This stage is difficult because it is hard to involve people in planning for the future. Moving out of the denial stage occurs when they see tangible evidence that things are different.

Stage 2: Anger and resistance

When it is no longer feasible to deny that something is happening or has already happened, people may move into a state of anger, accompanied by forms of resistance. Leadership is needed to help people work through this and on to the next stage. If leadership is poor, anger and resentment may last indefinitely.

Stage 3: Exploration and acceptance

This is the stage where people are beginning to develop a better understanding of the change and are more willing to explore further, and to accept it. They are more willing to participate in the process.

Stage 4: Commitment

This is the stage where people are willing to work towards making it succeed. They have adapted sufficiently to make it work. While some changes, for example downsizing, may never be accepted, eventually people do commit themselves to making the organization effective within the constraints arising from the change. The change process can take some time to stabilize.

The following insight highlights some of the problems that people leading change may face.

New or different ideas often run into trouble before they reach fruition. However, change leaders need to help teams overcome blocks to change.

Forecasts fall short A plan is needed but it is difficult to predict timing and cost. Change leaders need to accept departures from plans.

Expect the unexpected A new path is unlikely to run straight and every change brings unanticipated consequences. Change leaders need to respond, to make adjustments and to make their case.

Momentum slows You do not have solutions to problems, and the team is discouraged and enmeshed in conflict. Critics emerge. Even if a coalition has been built and key stakeholders are involved, you will be challenged. When the impact of change becomes clear, those threatened by it will formulate objections. This is when change leaders need to respond, remove obstacles and push forward. Actual progress will produce more believers than doubters.

Source: Adapted from (Kanter, Rosabeth Moss, 1999) The Enduring Skills of Change Leaders. *Leader to Leader*. 13 (Summer 1999): 15–22.

Change management: the skill requirements

Managing the kinds of changes encountered by and instituted within organizations requires an unusually broad and finely-honed set of skills, chief among which are the following:

Political skills
Organizations are first and foremost social systems. Without people there can be no organization. Organizations are intensely political. Change agents need to understand it.

Analytical skills
A rational, well-argued analysis can be ignored and even suppressed but not successfully contested and, in most cases, should be successful. If not, the political issues haven't been properly addressed.

Why do people and organizations resist change?

Many writers argue that constant innovation is the best way to secure both the individual and the organizational success. Roffe (1999) offers three scenarios:

1. Incremental change: here it is the little, unnoticed changes that make the biggest differences
2. Discontinuous change: it is different this time because the response needed is not related to a familiar pattern
3. Radical change: where 'upside-down' thinking is needed.

In a general sense, entrepreneurial-type managers are thought to be best suited to anticipating the need for, and then leading, productive change. Innovative firms take an 'integrative' approach to problem-solving by showing a willingness to see problems as a whole, and in their solutions to move beyond received wisdom, to challenge established practices and generally view change as an opportunity rather than a threat. This approach requires the skill to: persuade people to invest time and resources in new and possibly risky initiatives, manage problems arising from team-working and employee participation, and understand how change is designed and constructed in an organizational context.

Firms that use compartmentalized structures are more likely to see problems in isolation and out of context. Here, it is unlikely that organizational effort will be devoted to the problem as an integrated whole and the outcomes will reflect this.

Complacency at the top is also a common reason for poor performance. To break free, decentralization is important so that entrepreneurial managers in less senior roles feel that they have the authority and resources to exploit their ideas.

Decide exactly what you want – Unclear goals create unclear outcomes. Succumbing to the temptation to start work without thought and planning wastes energy and produces disillusionment. Clear goals direct energy, give a sense of purpose and provide a context for resolving any problems.

Decide that you really want the change – Don't see the change as an option, decide that it must happen. Believe that there is no alternative, no matter how busy the organization, no matter what might crop up two months from now. If there is an alternative, don't bother starting. Many change projects start life as 'a pretty good idea' that is 'probably worth the effort in the long run'. All too often, people begin with the intention of seeing if anything crops up later along the line. Such saintly efforts are easy prey for people keen to play the role of change assassins. Don't let your project take a mugging.

Own it – Someone must make this change happen and take responsibility for everything it produces – whether the consequences are anticipated and manageable, or not. Someone has to be clearly identified with the project, not only when it is fashionable and full of hope and the best players, but also when it begins to annoy people and your best people leave to work on something that 'cropped up later'.

Be realistic – The change may be as painful and costly for you as for the people around you. The pain and cost may come before, during or after the project – but come it will. Realism means understanding the volume of work involved in keeping individuals and organizations aligned with the change vision, especially when their instincts are screaming at them to get back to the old way of doing things.

Understand what blocks change – Become fascinated by the current practices or behaviours in your organization that resist change. Get to know them intimately. Give power to the strong and take power from the weak. In this context, strong means the positive things you want to achieve. Praise them, reward them, reinforce them, celebrate them, repeat them and publicize them when they happen. By contrast, punish old behaviours when they happen – and make it clear why you have corrected them.

Be positive – Attitude and self-belief are drivers of change. Don't play the 'but' or 'maybe' game; doubt slaughters change. Try not to be side-tracked by fear.

Be optimistic – 'If you want to achieve excellence, you can get there today. As of this second, quit doing less than excellent work'. So, allegedly, said Thomas Watson, the founder of IBM.

Deciding to make a change takes an instant – but sustaining it is the challenge. Most change programmes are long and complex. Some are so long that there's a good chance that you won't be around to see it end, while some change destinations alter as the project is in motion. So focus on the journey as well as the destination.

Be aware – raise awareness by asking key questions.

What is happening to take us towards the goal?

What happened last week that failed to move us forward, or took us down old paths that we agreed we wanted to change?

What can each of us do next week that will move us towards our goal?

Let it happen – It seems a contradictory thing to say, as I do, both that a clear sense of what you want gives you a motivating direction and purpose, and that you should let go of what will happen. Allowing your purpose to unfold as it will is an exhortation to 'stay flexible'.

Source: Adapted from (Firth, D, 2003) www.treefrog.ws

Internal marketing

Internal marketing is an important 'implementation' tool. It aids communication and helps to overcome resistance to change. It informs and involves staff in new initiatives and strategies. Internal marketing has a structure similar to external marketing. The main differences are that the customers are the employees.

The marketer's skills are traditionally associated with the interface between organization and customer/consumer. But management also have a need to communicate with those within the organization – and those stakeholders associated with it. It is unlikely that an organization will be truly successful unless these buy-in to management plans. There needs to be a common focus, and goals need to be understood and accepted. The prime marketing skills are communication – marketers are the specialists in identifying target audiences, assessing needs and in managing communications plans. Applying these skills internally means that a consumer-centred approach, with the employees identified as the consumers, needs to be adopted.

Managing the implementation of internal marketing (Jobber, 1995)

Set objectives for internal marketing, e.g. to persuade 100 staff to join a new Performance-Related Pay (PRP) scheme.

Tactics would include an internal application of the marketing mix, and could include staff forums, presentations, an intranet, away days, videos, personal visits by company directors or newsletters.

Evaluation would consider the take up of PRP against your objectives, attendees at away days, visits to an intranet page and so on.

Internal marketing

Internal marketing involves selling marketing plans to key internal staff or employees. Piercy and Morgan's model (Piercey N and Morgan N, 1997) of Internal marketing indicates the implications for the marketing mix.

Price – this relates to the benefit to the employee of taking this marketing planning information on board. It relates to the personal psychological cost of adopting different key values, and changing the way jobs are done. Often it requires asking managers to step outside their comfort zones with new methods of operation.

Place/Distribution – this concerns the physical and socio-technical venues at which organizations will have to deliver the product and its communications – i.e. where should employees be targeted, e.g. Internet, staff canteens, etc.

Promotion/Communication – this is the most tangible aspect of internal marketing – communication media and the messages used to inform and persuade employees. There will be work on the attitudes of the key personnel in the internal marketplace and two-way methodology must be employed.

Service quality is influenced by employees because of the inseparability of services production and consumption in relation to the provider, i.e. staff. Good communication, motivation and training are central to service quality, and this is influenced by internal marketing.

Internal marketing is like 'change management'. Firstly, internal customers need to be identified. As with external customers, they will have their own buyer behaviour, or way of 'buying into' the changes which you are charged to implement. As Jobber (1995) explains, three different segments, namely 'supporters', 'neutral', and finally 'opposers' can be targeted. Each segment requires a slightly different internal marketing mix to achieve the internal marketing objectives.

For example, if the change was that a company was to relocate closer to its market, 'supporters' could be targeted with information about lower property prices; 'neutral' internal customers could be targeted with incentives such as better rewards. With 'opposers', a choice would need to be made between inaction or forcing acceptance of change. It depends on a calculation of what the impact would be between these two courses of action.

How to plan for a change programme?

The approach needs to be properly considered before starting the implementation. The climate needs to be accepting of change.

Appoint a change agent, or champion for change that will help to ease changes through.

Audit the skills and capabilities of the team. Train and develop as necessary.

The change must be correctly marketed to your target audience.

Decide upon the plan.

Work out a realistic budget and keep to it.

Try to anticipate the arguments against change.

Activity 6.1

Think about a change which has recently been introduced in your organization. Would you say it was marketed effectively internally?

What was the change?

What was effective about this approach?

How could this approach have been improved?

Planning for internal marketing

Internal marketing requires a similar kind of approach to that used in external marketing. An internal marketing audit is needed to discover who comprises the target audiences and to identify what are their needs. Channels of communication, both formal and informal, need to be identified. The same kind of questions that are used in any marketing audit can be used. Payback will be in terms of commitment rather than cash. Objectives should be SMART but couched in terms of changed behaviour rather than increases in market share, etc.

Strategy

Establishing a strategy for change will require a long-term view to be taken. What is the long-term need, and what are the short-term issues? Within the long-term strategic goal(s) will be the short-term need to introduce new products, to change operating procedures and so on. New product introduction may not be seen as an internal issue but internal staff need to know about, and be familiar with, new products before the outside world is notified. (One can be sure the telephone calls will start within hours of a launch. Internal staff must not respond 'Is that one of our products? I didn't know.')

Targets

Just as in marketing communications, there is need to identify target audiences. These will range from internal groupings such as individuals, sections, departments, etc. to include those 'exterior' stakeholders such as the organization's shareholders, bankers, lawyers, agencies, consultancies and so on. An internal marketing communications plan can be far more complex than one used to promote a product. The target audiences are more diverse.

Promotion

Two-way communication means that the target audience members should be able to have some input into proposed change. Internal communication media includes meetings, newsletters and noticeboards, but there is a need to achieve impact. Change has to be marketed effectively, and training and development offers a good opportunity to do this.

Price

Faced with 'selling' an idea or proposal to senior managers, the same process should be adopted but the needs of the management team and the stakeholders need to be considered, and benefits such as raised profitability quantified and communicated. The price to an internal audience is measured in terms of inconvenience, extra work, coping with unfamiliarity and so on. The question 'Why bother?' must be answered, and answered well.

Product

The product consists of market strategies and the marketing plan. Therefore, the 'product' needs to be 'sold' in terms of values, attitudes and behaviour to employees so that they can buy into it.

Place

For the internal marketer, place can be interpreted as when and where a change will be introduced. For example, it may be better to introduce a new computer system in the off-season rather than at peak times.

Promotion As has been said above, promote the benefits to those in each target audience.

Process All aspects of the change need to be thought through carefully, piloted, evaluated, modified, and re-piloted. It should ease the burden of adapting to change and, if possible, should simplify an employee's task. The introductory process, similarly, should be timetabled and then managed so that what is announced actually happens when and how it should.

Participants All involved, from top management to junior staff must follow the same procedures. If a senior manager does not comply it is unlikely that others will bother.

Employees are the company. Particularly in the services sectors, they represent the culture, the brand and the customer experience with the company. Employees are the best form of marketing during change. If people don't feel good about the change, customers will know it quickly.

Segment the benefits of the change. What factors are beneficial to employees, shareholders, customers and other stakeholders? Use these benefits to create key messages about the changes to be marketed to the appropriate audience.

Be truthful and genuine. It only takes one example of misdirection or dishonesty to create employee distrust of management's messages. Spin is spin, and people generally know when they are being spun. Be willing to show that a particular change isn't necessarily 'good' for everyone.

Change requires strongly embracing the future and a quick release of the past. Keep the organization's 'eyes' looking forward. Keep it thinking about what the customer wants. Those who have worked at the company for a long time tend to pull the company back into issues of tradition. Customers care little about the past. What will you do for them today or tomorrow?

Focus communications around the people who will remain after any staffing cuts or changes.

Deal with 'survivor syndrome', i.e. the phenomenon of those who keep their jobs feeling guilty that they have kept their jobs while many lose theirs.

Focus the organization externally. Work to eliminate the inwardness that comes with change.

Recognize that change is a personal issue. It involves a loss of control and employees, once content with their careers, now have to ask 'Will I have a job when this is finished?'

Make changes quickly, decisively and as fairly as possible. Spreading bad news over a longer period is more painful than making that one decisive action.

Focus on customers. Show a true concern for customer issues, but the change is not a customer vote. Communicating to your people, who will in turn reassure your customers, is the best defence.

Source: Adapted from Change Marketing: The Universal Truths for Marketing the Benefits of a Merger/Acquisition (Bedford Consulting Group, June 2002).

Summary

Change is a natural part of the environment, but is seldom popular and is often resisted. Change, as a process, can and should be managed. It is as much subject to management planning and control as any other process. All change should be taken seriously, and planned and implemented with care. Major changes include a switch from a product/sales to a marketing/customer approach, and from a domestic to an international orientation. Internal marketing is of crucial importance in securing change and is best handled from a corporate level, possibly with marketers seconded for the purpose. Change always requires a price to be paid in human terms.

Bibliography

Enduring Skills of Change Leaders. *Leader to Leader* 13 (Summer) pp 15–22

Bacal, R., (2000). www.work911.com/articles.htm. Understanding the Cycle of Change and How people react to it.

Bedford Consulting Group, (June 2002). www.bedfordgroupconsulting.com.

Firth, D., (2003). 10 Rules of Change, *People Management*, (6th March).

Grove, Andrew S., (1999). Managing Segment Zero, *Leader to Leader,* Winter, (11).

Kanter, Rosabeth Moss, (1999). http://drucker.org/leaderbook/L2L/summer99/kanter.html.

Piercey, N. and Morgan, N., (1997). Internal Marketing, *International Journal of Bank Marketing.*

Whittington, P.R. and Mayer, M. (2002). *Organising for Success,* London: CIPD.

Sample exam questions and answers for the Marketing Management in Practice module as a whole can be found in Appendix 3 at the back of the book.

---

unit 7 marketing communications

Introduction

Marketing communications strategy is concerned with how an organization can successfully communicate and deliver its marketing strategy. The Marketing Communications units of the CIM syllabus are intended to provide the skills and knowledge that enable marketers to manage marketing communications and brand support activities within organizations. The Marketing Management in Practice Module builds on the underpinning knowledge developed in the CIM Marketing Communications module.

Designing a communications campaign

A communications campaign is the dissemination of messages using appropriate channels, to a well-defined audience in order to educate and create an informed public. Designing and implementing a communications campaign could be carried out entirely within house, or it could be devolved to an agency, or the campaign could involve a combination of internal and external input. Obviously the size of the campaign and that of the budget, as well as its aims and objectives will be important factors in determining which approach to use. The key barrier to integrating the communications mix is people, and the way they work. The best way to overcome this barrier is to motivate the key players to work as a team. An effective team is one that includes client and agency, across the entire communications mix.

Full-service agency

When using an external agency the most straightforward approach is to is to use the services of a full-service agency that is able to assemble a team including representatives from all the agency services that the client needs. Full-service agencies can provide a comprehensive range of services such as creative, strategic planning, production, media planning and buying, and market research. The advantage of using a full-service agency is the range of skills that can be drawn upon when needed, and the fact that all the elements of the promotional mix and marketing communications operation can be brought together making the whole process easier to manage and control. However, this strength is also a potential weakness because if the relationship breaks down, it will be difficult to find another agency to take on the work at short notice and still keep to the envisaged timescale.

Limited service agency

An alternative to the full service agency is a limited service agency that specializes in particular elements of the marketing communications process. For example, an advertising agency may specialize in the design of advertisements. The advantage in using a limited service agency is that a client can use different agencies for the different skills that best suit his needs. This gives choice and flexibility but it can take a lot of time to manage the different relationships involved. Selecting an agency should be based on explicit criteria based on the aims and objectives of the communications. Key issues are whether the agency fully understands the requirements of a brief, and whether it will be able to work with the client as a team. In some cases companies are establishing online communication services which may make it more difficult to tell whether or not the chemistry is right between the client and the agency.

Marni Media – integrated marketing communications

Marni Media is an online information and creative marketing service. The firm's services integrate marketing strategy and creativity into written copy, sales presentations, website design and media management projects. Marni Media's objective is to provide professional marketing and creative media expertise to a client's communication team. Effective marketing communications depends upon team work between marketers, designers and programmers. Marni Media provides marketing and creative services to small and medium size businesses, advertising agencies, corporate marketing departments, web design teams and web content producers. Our services integrate marketing strategy with written and visual content. We create and produce effective front-end website design and content based upon search engine marketing strategies. Marni Media's objective is to deliver the right message to the right audience for business clients. Our approach to marketing communications is based upon experience in creating and producing messages to customers in web-based, e-mail, print, trade show, radio and television formats. We start by clearly defining marketing objectives and target audiences before the creative process begins, and we follow-up with research and analysis to improve the efficiency of the media project. We believe that business should make it easy for customers to buy products and services.

Developing an agency brief

Elements that could be contained in an agency brief are:

Current situation – the history of the brand, previous campaign successes (or failures) and the reasons for mounting the new campaign.

Promotional objectives – Having set marketing objectives, the promotional objectives need to be identified. These will vary but could include, for example, encouraging product trial or direct sales or increasing distribution outlets.

Target markets – This should include socioeconomic details (e.g. age, class, sex) and also psychographic information on users. This will have a bearing on the focus and content of the promotional activity.

Product/service – In providing the agency with a detailed brief, this section should include any available research that has been used to establish the perceived benefits so that these can be promoted strongly.

Budget – The budget should include funds for the cost of the media and the production of promotional material.

Competitors – Find out about these and include the results of your findings in the brief.

Timescales – Media scheduling will play an important role at this stage.

The creative team will be responsible for the direction of the artwork, ensuring that visualization and copywriting match the needs of the organization, and they will be directed by the Account Manager within the agency who will also brief the media and planning functions.

When agencies are used, the process of briefing will be followed by the 'agency pitch'. An agency will carry out research into the marketing and communications situation, and then present creative and media plans to the client.

What type of campaign is it?

There are different types of marketing communications campaign. An educational campaign targets a specific audience with information that benefits the consumer, for example, health related matters, or how to obtain benefits. A marketing campaign promotes, for example, a new service or product, or repositions an old service or product, and focuses on price, promotion and product. A public relations campaign would focus on image and name recognition. The following is an example of an integrated campaign that was the result of extensive research carried out over a year involving marketers and professionals working in the anti-drug field.

National youth anti-drug media campaign

The campaign's five-year initiative to reduce and deglamorize youth drug use targets middle-school-age adolescents (approximately 11 to 13 years old), parents and other influential adults. The integrated communications campaign delivers anti-drug messages to kids and parents where they live, work and play through advertising, the Internet, movies, music and television, public education efforts and community partnerships. The campaign will spend about $180 million per year in advertising – and receive a pro bono match of equal value from the entertainment industry, media, corporations and other advertisers – to expose young people to innovative anti-drug messages that reinforce the ads. For more than a year, TV ads have run nationwide during prime time. Nearly a year of research went into designing the campaign. Hundreds of specialists were consulted, including experts in behaviour change, drug prevention, teen marketing and advertising communications, as well as representatives from professional, civic and community organizations. The campaign will be constantly monitored, evaluated and updated to ensure that it effectively reaches teens and their parents.

Who is the target audience?

Communication should be tailored to meet the needs and interests of a given audience. Is the audience potential buyers, current users, deciders or influencers, individuals, groups, or the general public? Are the members of the target audience consumers, businesses, nonprofit organizations, or government agencies? The target audience is a critical influence on decisions about what to say to whom, when and how.

What are the aims and objectives of the campaign?

Try to devise both quantitative (measurable) and qualitative objectives. A quantitative objective would be, for example, to increase the number of users by twenty per cent per year. A qualitative objective would be to improve public understanding of the benefits of recycling by the autumn, measured by pre- and post-survey responses. The campaign may be trying to elicit a cognitive (attention), affective (feeling) or behavioural (doing) response.

Designing the message

This is concerned with what to say, how to say it and who should say it. The aim is to find a theme, idea, appeal or unique selling proposition. The message can try to appeal on moral, rational or emotional grounds. Rational grounds emphasize the benefits of a product or service such as quality, value or performance. Emotional appeals try to stir up negative or positive emotions to motivate purchase. Moral appeals to an audience's sense of propriety and the right way to behave. The structure of a message is important, that is whether it is a one sided or two sided presentation mentioning benefits and shortcomings, and the order in which arguments are presented. The credibility of the message source depends on expertise, trustworthiness and likeability.

Select the channels

This involves choosing between a range of personal communication channels, for example, face to face or through telephone or e-mail and non-personal communication channels which include the media.

Activity 7.1

Think of a marketing campaign that you have been involved in or which is memorable to you.

What type of campaign was it?

Who do you perceive was the target audience?

What was the key message?

What channels were used?

What made it stand out for you?

Determining the marketing communications budget

A key task within the framework of marketing communications is the appropriate determination of the levels of expenditure required to fulfil the task established. The amount of money spent on marketing communications differs widely among companies, even within the same industry. There are various methods to choose from, each with a slightly different focus, and different advantages and disadvantages.

Percentage of sales – A widely used method of budget determination is based on the calculation of a ratio between past expenditure and sales. The model creates a situation in which the budget only increases against an expectation of higher sales and fails to acknowledge that marketing can create sales for a brand.

Percentage of product gross margin – A percentage of either the past or expected gross margin – net sales less the cost of goods – is used.

Percentage of anticipated turnover – This approach is based on the allocation of a fixed percentage of future turnover to the marketing communications budget.

Unit or case/sales ratio method – This method is based on estimating sales volumes, and a fixed sum per unit is allocated towards marketing communications expenditure. Multiplying the expected sales volume by the fixed allocation gives producers the size of the budget. The expenditure patterns reflect past achievement and tends to benefit growth brands and disadvantage those that are declining.

Competitive expenditure – Another frequently used approach is to base a brand's expenditure levels on an assessment of competitors' expenditures. However, the difficulty is how to make an accurate assessment of the level of competitors' spend. While it is possible to obtain a reasonable fix on advertising spend from published information, the same is not true of sales promotional spend and other categories of marketing communications.

Share of voice – This approach is based on the relationship between the volume share of the product category and the expenditure within the category as a whole. It is primarily related to advertising expenditure.

Media inflation – This makes the assumption that the previous year's budget should be increased in line with the growth in media costs.

Objective and task method – This method is based on the specific objectives that the marketing plan needs to achieve. The objective and task method requires that specific objectives for the campaign are defined; for example, increasing brand awareness, encouraging sampling and trial, promoting repeat purchase and so on. A numerical target is given and the costs of achieving this target are calculated. The budget is based on present goals rather than past or future results.

What can be afforded – This is based on a management assessment of, for example, the return on investment, and the marketing communications budget is the amount that remains after calculating that level and other claims on the budget.

Deciding on a marketing communications mix

There are many different terms used to describe the various methods used by organizations to communicate with customers and other stakeholder groups.

Advertising

Advertising is one of the most influential forms of communication within the promotional mix and is particularly effective at reaching large audiences with specific messages. Depending on the media used, costs of reaching individuals can be lowered compared to other forms of communications. It can be used at different stages of purchasing, or for awareness creation at the early stages of a new product launch. Its main purpose is to inform, persuade and remind customers to purchase products and services. Advertising objectives are expressed in terms of promoting products, organizations and services, or stimulating demand, increasing sales, brand and product awareness, and reminding and reinforcing perceptions of a product or service.

Sales promotions

Sales promotions often complement advertising, and may be planned and executed in parallel with associated advertising and possible public relations campaigns. They are used to encourage customers to trial products and services, and then to purchase them. The main aims and associated objectives of sales promotions are, for example, to increase brand and product awareness, attract new customers, increase trial and adoption of new and existing products, increase brand usage and to encourage trading up to the next size or the next range. Sales promotions can be a highly targeted and flexible form of communications and evaluation of their effectiveness is usually an integral part of the communication through, for instance, coupon redemption, money-off vouchers/coupons, buy one get one free, discounts, trial-sized products, etc.

Trade promotions

Good trade promotions, i.e. a good 'push strategy', highly incentivized, backed up by appropriate merchandising and appropriate advertising, may be advantageous. Specific methods might include, for example, allowances and discounts, free merchandise, selling and marketing assistance, co-operative advertising, merchandising allowances, market information and product training. The following Case Study from Nortel demonstrates a range of incentives available if the value of sales is forecasted to be more than $1million.

Nortel Networks

The Nortel Networks Partner Support Plan is designed to simplify your relationship with the Company and make it easier for both parties to work together. The end result is that meshing your business goals with Nortel Networks is easier, more cost-effective and more advantageous than ever before. The Nortel Networks Premium Partners is associated with specific plan criteria that establish the basic guidelines for the relationship. Participants with annual forecasted purchases of Nortel Networks products greater than $1 million are eligible to register as a Premium Partner – the highest level within the plan. Premium Partners have access to the broadest spectrum of products, services and support programmes including:

- Eligibility for the Volume Discount Plan
- Assigned resources for sales and marketing support
- Access to new or restricted products if authorization requirements are met
- Marketing support funds
- Participation in all channel partner events.

The Nortel Networks Enterprise Solutions Co-op Fund is available to reimburse Premium Partners for pre-approved marketing activities. The funds can be used to create market and product awareness, increase sales and support your marketing efforts through a wide variety of marketing communications including advertising, direct mail, trade shows, promotional items and other marketing communications. Having access to new products can enable you to be first to market.

You will have access to:

Volume discounts, Promotional Funds, Direct purchase, Indirect purchase, Assigned resources, Access to restricted products, Marketing programmes access, Pre-sales support, Post-sales support and Partner event access.

Retailer to consumer sales promotions

The key aims and objectives of this process will be to increase sales through a range of promotional techniques such as increasing in-store trade and customer traffic through, for example, the use of coupons and money-off vouchers, discounted promotions for next purchase, the use of storecards and rewards systems.

Manufacturer to consumer sales promotions

Typical sales promotion activities might include encouraging trials through the use of samples and gifts, disseminating information packs door-to-door and encouraging customers to trade up from their existing models.

Personal selling

Personal selling is the most expensive element of the marketing communications mix because it is resource-intensive, and involves high contact and customer maintenance costs. In some instances, personal sales have been replaced by direct mail, telemarketing and e-mail. Personal selling includes activities such as:

Prospecting – Gathering information in order to gain sales leads and prospective clients

Communicating – Being the provider of information about the organization, its products, services and after-sales care

Selling – Persuading a potential customer to adopt the product

Market research/information gathering – Environmental scanning, competitor intelligence, customer intelligence

Servicing of accounts – Maintaining and providing ongoing customer service, including technical support, financial contractual arrangements and logistical arrangements

Allocating – Ensuring that the allocation of products to customers is undertaken at all times, in particular, in times of production shortages

Customer relationship building – Building and sustaining long-term customer relationships.

Co-ordinated marketing communications mix

The communications mix is the use of these elements in a co-ordinated way so as to achieve the promotions' objectives. Usually, a combination of marketing communications tools are used to meet specific campaign objectives. For example, advertising campaigns are often supported with sales promotions activities, or public relations or both. The role of marketing communications is to:

- o differentiate a product/brand (to make it different to a competitor's brand or seem different through effective positioning)
- o remind and reassure a target audience with regard to benefits (to encourage (re)purchase)
- o inform a target audience by providing new information (e.g. of a new brand or flavour)
- o persuade an audience to take a particular set of actions (e.g. visit a theatre, stop smoking)

The following Case Study shows the wide range of responsibilities of a marketing communications manager.

Senior marketing communications manager

Responsibilities:

Actively help to develop and implement a marketing communications plan that effectively reaches target users, and facilitates the job of product marketing and business development teams by generating quality customer and partner leads.

Design, co-ordinate production and implement ongoing advertising, direct mail and other promotional programmes.

Maintain overall responsibility for management of and changes to company website.

Actively contribute to the development of and regular updates to corporate and product messaging, as well as to public relations materials.

Track newsworthy events and co-ordinate with public relations agency to publicize.

Gather information for press releases and co-ordinate approval and distribution processes.

Help co-ordinate the creative process, development and production of the company's collateral materials.

Help manage development, writing and production of company newsletter.

Co-ordinate with sales teams to collect leads, integrate with salesforce and manage the appropriate follow-up.

Manage development of the process to measure marketing communications results, including quality of leads generated, etc.

Hold primary responsibility for managing the company's various advertising, design and public relations agency relationships, including negotiating contracts, managing administrative and billing issues, etc.

Review and evaluate the effectiveness of communications activities

Many organizations measure the effectiveness of their marketing communications, and there are a range of techniques and procedures available. Increasingly, it is the synergy that derives from effective co-ordination of all activities that determines overall success. Single elements of the communications mix are not used in isolation. Different parts of a campaign can be assessed and the evaluation process can be carried out at different stages of a marketing campaign, i.e. before, during and after a campaign has been launched. However, the overall impact of a co-ordinated marketing communications campaign and the degree to which the promotional objectives have been achieved are key measures that interest stakeholders.

Whilst the primary focus is upon ascertaining whether objectives have been met and the strategy has been effective – efficiency is also of interest. There should be a strong emphasis on 'efficiency', 'effectiveness' and 'value for money', which means making the best use of the available resources to achieve the best possible outcomes. However, some aspects of marketing are notoriously difficult to evaluate; for example, advertising. Whilst communications is one element of the marketing mix, the other elements should be evaluated as well.

Pre-testing is about showing unfinished advertisements, often to focus groups to gather their reactions and to understand their reasoning. Post-testing is concerned with the evaluation of a campaign once it has been released. A typical measurement is the number of enquiries or direct responses elicited by a single advertisement or campaign. Recall and recognition tests are common post-testing procedures for advertisements.

Tracking studies involve collecting data from buyers on a regular basis in order to assess their perceptions of ads. Sales promotion evaluation includes methods such as *consumer audits* and general s*ales information*, *retail audits* including, for example, changes in stock levels, distribution, market share, etc. immediately after a promotional campaign. *Sales force feedback* is also a common measure.

Voucher/coupon redemption – Usually coded so that the different response rates in different media can be tracked.

Public relations

Some commonly used measures of results are:

Budget – Has the planned activity been achieved within budget and timescale

Awareness – Established through using market research activities

Attitude – Positivity or negativity and whether there is any change in consumer behaviour

Media coverage and tone – Coverage in a range of media – number of column inches, key headings and the tone

Positioning – Comparative information about the relative position of the organization and the competition

Response generation – Enquiries or leads linked to reference codes or enquiry sources, for example, a particular newspaper

Share price – Recent highly publicized scandals such as Enron and WorldCom show that share prices can be manipulated, especially when exceeding a particular level is a management target, the achievement of which means that large bonuses can be earned. During the so-called Dotcom boom, some worthless stock was also heavily promoted by brokers. A share price can also be affected by a myriad of external factors outside a company's control so, all in all, a healthy degree of scepticism is needed before relying on share price as a guide to anything

Sales – When an organization suffers from negative perception, sales tend to drop. The challenge is to rehabilitate the image in order to increase sales.

Direct marketing activities

Evaluation of direct marketing activities is based upon the pre-determined objectives of the campaign. Typical measures for successful implementation of the direct marketing campaign will include:

- o Response rate
- o Conversion rate
- o Order value
- o Repeat orders.

Often, this information will be gathered through a range of voucher and campaign response codes that will be able to distinguish the source of the direct mail or promotion. However, the cost per enquiry and per order needs to be identified. Click-through rates are a common online measurement.

Calculating ROI

Obviously, the power of metrics diminishes if the information is merely distributed, and not intelligently assessed and acted upon by management. ROI is the most critical measure of marketing programmes for making decisions that will help maximize company profits. ROI in its simplest form is: {Net Profit (pre-marketing investment) – Net Profit (post-marketing investment)} – Investment = Return. Return/Net Profit (pre-marketing investment) = ROI.

Planning a social marketing campaign

When planning programmes or awareness campaigns, it is important to target programmes and messages to reach and meet the needs of the intended audience. In health communications, these concepts take on the following meanings:

Product – is the knowledge, attitudes or behaviour you want the audience to adopt

Price – can be interpreted as what the target audience must give up in order to receive the programme's benefits

Promotion – is the means for persuading the target audience that the product is worth the price

Place – refers to how the message is disseminated, such as through electronic or print media, or community programmes.

Stage 1 – Planning and selecting the strategy
This stage provides the foundation for the entire social marketing process. An assessment of the problem, the target audience and the available resources is conducted before moving ahead. During this planning process, the target audience should become increasingly segmented. This segmentation will aid in the development of appropriate messages. Goals and objectives for the programme will be developed at this time.

Stage 2 – Selecting channels and materials
Channels are how the message will be delivered, whether it is face-to-face, group, mass media, or a combination of channels. The more the channels selected, the more the target audience will be exposed to the message. Determining the channel prior to producing materials is important because different materials work better in different channels.

Material selection involves using what you have learned about your target audience to your advantage. Time and money can be saved by selecting materials that are specific to the audience you are trying to reach.

Stage 3 – Developing the materials and pretesting
Draft the materials, pretest them with the target audience and, if necessary, revise them. Determine if materials get the intended results, or revise them accordingly. Pre-testing adds time to the project but it can help to avoid producing materials that the target audience do not read.

Stage 4 – Implementing the programme
A method for tracking and evaluating the programme should be in place before it starts. The tracking method should help to identify those areas where changes may be needed.

Stage 5 – Assessing effectiveness
The type of evaluation conducted at this stage will depend upon several factors, including: money, time, policies regarding the ability to gather information, the level of support for evaluation and the overall design of the programme.

Types of evaluation

- **Formative evaluation** includes pre-testing of materials, and is designed to test the strengths and weaknesses of a programme before it is ready for implementation
- **Process evaluation** reviews the tasks of implementing the programme
- **Outcome evaluation** is used to gather descriptive information. It gathers information about knowledge and attitude changes, expressed intentions of the target audience and the initiation of policy changes
- **Impact evaluation** is the most comprehensive of the four types of evaluation. It focuses on the long-term outcomes of the programme and long-term behaviour change.

Stage 6 – Refining through feedback
If the programme is to be continued, revisions of the programme should be undertaken. If this is the end of the programme, documentation of what was learned should be made so as to assist others who may undertake a similar project in the future. An evaluation report should be prepared that could be used to secure funding to continue the programme and assist others conducting similar activities.

Customer service

For companies facing increasing competition and more demanding customers, customer service is a necessity. Customer service can be thought of as comprising technical and personal service. The technical quality of goods is subject to various quality control methods aiming to 'get it right first time' and guarantees that if a product doesn't live up to what is promised, it can be replaced. Personal service refers to the way in which the product or service is delivered and is the most visible aspect of service on which a company is judged. It is much more difficult to ensure consistency, and a bad service experience cannot be replaced so easily as a tangible product. It is influenced by, for example, organizational culture, attitudes, behaviour and relationships. Understanding and meeting customer needs is a central aspect of marketing, and one of the factors that has led to an increasing emphasis on relationship marketing is the need to look at customer retention on a long-term basis.

Customer care needs to be an integral part of the business strategy and effective customer relationship management means focusing on the needs of customers. A myriad of factors will affect customer loyalty:

- o Satisfaction among employees is often a driving force behind customer satisfaction, since customer interaction with staff is often central to their experience
- o If an organization's operational processes are not coherent, this will affect the customer's experience.

Employees who deal with customers need to be empowered to make certain decisions independently. Service standards should be used wherever customers have direct contact with the organization, for example, speed and courtesy when answering phone calls.

- o Find out about different customer segments
- o Collect information about what and when customers purchase and use it for improving customer service
- o As part of a sales and marketing strategy, set out the levels of service that will be offered to different customer types
- o Enable customers to give feedback.

Developing customer service

The basis of good customer service is the culture of the organization because this embodies the values of the organization, including how customers and employees should be treated. Motivated and valued staff is a prerequisite of good customer care. All employees can have a positive or negative impact on customers, and this needs to be understood and monitored. A clear understanding by staff of the purpose of the business and the customers is required.

Customers encounter a company in a number of different ways and may interact with a number of different people during any transaction. The pre-transaction, transaction and post-transaction activities can be described as the customer's chain of experience. An organization committed to customer service will take steps to try to understand and gain feedback about the customer's chain of experience and their expectations of service. Sometimes, customer-care training focuses on superficial issues such as 'have a nice day' and doesn't look at the underlying causes of poor service; for example, management style, lack of empowerment of customer facing staff and lack of continuous training.

Customers' expectations are determined by a number of factors, some of which are within the control of the organization and some of which are not. Strategies for managing expectations should be incorporated within the marketing plan with marketing having influence on areas of the business that impact on customer expectations and experiences.

Essentials of customer care

If employees are expected to deliver high-quality customer care, their views should be canvassed for ideas about how customer service could be improved. They also need access to good quality training in areas such as dealing with telephone calls and managing customer complaints efficiently and effectively. A website can be used to give customers the services and information they want. A good database can also help with the organization and planning of customer contacts.

Moments of Truth by Jan Carlzon (Carlzon, J., 1987) is an account of how the Scandinavian airline SAS, was saved by promoting excellence in customer service. He put forward the view that any time a customer comes into contact with any aspect of a business, it provides an opportunity to form a good or a bad impression. Carlzon identified a series of critical transactions, for example, initial contact, first use, ongoing support and further purchases that he called 'Moments of Truth' because they had the potential to affect customer satisfaction and value. He sent SAS managers on training courses so that they would be able to better manage these moments of truth and this had a positive effect on the company.

Ways to improve customer service

Personalize communications – For example, greeting a customer by name, personalize the e-mail addresses of customer-facing employees.

Create opportunities for feedback

Find out from new customers why they chose the company over the competition. Ask existing customers what could be better. Enable online feedback by putting an e-mail response form or newsgroup on the website. Encourage complaints, as only one in ten dissatisfied customers bothers to complain, usually dissatisfied customers just take their custom elsewhere. Carry out occasional customer satisfaction surveys. Contact any customer who has stopped buying and keep a record of customer feedback to help identify problem areas.

Establish a customer hotline, and make sure the number is on every piece of paper sent out.

- o Monitor and analyse the contact you have with customers
- o Use software to discover which webpages are most popular.

Differentiate between different customer segments

When marketing, if appropriate, differentiate between different market segments.

- o Potential customers who have not yet purchased anything. For example, someone who has made an enquiry as a result of an advertisement where the aim is to build interest in what you have to offer

- o Another segment is customers who have already made a purchase, where your aim is to increase the frequency of their buying and to sell them other products and services

○ Premium customers who already make regular purchases. Sometimes, a few large customers generate a high proportion of profits and it is important to make sure that their needs are being met. Invite key customers to special events. Try to reinforce the idea that they are valued customers but without being unduly obtrusive or obsequious. Above all, don't be like Uriah Heep who was 'ever so..umble'.

Added-value schemes

A successful loyalty scheme pays for itself by encouraging more frequent purchases. The most common loyalty schemes are based on offering rewards to loyal customers. Several businesses can collaborate to support the same loyalty scheme. An accounting system may need to track the purchasing activity of each customer and recognize when discounts have been earned.

The following Case Study is an example of service standards and also shows how customers with special needs are catered for.

Inland revenue customer service standards 2002–2003

We aim to provide a prompt, efficient and courteous service to our customers.

Our aims and what they mean – We aim to provide you with the best possible customer service and we set targets to measure our success in providing that service.

Answering the telephone – We aim to answer 90 per cent of all calls to local offices within 20 seconds.

Answering post – We aim to respond fully to 80 per cent of post within 15 working days. Where we cannot do this, we will let you know the reason for the delay, and when you can expect a full reply.

Attending to callers at our Enquiry Centres – We aim to see 95 per cent of our callers without an appointment within 15 minutes.

Attending to repayment claims – When tax has been correctly taken at source from investment income but the recipient is not liable to tax, we aim to repay that tax within 20 working days of receiving a claim.

If you have a complaint, you should write to the area director of the office you are dealing with; most problems can be settled at this level. You can get his or her name from the people who have been dealing with your complaint, or at any Inland Revenue office.

Customers with special needs

We will do everything reasonably possible to help you. The full range of services include:

○ the use of Textphones, their locations and telephone numbers
○ handling Typetalk and Minicom calls from deaf customers through a telephone operator
○ providing an induction loop for people with hearing aids and lighted magnifier for the partially sighted in all of our Enquiry Centres
○ our website at www.inlanderevenue.gov.uk is compatible with speech output software used by people with impaired vision
○ Specialist help, such as sign language interpreters and other language interpreters

> o publishing leaflets in other languages
> o providing some forms and leaflets in braille, large print, on audio tape and disk
> o home visits to customers who are unable to call at our offices and cannot be helped over the phone or by correspondence.

Relationship marketing

Key dimensions that provide a basis for a relationship:

Reliability – ability to perform the promised service dependably and accurately

Responsiveness – willingness to help customers and provide prompt service

Assurance – knowledge and courtesy of employees, and their ability to inspire trust and confidence

Empathy – caring, individualism, attention the firm provides its customers

Tangibles – physical facilities, equipment and appearance of personnel.

Customer retention management

There are a number of techniques for measuring customer satisfaction linked to profitability. Established customers tend to be more profitable because:

- o They place frequent, consistent orders, and cost less to serve
- o They tend to buy more
- o Satisfied customers may sometimes pay premium price
- o Retaining customers makes it difficult for competitors to enter a market or increase their share
- o Satisfied customers often refer new customers to the supplier at no extra cost
- o A higher retention rate implies fewer new customers need to be acquired.

Customer retention in business-to-consumer (b2c) markets

In consumer markets, customer retention schemes are focused around loyalty cards. Loyalty schemes are based on accessing information from customer databases, and making use of direct response media such as direct mail and telemarketing. Product-based sales promotion advertising is more widely used by retailers who do not use loyalty schemes.

Retaining customers in business-to-business (b2b) markets

The basic principles that a b2b market should consider in relationship development:

Technical support – providing added value to clients in industrial markets

Technical expertise – providing expertise can be a good selling point for the organization

Resource support – making available a range of cost-effective resources to support the relationship

Service levels – these appear to be of growing importance and will relate in particular to time, delivery and product quality

Reduction of risk – using exhibitions, trial use and product delivery guarantees.

The relationship marketing plan

It is essential that an organization manages the scope and range of relationships within the marketing environment in order to achieve success.

Relationship marketing and mass customization

Mass customization enables companies to focus on what customers want, rather than what the company can produce. It also allows companies to produce individually tailored products. There is a longer history of using this approach with services such as banking stockbroking rather than products. Mass customization is also more common in b2b and the simplest approach is to design a product that buyers can customize themselves. Dell Computers allows the buyer to design an individual computer and then track it through to delivery. Much of Dell's production, up to the point of final assembly, is outsourced which means that suppliers at every link in the chain need good timely information about what customers want, and when. Speed and good communications are essential if mass customization is to work.

The Age of E-tail (Birch, A., Gerbert, P. and Schneider, D., 2000) conveys the message that the future of shopping is online and the result of this will be the need for companies to offer almost everything in ways that are specifically tailored to the customer. Personalized products such as cars and PCs are made to individual specifications and soon all successful e-tailors will offer almost everything tailored individually to the customer. E-tailors need repeat business to achieve profitability but e-customers are fickle.

Plan for introducing better customer service

1. Review other organizations with good reputations for good customer service. Look at how this compares with practices in the target organization
2. Agree what customer service means and how it will be interpreted in the target organization
3. Agree customer service standards and procedures
4. All staff should participate in the process of change. Establish a working group or project team that has representation from all the parts of the organization that have an influence on customer service
5. Review strengths and weaknesses
6. Agree and communicate customer satisfaction performance targets
7. Develop plans to implement changes, including an internal marketing plan
8. A training programme aimed at everyone who has an influence on customer service should be devised or outsourced and implemented.

Marketing channels

Increasingly, organizations are examining the whole demand chain that links raw material, components and manufactured goods, and how they are moved to their customers. The starting point should be the customer needs for which the organization needs to mobilize its resources. However, the term 'supply chain' is challenged because it suggests too linear a view of purchase, production and consumption. A more contemporary term is 'value network'. Philip Kotler in his book *Marketing Management* (Kotler, P., 2003) expresses the wish that marketers will look more widely than the customer side of the value network and participate in upstream activities. This would mean that they became network managers, not only customer and product managers.

Marketing channels are an integral part of the marketing mix, and they provide the means by which products and services are made available to end-user customers. They link manufacturers with their target markets, and are the means by which customers can access the products and services that they want. They consist of a number of different organizations each of which fulfils a particular role. Typically a conventional channel will consist of a producer, wholesaler, retailer and end-user customer who need to collaborate and cooperate with each other. Intermediaries assume particular roles in relation to the other members of the marketing channel according to their position.

Hybrid channels

There are also 'hybrid' channels with different strategies used to reach different types of customers. For example, IBM uses its sales force for its largest accounts, telemarketing for medium sized accounts, direct mail for small accounts, retailers to sell to even smaller accounts and the Internet for speciality items. The Internet has had a major impact on established marketing channel structures because it allows direct contact between, for example, a service provider and the customer. Low-cost airlines is an example of this. Overall, the effect of more direct selling has been to reduce the number of intermediaries.

Distribution channels

A distribution channel consists of individuals and organizations who ensure that a product or service is available to the customer at the right place and time. A channel comprises marketing intermediaries, for example transportation companies, merchants, agents, wholesaler, warehouses and retail outlets. The successful management of the supply chain depends on motivating and controlling distributors and distribution outlets. Investing in intermediaries and their activities motivates them to undertake marketing within their network, thus adding value to the customer-supplier relationship. Traditionally, manufacturers operated within the area of production and marketing of brands, and retailers focused on selling activities. Interaction between the two was often based on manufacturers acting as 'order takers' and retailers as sales outlets.

The challenge of making products and services available to customers around the world when, where and how they want them is complex. Technology transfer has made product advantages difficult to maintain but distribution is seen as having the potential for achieving a competitive advantage if marketing channels can be designed to provide excellent customer service. This means that members of the channel need to work together to create added value. A competitive advantage gained through better distribution is not so easily copied and may offer more of a sustainable competitive advantage. The main objective of physical distribution is to decrease costs while increasing service to the customer. The manager will need to consider the order processing, materials handling, warehousing, inventory management and transportation issues. Managers strive for a good balance of service, costs and resources. Therefore, effective planning is paramount to ensure that this happens by determining what level of customer service is acceptable, yet realistic in terms of costs. As physical distribution affects every element of the marketing mix, it is important that the customers' needs are at the top of the list. An effective physical distribution programme should have a positive impact on customer satisfaction; for example some companies offer guaranteed 'next day' delivery.

The following Case Study shows how 'category management' in the small convenience store sector is based on a collaborative approach between manufacturer and retailer.

Category management

Category management is based on a more collaborative approach and means that manufacturer and retailer interact actively together. Together they evaluate sales data to determine who buys what in a particular category, how often and how much they spend. Based on this shared data, they are able to develop customized strategies for individual categories in specific stores so that shelf-space, pricing, promotions, etc., maximize sales and profits. This means that manufacturer and retailer share, and are committed to, common goals.

Retailers should consider several criteria when evaluating the impact that categories have on their businesses, including: category sales, category gross profits, the category's ability to draw store traffic, and the impact on store image. Selecting the right supplier partner is critical. An ideal supplier partner should possess the following qualifications:

- Track Record – The supplier partner should have a history of successfully driving the retailer's business
- Data Management – The supplier partner should have the skills and resources to deliver state-of-the-art, business-building information, insights and ideas
- Does the candidate have access to data for use in better understanding category dynamics and benchmarking performance?
- Can the candidate interpret data and develop business-building recommendations?
- Personnel – Does the proposed team have high-quality members? Do you get along with the candidate's team members?

Wholesaler
Wholesalers buy products from the manufacturer, store them within their warehouses and sell the products on to the trade. Producers try to increase demand, and support marketing activity through various push and pull strategies. Both wholesalers and retailers want their respective customers to perceive a high level of service and value in the goods and services they purchase.

Retailer
Nowadays, retailers often have a presence on the high street and the Internet. They provide the link between the customer and the producer, and may require a lot of technical support, customer services backup, stock ordering facilities, systems underpinning the sales process, information and merchandise. Retailers provide wholesalers with sales contacts and outlets and help them by purchasing small quantities of stock on a regular basis. Retailers focus on end-user consumers and consider their buying motivations.

Distributors/dealers
Distributors and dealers stock products for manufacturers and sell them on, including after-sales service, warranties and credit facilities. Dealers often specialize in a particular brand and sell to the end-user, making the channel shorter.

Agents/brokers/facilitators
Agents and brokers act on behalf of the manufacturer and bring buyers and sellers together.

Franchisee

A franchisee holds a contract to market and supply a product or service that has been very strictly designed and developed by the franchiser. There are often restrictions on store design and layout, and what is sold within the retail outlet.

Licensee

A licensee pays royalties on sales or supplies to the licensor. The licensor is often the manufacturer of the product.

Merchandiser

Merchandisers are responsible for promotional displays in stores relating to different products.

Value-added activities

Examples of the kinds of value-added activities that intermediaries can undertake is: analysing information such as sales data, evaluating channel activities, co-ordinating advertising, personal selling, promotions, etc., facilitating communication, maintaining relationships between manufacturer and retail outlets, and providing advice, technical support, after-sales service and warranties.

Channels perform most effectively when they co-operate, co-ordinate and integrate their activities. Vertical channel management is where two or more channel members are connected by ownership or legal obligation. Marketing mix activities are more integrated, and often more effective because of this. Horizontal channel integration is the merging of organizations at the same level of channel operation under one management, for example, through mergers and takeovers.

Conflict in marketing channels

Conflict in marketing channels can occur for a variety of reasons over issues such as stock levels, pricing and sales order processing. Sometimes it is because channel members have different priorities, and are focused on different business elements. A manufacturer might be focused more on products and processes, and a retailer may be focused more on customers and the processes necessary to meet their needs. Poor communication between channel members can be a cause of conflict but communication is an important co-ordinating mechanism for all members of a marketing channel. The willingness of members to share information and associated resources is an important factor because it enables an openness between parties, through which full information can be exchanged. This means that the producer must be willing to share sensitive information, and the distributor must be willing to share information about themselves, their customers and markets.

Extranets

Extranets can be used to engage distributors and producers, and allows for fast, accurate, low cost exchange of information. It involves building bridges between the public Internet and private corporate intranets, and can be seen as part of a company's intranet that is made accessible to other companies, to the public, or comprises components that enable the collaboration with other companies. Maximizing accessibility will mean that many partners can be involved and the more the participants, the greater the rates of return from the system. Extranets can also help companies to finally realize the benefits of Just-In-Time (JIT) inventory systems.

Other uses of extranets include:

- Private newsgroups that co-operating companies use to share valuable experiences and ideas
- Groupware collaboration in the development of new products or services

- ○ Training programmes that companies develop and share
- ○ Shared product catalogues accessible only to wholesalers or those in the trade
- ○ Project management and control as part of a common work project.

The following Case Study shows examples of extranets.

Automotive Network eXchange (ANX)

Chrysler, General Motors and Ford Motor Co. have a collaborative extranet called the Automotive Network exchange (ANX) which links them to their suppliers. Communications between suppliers and manufacturers are quicker, and the system is used for product shipment schedules, order information, files for product designs and purchase orders.

Federal Express' Tracking System (www.fedex.com)

On FedEx's public site, a tracking number can be entered and any package still in their system can be located. In one session all the information needed to prepare a shipper form, obtain a tracking number, print the form and schedule a pick-up can be entered. The processes on their site have been copied by many other companies.

The promotional mix in the marketing channel
The role of marketing communications in the distribution channels is different to that used in consumer markets because the target audience and the information needs are different.

Differentiation	Channel members need to understand how a manufacturer (and/or products) adds value and is different from other products that they carry. It is also needed upstream to secure stock, support and resources.
Reinforcement	This reminds downstream members of superior product features benefits plus support facilities, reassuring them in terms of continuity, value and reliability. This focuses on reassuring upstream members that their interests are being looked after.
Information	To provide downstream members with suitable levels of customer support, and upstream members with market and performance information.
Persuade	To encourage downstream members to carry (extra) stock, provide facilities and to meet required service levels. Upstream members need to be persuaded to allocate stock, promotional support and financial conditions in the favour of downstream members.

The promotional mix has to deliver messages that relate to product features and benefits. Personal selling is the main tool because it is through face-to-face meetings that relationships between organizations are developed and maintained. This is often supported by direct marketing, sales promotions and public relations. Advertising is used to a much smaller extent because it is expensive and relatively inefficient in achieving these aims. As mentioned above, the Internet has transformed a large part of marketing communications activities and enables organizations to share information. Personal selling, supported by direct marketing and the Internet, plus exhibitions and sales literature can provide an effective mix.

Evaluating channel effectiveness

It is essential that having selected an appropriate distribution channel and intermediaries, their efficiency, effectiveness and performance are continually managed.

Key performance and evaluation measures include:

o Regular reviews
o A forum for problem review and solution
o Monthly, quarterly and year sales data analysis
o Average stock levels
o Lead and delivery times
o Zero defects
o Customer service complaints
o Marketing support – achieving marketing objectives, level of marketing activity, sales promotions, distributor incentives
o Spot-check of distributions further down the supply chain
o Annual performance audit.

From an Internet perspective, typical evaluation methods of marketing effectiveness might include:

o Number of leads
o Increased sales
o Customer retention
o Increased market share
o Brand enhancement and loyalty
o Customer service.

The following Case Study shows a typical working day for a marketing channel executive in a mobile phone manufacturing company.

Channel Marketing Executive: a day in the life

Toria works for a mobile phone company as a Channel Marketing Executive. She provides channel marketing/retail support to dealers and channel members (managing & planning merchandiser programme, dealers' road show and events, POS fulfilment, etc.). She manages product launches and marketing collaterals' fulfillment to channel members.

9:00 a.m. – My morning begins with replying to dealers' fax and e-mail requests of the Company's channel marketing/retail support. The most exciting part of my day is when we have an active discussion with channel members on how to implement activities and formulate strategies.

10:00 a.m. – Meeting with channel members to discuss new promotional activities or events. Today, we discuss the upcoming dealer road show.

11:00 a.m. – I am contacting dealers about any updates pertaining to The Company or their shops. I work with the rest of my colleagues as a team to implement dealer events and sales training. My time is mostly spent meeting with channel members to work out dealer events. I also visit them at retail shops to ensure that there's retail support and wide exposure of the Company's brand presence.

3:00 p.m. – Meeting with a dealer to discuss his road show.

7:00 p.m. – Time to go home. This is the usual time I leave from the office. However, when I'm on site at a roadshow, I leave around 9 p.m. so that I can ensure logistic arrangements are met before the event starts.

Internal marketing

The basis of internal marketing is focusing on the relationship that exists between the organization and its employees. One of the success factors for the implementation of the marketing plan is to treat internal staff as if they are customers who all need the same consideration and attention as external customers. The aim of internal marketing is to develop a unified sense of purpose among employees. It plays an important role in ensuring that the organization is marketing- and customer-focused. Internal marketing is based on a communications programme, and there are a number of steps that an organization can take in order to achieve internal synergy and employee co-operation:

- ○ Creating an internal awareness of the corporate aims, objectives and overall mission
- ○ Determining the expectations of the internal customer
- ○ Communication to internal customers
- ○ Changes in tasks and activities
- ○ Internal monitoring and control.

It is as important to segment the market internally, as it is segmented externally. A key aim of the marketing plan should be the successful motivation and retention of the internal customer so that the organization can meet the needs of the external market.

Consumer and business-to-business marketing communications

The importance of b2b communications is underpinned by buoyant Internet-based marketing communications compared with relatively slow growth in the b2c market.

The most important difference, however, is that organizational buying decisions are taken by *groups* of people rather than individuals. A key issue is to identify the individuals who comprise the decision-making unit.

Communications in marketing channel networks

A planned, channel-orientated communications strategy should contribute to and reinforce the partnerships in the network. There are many factors that can influence channel communication strategy, for example:

- ○ Power – are some organizations more important than others?
- ○ Direction – are communications one-way or two-way?
- ○ Frequency – how often should messages be sent?
- ○ Timing – messages should be sent to all members simultaneously or serially?
- ○ Style and content – messages should be formal/informal? What must be included?
- ○ Distortion – will messages be received, stored and acted upon as the originator intends?
- ○ Information sharing – is there a willingness to share information in the marketing channel?

Summary

There are a variety of approaches to planning the design, implementation and evaluation of communications campaigns. Marketing communications are used to develop relationships or communicate with a range of stakeholders including the provision of support for members of a marketing channel. There are also a variety of ways to review and evaluate the effectiveness of communications activities.

Bibliography

Birch, A., Gerbert, P. and Schneider, D., (2000). *The Age of E-tail*, Milford CT: Capstone.

Carlzon, J., (1987). *Moments of Truth*, Harper.

Kotler, P., (2003). *Marketing Management*, New York: Prentice Hall. 11th Edition.

> Sample exam questions and answers for the Marketing Management in Practice module as a whole can be found in Appendix 3 at the back of the book.

unit 8
developing marketing plans

Learning objectives

○ Develop an operational marketing plan, selecting an appropriate marketing mix for an organization operating in any context such as FMCG, business-to-business (supply chain), large or capital project-based, services, voluntary and not-for-profit, or sales support (e.g. SMEs)

○ Use the main techniques available for planning, scheduling and resourcing activities within the plan

○ Identify appropriate measures for evaluating and controlling the marketing plan

○ Review and evaluate the effectiveness of planning activities.

Introduction

The Marketing Management in Practice module is intended to give participants some practice in developing and implementing marketing plans at an operational level in organizations. A key part of this is working within a team to develop the plan and managing teams implementing the plan by undertaking marketing activities and projects. Its aim is to encourage you to integrate and apply knowledge from all the modules, particularly as part of a team. The focus should be on implementing a marketing plan as a team activity and careful attention needs to be given to the issues surrounding the actual implementation of a plan.

Planning

In his book, *The Rise of Fall of Strategic Planning*, Henry Mintzberg describes how strategic planners make the mistake that the future will resemble the past and tend to gather 'hard' data on their industry, markets and competitors, whilst ignoring 'soft' data such as talking with customers, suppliers and employees. Many organizations now make use of the term 'Strategic Intent' defined by Gary Hamel and C.K. Prahalad in their book *Competing for the Future* as 'an ambitious and compelling dream that provides the emotional and intellectual energy for the journey to the future, conveying a sense of direction and destiny'. Strategic intent is more flexible than a strategic plan and recognizes that the best laid plans may need to change in response to market conditions. The pace of change means that it isn't always possible to anticipate change and, for example, cataclysmic events such as September 11th and its

191

aftermath which wasn't and couldn't have been anticipated, can completely transform the business context. The upshot of this is that planning is important but it needs to incorporate flexibility. The days when vast resources were put into creating gigantic strategic plans that were out of date by the time they had been produced are probably over for the present.

The core ideology of the Houston Independent School District outlines the direction of the school district and the expectations we hold for all employees. By defining our organization's purpose, we define what we are. Our core values define who we are, and our strategic intent and goals define what we intend to do to achieve our purpose.

Marketing plan components

Marketing plans tend to vary by industry, size of company, stage of growth and organizational goals. The process of preparing it is as important as the particular form it takes. The process should make you think about goals and the marketing strategy that will be used to achieve them. A marketing plan may contain all or just some of the following components.

Executive summary

Introduce the organization:

- explain the major points of your plan
- describe briefly the nature of the business and the products or services offered
- include a mission or values statement and objectives
- list the structure of your organization and the senior management team
- summarize the marketing objectives and strategies that are in the plan.

Marketing audit

A good marketing audit is:

- **Systematic** It follows a logical, predetermined framework – an orderly sequence of diagnostic steps
- **Comprehensive** It considers all factors affecting marketing performance, not just obvious trouble spots. Marketers can be fooled into addressing symptoms rather than underlying problems. A comprehensive audit can identify the real problems
- **Independent** To ensure objectivity, outside consultants are used sometimes to prepare the marketing audit. Using outsiders may not be necessary, but having an objective auditor is important
- **Periodic** Many organizations schedule regular marketing audits because the environment for marketing is dynamic.

A typical marketing audit consists of a number of sections, for example:

Marketing environment audit

This is based on an analysis of the internal and external environment. It should include information about target markets, including information about other individuals or organizations that offer similar products and services. Identify key issues in the competitive environment, for example, challenges, such as new legislation or the impact of technological changes.

The marketing audit is important to the planning process because it provides the analysis that supports the corporate and the marketing decision-making process. An audit should provide information on the external (macro) and internal (micro) environment. Understanding trends and trying to anticipate changes that will have an impact on markets, customers, suppliers and competitors are important aspects of strategic development. Decisions about product and service development and investment decisions should be informed by the outcome of the marketing audit. The challenge is to use data intelligently and be prepared to respond to changes that influence consumer preferences and behaviour as well as to be proactive and try to influence that behaviour.

Environmental scanning

This is the systematic collection and evaluation of information from the wider marketing environment that might affect the organization and its strategic marketing activities. It is undertaken by marketing planners.

Key issues are:

- Making sure that data is up-to-date, particularly for markets that are volatile and where consumer behaviour can change quickly
- The ability to identify what is significant amongst a myriad of detail. It is important not to drown in a sea of information
- Collecting data on a regular basis may be too expensive for an organization to undertake itself but the data that is available to purchase from market research analysts may not be specific enough about particular markets and products
- Marketing managers need to be able to understand the environment in which they are operating.

Marketing analysis tools

Analysis tools commonly used for this purpose are PESTLE, Porter's 5 force analysis, gap analysis, BCG matrix, GE matrix, etc.

A PESTLE (Political/Policy, Economic, Social/Societal, Technological, Legal and Environmental) analysis is a logical framework for identifying and assessing the various influences on the present and future development of the organization. It is usually a precursor to developing a SWOT analysis of the internal strengths and weaknesses of the organization compared with the opportunities and constraints in the external environment.

Political factors Such as a changes in government and the ramifications of their strategies such as tax levels, education and training issues, employment legislation, etc.

Economic factors Such as the impact of the trade cycle, levels of disposable income and inflation.

Typical questions are:

What are the effects of competitors (their products, services, technologies) on your operation?

What major developments in income, prices, savings, taxation and credit will affect the organization?

Social/cultural Issues Such as the ageing consumer, increases in one-parent families, changing values, attitudes and beliefs to smoking.

Typical questions to ask are:

What population trends are expected to affect existing and planned strategy?

- What social and psychological patterns (attitudes, lifestyle, etc.) are expected to affect buyer behaviour patterns? How are environmental trends monitored?
- How are present and pending legal developments affecting your operation?

Technological factors Such as the increased rate of computer capability, production methods, etc.

Legal issues Such as changes in advertising legislation for tobacco, regulations and codes of practice for promotions, etc.

Environmental issues Such as attitudes towards pollution, energy use, fair trade, slave labour, etc.

The following Case Study is an extract from a PESTLE analysis carried out by a national training organization that was faced with the loss of government grant and the need to become a commercial organization dependent on winning contracts.

The future development of a training organization: PESTLE analysis

Political issues

Learning and skills are regarded as central to economic growth and prosperity, and underpinned by government resources.

Employers are central to the Government's agenda but UK employer networks and institutions are weak, limiting opportunities for information sharing, best practice and collaboration.

The environment of audit inspection, information and regulation will become more intense and sophisticated. Developing standards, benchmarks and quality assurance procedures will continue to be important.

Economic issues

Globalization

There will be global markets in skilled workers as well as in investment and trade. Taking advantage of globalization will require people who are able to access the resources of other people and organizations around the world.

Flexible labour markets

Non-standard employment, i.e. part-time work, flexi-hours, self-employment and home working will become more common.

The Information economy

The information economy will be a small business, entrepreneurial economy and small firms will become more important. Knowledge is seen as a resource by businesses, governments, and individuals.

Social

Skills

UK labour productivity currently lags behind that of other major industrialized countries. The need for 'softer skills' such as communication and team working is likely to increase because of flatter structures, more team-based operations, greater diversification of job roles and other changes to the workplace.

Demography

Young and skilled people are becoming a scarce resource, particularly in countries with tight labour markets. There is an ageing workforce.

Qualifications

A significant number of individuals and employers are not engaging with the qualifications system at all.

Developing the supply side of training

In a demand-led system, private providers, voluntary sector providers and companies' in-house training facilities will be able to compete with public sector providers.

Technological

Technological developments will mean that the provision of education and learning will become more diffuse, informal and user-driven. The Internet's use as a source of information and education will grow significantly.

Legal

Legal issues concern the status of NTOs, ownership of Occupational Standards and whether there are any obstacles that might impact on the transition of NTOs towards becoming commercial organizations.

SWOT analysis

This should be a summary of the marketing audit and indicate the key issues which need then to be considered further. A SWOT analysis is undertaken to help plan the marketing mix, which includes:

- ○ Strengths of the product/ service/ organization
- ○ Weaknesses of the organization
- ○ Opportunities available to the organization (external factors)
- ○ Threats which may come from the competition.

One way to improve upon the basic SWOT is to include more detailed competitor and business environment information in the analysis. SWOT analysis can also be augmented through surveys, for example, customer awareness, interest, trial and usage levels.

GAP analysis

A gap analysis is something which needs to be monitored and considered in terms of filling the gap, should one occur. A gap is where corporate sales and financial objectives are greater than the current long-range forecasts in marketing planning. A gap could be filled in various ways, for example, by improving productivity, reducing costs, increasing prices, stimulating increased usage, increasing market share, finding new user groups, developing new market segments, product development.

The marketing audit should ensure that the method chosen to fill the gap is consistent with the company's capabilities and builds on its strengths. For example, it would normally prove far less profitable for a dry goods grocery manufacturer to introduce frozen foods than to add another dry foods product. Likewise, if a product could be sold to existing channels using the existing sales force, this is far less risky than introducing a new product that requires new channels and new selling skills.

Marketing objectives

Corporate objectives are derived from the corporate plan, and inform the direction and focus of the marketing plan. Marketing objectives cover issues such as increasing the awareness of your product or service among your target audience in a particular time frame. The marketing objectives are likely to be linked to market share or sales targets. Long-, medium- and short-term objectives should be identified, some of which should be SMART. Examples of objectives are:

1. Profitability objectives – To achieve a 25 per cent return on capital employed by August 2007

2. Market share objectives – To gain 30 per cent of the market for umbrellas by September 2006

3. Promotional objectives – To increase awareness of the dangers of Hepatitis to travellers from 15 per cent to 30 per cent by April 2005

4. Objectives for survival – To survive the current double-dip recession

5. Objectives for growth – To increase the size of our German Brazilian operation from $200,000 in 2002 to $400,000 in 2003

6. Objectives for branding – To make Y brand of bottled beer the preferred brand of 21–28-year old females in North America by February 2006.

Goals and aims tend to be more vague and focus on the longer-term compared with objectives. They will not be SMART.

Marketing strategy

Segmentation – targeting and positioning The key area in the strategic section of the marketing plan will consider these issues. The corporate plan may indicate the markets in which the company will operate, but the marketing plan will consider the segmentation strategy, targeting and resulting positioning strategy. This will be linked to the branding decisions.

Marketing mix decisions The strategy will inform the decisions in relation to pricing, product, place and the extended Ps – people, process and physical evidence. Here, the marketing communications plan will be developed.

Budget decisions will need to be taken throughout the strategic and operational areas of the plan. The methods of determining the marketing plan will be considered.

This describes how you intend achieving your marketing objectives. It is, essentially, the heart of your marketing plan and covers the 4 Ps of marketing.

Product – Describe your product or service in detail. Include product features and benefits.

Price – Describe your pricing strategy and payment policies. There are a range of approaches to pricing strategies considering cost, volume and profit.

There are four key factors that affect pricing decisions, also known as the 4 Cs:

- ○ *Cost* Related to the actual costs involved
- ○ *Consumer/customer* Related to the price the consumer will pay
- ○ *Competition* Related to competitors' prices for substitute or complimentary products
- ○ *Company* Related to the company's financial objectives.

Promotion – Describe the promotional tools or tactics (a promotion plan) you'll use to accomplish your marketing objectives (See Unit 7).

Place – Describe how and where you will place your product so that customers have access to it and how you'll make the sale – your sales and distribution methods.

Action Plan – Describe what will be done, when it will begin or be completed and who will accomplish the tasks.

Budget – List the cost of the marketing activities you are describing in the marketing plan.

Measurements – Describe the specific numerical targets that will be used to measure the results of implementing your plan. Control involves setting standards and comparing progress against them. Corrective action needs to be taken if it looks like the standards won't be met. Include time limits for achieving goals.

Monitoring and control – The plan will need to identify the methods of monitoring and evaluating the plan. Decide which controls are important, how they should be implemented and who should be involved.

Control factors – There are four main areas where control mechanisms should be considered within the marketing plan, i.e. management control, financial control, efficiency control and strategic control.

o   *Management control* This includes areas such as performance appraisal for staff and the workforce, benchmarking procedures, etc. against other organizations
o   *Financial control* This includes financial controls which most companies are adept at calculating. It could include trend analysis, comparison, liquidity ratios, debt ratios, activity ratios, etc.
o   *Efficiency control* Here, this area considers the optimum value from marketing assets
o   *Strategic control* The easiest method of control is to measure marketing activities against market performance or objectives set.

Some organizations group their analysis into the following areas:

Financial analysis

This would include ratio analysis, variance analysis, cash flow monitoring, and capital expenditure monitoring. Financial analysis of competitors is relatively easy to perform because the financial accounts should be readily available. The main problems arise when the competitor is a division of a major corporation, and is not a limited company in its own right, and so is not obliged to publish its accounts, or when the company is present in markets where accurate financial reporting is not in evidence.

Market analysis

This would cover analysis of total market demand and market share. Market share information may not be as easily obtainable, although most organizations have access to some means of measuring this, such as through marketing database companies, market research periodicals, trade associations and journals.

Sales analysis

Analysis of sales targets and selling cost budgets. As with market share, this information may not be easily obtainable. Checking out the effectiveness of a marketing campaign from a product sales standpoint is critical. Begin the review process early, and repeat it often. The plan can be tweaked along the way to eliminate or shift schedules if some element of the mix is not working.

Physical resource analysis

This would involve analysis of plant and equipment utilization together with other measures of productivity and product quality. Operational effectiveness, e.g. process technology, people, information systems, etc. impact on operational efficiency. This affects costs and business performance, including the speed and efficiency of service, customer perception, quality and reliability of product or service and warranty claims.

Systems analysis

The effectiveness of strategic implementation and analysis of marketing resource applications.

Companies may benchmark best practice at different levels of the organization in a variety of ways:

- o in an organization in another industry
- o internally, e.g. comparing operations in business units in different locations
- o with competitors, though they may be unwilling to share the secrets of their success.

The way an organization prioritizes these factors has a bearing on its performance.

This leads to the following questions:

- o Which factors are absent from your organization? Do these need further investigation?
- o Which factors do competitors pay more attention to, compared to your organization and why?
- o Which factors are given low priority by your organization? Do these indicate areas for improvement?

Tracking procedures

This section of the plan should include plans and procedures for tracking each type of media you are using and which seems to be the most effective.

Display advertising With traditional consumer publications, tracking can be done through the use of different phone numbers, special offers (specific to that advertisement or publication), or reference to a specific department to call for information.

Many trade publications also include Reader Service Cards that allow the reader to circle a number that corresponds to your ad on a mail-in postcard in order to get more information about your product or service.

Direct marketing With postal mailings, tracking is relatively simple. Include on the mailing label a code (called a key code or a source code) that corresponds with the mailing list. For telemarketing campaigns, tracking is also relatively simple since someone is communicating with the customer throughout the entire process in most cases.

Internet marketing Usually this is easily tracked because it is based on click throughs, or page impressions.

Promotions Most closed promotions are basically 'self-tracking' because they require the customer to do something such as fill out an entry form (trackable), turn in a coupon, return a rebate slip (trackable), or log-on to a website to claim a prize (also trackable).

Tools for monitoring and control
There are many tools to help with control and monitoring:

- o Market share analysis
- o Sales analysis
- o Budgets
- o Marketing research
- o Marketing information systems (MkIS)

199

- ○ Feedback from customer satisfaction surveys
- ○ Cash flow statements
- ○ Customer Relationship Management (CRM) systems
- ○ Activities of competitors to aspects of your plan
- ○ Distributor support
- ○ Performance of any promotional activities.

Supporting documentation

Include any supporting documents referenced in other plan sections here, such as CVs or key management resumés, spreadsheets, market research results, etc.

Activity 8.1

Read and compare the case studies below and critically appraise them as marketing plans. They differ from each other in some respects. Your task is to decide whether these differences are because the organizations are different in size, etc. and serve different markets with different products and services, or is it because of differences in the usefulness and comprehensiveness of the Plan?

Would either of the plans benefit from some of the strengths of the other plan, or is the same level of detail not necessary for both plans?

Use the components of a marketing plan from above and decide:

- ○ Are there components that haven't been used in one plan which would improve the other plan if they were included ?
- ○ What gaps are there in the plans?
- ○ How could either or both plans be improved?

Case Study 1 – Diamond Badges

Marketing plan

The following marketing plan is written by the solo owner of a small business. Names of some businesses and cities have been fictionalized at the owner's request.

Mission statement

Technically, the mission statement is in the opening of the entire Business Plan, of which the Marketing Plan is a part. It's included here for the reader's information.

Diamond intends to supply Oxford with the most visually interesting Badges available today. They will delight their users and provide a springboard for creative activity. Diamond believes artistic expression enhances life. It appreciates the skill of human hands and the sensitivity of human hearts. It regards Badges as small works of art in which we are able to see ourselves.

Diamond's marketing plan

Diamond is a specialty retail store offering a collection of antique, contemporary and hand-crafted Badges from around the world. These Badges are distinguished from those available in the marketplace by the quality of materials, workmanship and design.

Diamond addresses the need to have fun! Badges are wonderfully expressive objects that add unexpected vitality to clothing. Apparel manufacturers are witnessing a competitive advantage to using fun and distinctive badges.

With growth, Diamond will also establish a working studio.

Diamond opened for business on 5 August 1999, with an inventory valued at £2,050. In the first eight months of operation, another £2,290 of inventory was added. Sales totalled £2,376 for the same period with the average monthly total being £172. Sales have increased steadily over this eight month period.

Organizations and businesses served include:

Oxford Badgemakers Guild

Badge for Profit of Oxford

Intercom Designers

The Workroom.

Funding for the company has come from the personal income of the sole proprietor and from the income generated by sales. Additional funding is sought for the expansion of inventory and for advertising.

Product or service description

Diamond offers hand-crafted and manufactured badges in a range of materials and finishes. A high percentage of these Badges are made of natural materials such as horn, bone, wood, glass and clay. These Badges are hand-crafted by artisans throughout the world and are of original design. Manufactured metal and synthetic Badges are also offered, together with a collection of vintage and antique Badges.

Badges are often purchased for their beauty, and collections of antique Badges represent a significant investment and historical rise in value.

Location

Diamond is located in Oxford on the second floor of the Tower Building. With growth, it would like to relocate to the building's south end. The benefits of this location are first floor access, room for expansion, higher visibility from large arched windows, more convenient parking, closer proximity to area retailers and reasonable cost.

Market analysis

The industry

According to the British Badgemakers Craft Association, the home Badge-making industry contributes £2.5 million in retail sales to the economy. In the five years from 1995–2002, first-time buyers of Badge-making machines increased from 40 per cent to 55 per cent. In the last five years (1991–1996), membership in the British Badgemakers Guild has doubled in size with a 55 per cent increase in the number of local chapters. Today's Badge-making is technologically advanced and computer memories have also enhanced the creative potential of the Badge-making machine.

Badge-making is one of several creative industries served by Diamond. As this country reassesses its priorities, home-oriented leisure activities enjoy increased levels of interest.

The target market

The Badgemaker's profile, as reported by the British Home Badge making and Craft Association, looks like:

- o   75 per cent female
- o   35 to 64 years of age
- o   household income of £35,000 and more
- o   artistic, values originality.

This profile is supported by direct observation of Diamond's customers.

People who pursue the creative industries value objects made by hand, and purchase them for themselves, their friends and their families. They are deeply involved in home-based leisure activities such as reading and gardening. Badges are used increasingly in the home as an element of interest and design.

The competition

Direct competitors exist in three nearby cities. They are the Badge Factory, a high-end of the market shop located in York and two badge shops in Bath – Antique Badges and Renewal Badges. The strength of these competitors lies in the length of time they have been in business. Awareness of their product is well established.

Badges are displayed prominently at Diamond in a manner consistent with their quality and character. Again, Diamond will compete by focusing on Badges. The company will also compete on the basis of location.

Antique Badges and Renewal Badges offer a product impressive in its range of quality, price and character. They are both centrally located and are the model upon which Diamond patterns itself.

Diamond will entice fans away from these shops by diligently procuring Badges of high originality. Independent Badgesmiths will be showcased whenever possible. Diamond will also maintain a large collection of vintage and antique badges. Indirect competition comes from Northeast Fabrics. Diamond offers Badges that cannot be found in these stores and priced generally higher. Diamond will attract customers who may be willing to spend more on Badges than on fabric to achieve a higher level of style and expression.

Promotional objectives and strategies

One of the greatest challenges facing Diamond in its first year of operation is lack of awareness. At this time, the customer base is 200 people. The company's goal is to double this number over the months of June through October for an overall goal of 400 customers.

Strategies for achieving this goal include:

- o Establishing an auxiliary sales display at the local farmer's market on Saturdays throughout the summer. This can be done at a cost of £110
- o Distributing business cards and reprints of an article about Diamond which appeared in *Lifelike Magazine*. Distribution points will be the farmer's market, the Arts Alive Gallery and the Underground Studio
- o Publishing a quarterly newsletter to existing customers and selected businesses. The newsletter will solicit referrals, advertise additions to inventory and notify readers of current sales promotions
- o Establishing quarterly sales promotions in May, August, November and February
- o The April sales promotion will be in honour of Mother's Day. Customers will be treated to an afternoon tea; discounted gift certificates for mothers will be offered
- o November will focus on year-end festivities
- o February will highlight Valentine's Day
- o Advertising in the newsletters of the Woodbrook Weavers, the Oxford Guild. Costs range in the area of £10 per issue
- o Continuing to advertise in the Yellow Pages at a cost of £15.75 per month
- o Another goal which Diamond needs to address is that of building inventory. Summer months will allow a greater portion of the company's resources to be directed toward augmenting inventory
- o Diamond will advertise in the area weeklies, such as *Retreat*, as wanting to buy old Badges
- o Diamond will solicit handmade Badges by advertising in the 'Opportunities' section of *The Art Calendar* as a consignor.

Pricing policy

Three categories of Badges are purchased by Diamond for resale. They are hand-crafted Badges, manufactured Badges and antique Badges. The standard industry mark-up is 100 per cent.

The average retail price of hand-crafted and antique Badges is £4.25. Manufactured Badges range in price from £1.45 to £2.00, depending on what material is used. Badges of natural materials are more expensive.

Case Study 2 – Stormbreaker

Stormbreaker is a small but profitable company in the extremely competitive sportswear market. In order to grow and become even more profitable, it needs to expand its products to a wider market and consider segmenting specific areas of the marketplace. In 2000, Stormbreaker introduced a fully waterproof, fully breathable outer clothing system, virtually eliminating the condensation problems normally associated with waterproof clothing.

Turnover in 2000/2001 was £16 million, with a net profit of £182,500. R&D investment is £250,000 with other costs being covered by co-operation with suppliers and customers.

203

The market environment

It is clear that many individuals will have specialist sports shoes for specialist sports (tennis, running, cycling, etc.). There are many other companies that are now well established in this market. Some specialize in sportswear alone, unlike Stormbreaker, who have a wide range of sports shoes and sportswear.

Distribution

Stormbreaker has recently been considering some options regarding the way their goods reach the final consumer. Although their goods have an established identity amongst the key consumers, most of the goods are actually sold through specialist retail outlets and catalogues to whom they supply leaflets and posters.

With the advent of e-commerce and the possibility of expanding their network, the company has recently been considering web-based activities much more seriously.

Stormbreaker continues to be highly active in pioneering the use of new materials in their product range. The use of 'smart' materials is particularly interesting them at present. The development of heating and cooling the wearer, utilizing specially bonded fabrics is currently being explored.

SWOT analysis

Strengths

- o Good brand
- o Good range of outdoor items
- o Specialist products
- o New waterproof material
- o Good TV exposure and PR in general
- o Innovative organization.

Weaknesses

- o Not well known
- o R&D base small
- o Marketing and branding budget too small
- o Manufacturing UK oriented
- o Limited range.

Opportunities

- o Expand manufacturing base
- o Creating strategic alliances with companies that have produced new materials and used chip technology
- o More expenditure on marketing and PR
- o Segmentation and targeting.

Threats

- o New entrants with products based on chip technology
- o Aggressive branding by more established companies
- o Me-too products.

PESTLE analysis

Political

There are hardly any political issues impinging on the company. The only thing it needs to consider is the possible ethical impact of manufacturing in the Far East. If they handle this sensitively and well, then they will be able to use this in their marketing strategies.

Economic

The possible plateauing of running shoe sales. Also, any impending recession will mean that consumers will rein back spending on possible luxury items.

Social

Society is ageing ... certainly in Europe. In considering marketing strategies, the company will have to take into account grey buying power and its impact on their marketing segmentation policies.

Technological

The technology for sports clothing is continuously developing and improving. In the long run, one can see how 'computerized/smart' materials-based clothing will come into being. Various information links within the case show how this technology is evolving. Technological changes are likely to have a far-reaching impact on the company's sportswear. They need to scan the environment continuously to monitor these changes.

Legal

Not too important, unless they produce sub-standard goods or infringe copyright.

Environmental

This usually relates to the production of the sportswear, whether it is environmentally friendly or not. This does not appear to be an issue for Stormbreaker.

However, their products allow a person to visit previously unexplored places, which affects the environment.

Porter's Five Forces Analysis

Threat of new entrants

This could be a significant issue for Stormbreaker. New entrants could appear:

- through the web
- new brand development by some of the major companies: for example Boots introduced their Botanics range to compete with Bodyshop products.

Power of suppliers

Supplier power largely depends on their strength in bargaining. It appears that this is not a significant issue for Stormbreaker, as the main items of use are leather and other generic materials.

Many new items such as self-wicking clothing are developed by the company itself, or in co-operation with suppliers.

Power of buyers

This is a significant area for Stormbreaker to consider and also impacts on the generic strategies they adopt (see later questions).

The customers have considerable power – whether they are the end-consumers or the retailers.

Threat of substitutes

The threat of substitutes is forever present. 'Smart' materials and 'computerized' clothing accessories could be the future for outdoor pursuits. The company, however, may not have enough R&D clout to undertake product development in this area.

Rivalry between firms

The market is *very* competitive.

Product	Stage of the Product Life Cycle
'Smart' clothing	Introduction
Clothing and accessories	Growth
Walking and climbing boots	Maturity
Sports shoes and football boots	Decline

To gain a deeper understanding of the issues and factors affecting planning and control issues for Stormbreaker, utilize the following as the basis for your group discussions.

- o Product Life Cycle analysis
- o The Ansoff Matrix
- o The General Electric Matrix
- o Innovation/value Matrix
- o The BCG Matrix
- o Core Competencies
- o Gap Analysis.

The life cycle model helps to show how a product may grow and then eventually decline. The Adopter Categorization of innovators, early and late majority and laggards should also be considered in conjunction with this model. Decline is not inevitable and a number of companies halted their decline in sales in the mid–eighties by repositioning their brand and revitalizing their offer to the consumer. Improved marketing and product development, and more investment can help to halt decline.

		Products	
		Existing	**New**
Markets	***Existing***	Football/Running shoes Climbing/Walking boots Accessories/clothing	New waterproof attire Elasticated clothing 'Smart' clothing
	New	Clothing for cyclists	'Smart' clothing for different markets, including the health market

Figure 8.1 Ansoff Matrix for Stormbreaker

This analysis helps you to ascertain whether the company actually has competences within attractive sectors.

Figure 8.2 Industry/Product Matrix for Stormbreaker (General Electric Matrix)

Figure 8.3 The Innovation/Value Matrix.

Stormbreaker needs to consider the Innovation/Value Matrix in terms of the possible threats from the Me-too and Migrator competitors. If it is to keep its lead then it must innovate. Its large R&D budget is indicative of this. The dotted arrow shows the threat from me-too companies. It is important for Stormbreaker to protect its innovations with a patent.

BCG matrix

A possible BCG analysis is presented for Stormbreaker, taking into account industry growth and potential growth for Stormbreaker products. In undertaking this analysis, it would be hopeless to consider the whole market. We have to make the assumption that Stormbreaker is competing within a small sector of the specialist market and therefore the idea of a market share actually makes some sense! The potential trajectories for the products are shown in the matrix.

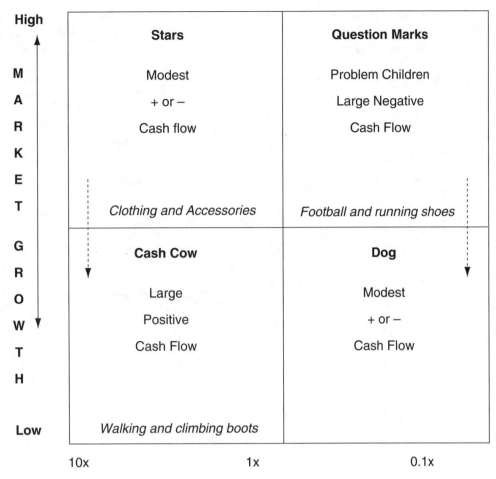

Figure 8.4 Boston Matrix

Market share

In addition to this, it is useful to gauge what products/markets meet the above criteria. Whatever strategy Stormbreaker undertakes, these criteria should be met to ensure continued success in the marketplace. The above analyses show the positioning of the company *vis-à-vis* its product portfolio and market attractiveness. You could continue analysing a company's situation *ad nauseum*, ending up with paralysis through analysis. You should consider issues such as available time and the most relevant models. From these analyses, Stormbreaker has several potential routes that it could follow. The route chosen will depend on the strategies that it is likely to follow.

a) Possible mission statement
Stormbreaker's mission is to be the leading niche player in the outdoor footwear, clothing and accessories market, providing high quality differentiated products that delight the customer.

b) SMART objectives
SMART objectives have to align themselves to the longer term strategy. Examples of these would be:

- Achieve a 5 per cent return on sales
- Increase the R&D budget by 5 per cent
- Increase marketing spend by 10 per cent
- Increase turnover by 10 per cent
- Increase accessory and climbing boot sales by 20 per cent.

All these should be achievable within one year. Market forces may lead the company to change direction in the future. It is therefore sensible to have tight boundaries for one year and more flexible ones for the ensuing years.

Figure 8.5

c) Possible option for Stormbreaker to follow

- o Drop the football and running shoe market
- o Expand research into 'Smart' clothing technology (computerized clothing)
- o Consider a strategic alliance
- o Concentrate on pushing forward the focused strategy (Porter)
- o Improve return on sales by concentrating on the most profitable items
- o Develop a communications plan that fits with the strategies adopted.

The company could decide to follow all these options or some of them, depending on its resource base. A differentiated strategy, with more manufacturing taking place in the Far East, would certainly help to increase its market share, but would it then have a negative impact on its specialist market? Once an option has been decided and the strategy set actions need to be considered. For instance:

- o Dropping the football and running shoe market will mean considerable loss in revenue
- o No one can predict the potential market for 'smart' clothing. A basic calculator now has more computing power than the Apollo spacecraft which landed on the moon in 1969. Mobile phones, smart cards, digital cameras and many more everyday items are the results of continuing developments in, and combinations of technology
- o Alliances are usually within distribution networks for the sports and clothing industry. Whilst Stormbreaker collaborates with suppliers in the development of materials, it does not have sufficient volume of output to have exclusive use of such materials. Stormbreaker gains a reputation for innovation from these relationships
- o Concentrating on the more profitable items can improve return on sales, but not always. Porsche improved their position by cutting back on diversity in the mid 1990s and improved

their position considerably. Triumph motorcycles withdrew from the smaller bike market in the 1970s. The consequent loss of 'novice' customers led to a decline in sales of larger bikes.

Stormbreaker should not only set targets and measure performance against them, but should also benchmark these against the industry, specific competitors and best practice. Any aspect of the business can be benchmarked, providing opportunities for measurement and improvement at the tactical and local level. From this comparison, the essential attributes for delivering value to customers can be derived.

Activity 8.2

Implementation

It is important to schedule the events in your plan and assign responsibilities for implementation. Using some of the components of a marketing plan above and previous chapters in the book, draw up a simple action plan for implementing the Stormbreaker marketing plan. Try using a GANTT chart to schedule the activities.

Pay particular attention to who should be involved in the implementation. Identify the positions of people involved, for example, finance manager, marketing manager, etc.

The plan should include information about:

o   What needs to be done (tasks and activities)
o   Who needs to do it (assembling the team)
o   When does it need to be done (scheduling).

Summary

This Unit has provided examples of marketing plans and demonstrated that there is no uniform pattern. However, there are key issues that a marketing plan needs to address even if the formats are sometimes different.

Sample exam questions and answers for the Marketing Management in Practice module as a whole can be found in Appendix 3 at the back of the book.

appendix 1
guidance on examination preparation

Preparing for your examination

You are now nearing the final phase of your studies and it is time to start the hard work of exam preparation.

During your period of study you will have become used to absorbing large amounts of information. You will have tried to understand and apply aspects of knowledge that may have been very new to you, while some of the information provided may have been more familiar. You may even have undertaken many of the activities that are positioned frequently throughout your Coursebook, which will have enabled you to apply your learning in practical situations. But whatever the state of your knowledge and understanding, do not allow yourself to fall into the trap of thinking that you know enough, you understand enough, or even worse, that you can just take it as it comes on the day.

Never underestimate the pressure of the CIM examination.

The whole point of preparing this text for you is to ensure that you never take the examination for granted, and that you do not go into the exam unprepared for what might come your way for three hours at a time.

One thing's for sure: there is no quick fix, no easy route, no waving a magic wand and finding you know it all.

Whether you have studied alone, in a CIM study centre, or through distance learning, you now need to ensure that this final phase of your learning process is tightly managed, highly structured and objective.

As a candidate in the examination, your role will be to convince the Senior Examiner that you have credibility for this subject. You need to demonstrate to the examiner that you can be trusted to undertake a range of challenges in the context of marketing, that you are able to capitalize on opportunities and manage your way through threats.

You should prove to the Senior Examiner that you are able to apply knowledge, make decisions, respond to situations and solve problems.

Very shortly we are going to look at a range of revision and exam preparation techniques, and at time management issues, and encourage you towards developing and implementing your own revision plan, but before that, let's look at the role of the Senior Examiner.

A bit about the Senior Examiners!

You might be quite shocked to read this, but while it might appear that the examiners are 'relentless question masters' they actually want you to be able to answer the questions and pass the exams! In fact, they would derive no satisfaction or benefits from failing candidates; quite the contrary, they develop the syllabus and exam papers in order that you can learn and then apply that learning effectively so as to pass your examinations. Many of the examiners have said in the past that it is indeed psychologically more difficult to fail students than pass them.

Many of the hints and tips you find within this Appendix have been suggested by the Senior Examiners and authors of the Coursebook series. Therefore you should consider them carefully and resolve to undertake as many of the elements suggested as possible.

The Chartered Institute of Marketing has a range of processes and systems in place within the Examinations Division to ensure that fairness and consistency prevail across the team of examiners, and that the academic and vocational standards that are set and defined are indeed maintained. In doing this, CIM ensures that those who gain the CIM Certificate (Stage 1), Advanced Certificate (Stage 2) and Postgraduate Diploma (Stage 3), are worthy of the qualification and perceived as such in the view of employers, actual and potential.

Part of what you will need to do within the examination is be 'examiner friendly' – that means you have to make sure they get what they ask for. This will make life easier for you and for them.

Hints and tips for 'examiner friendly' actions are as follows:

- Show them that you understand the basis of the question, by answering *precisely* the question asked, and not including just about everything you can remember about the subject area
- Read their needs – how many points is the question asking you to address?
- Respond to the question appropriately. Is the question asking you to take on a role? If so, take on the role and answer the question in respect of the role. For example, you could be positioned as follows:

'You are working as a Marketing Assistant at Nike UK' or 'You are a Marketing Manager for an Engineering Company' or 'As Marketing Manager write a report to the Managing Partner'.

These examples of role-playing requirements are taken from questions in past papers.

- Deliver the answer in the format requested. If the examiner asks for a memo, then provide a memo; likewise, if the examiner asks for a report, then write a report. If you do not do this, in some instances you will fail to gain the necessary marks required to pass.

- Take a business-like approach to your answers. This enhances your credibility. Badly ordered work, untidy work, lack of structure, headings and subheadings can be off-putting. This would be unacceptable in the work situation, likewise it will be unacceptable in the eyes of the Senior Examiners and their marking teams.

o Ensure the examiner has something to mark: give them substance, relevance, definitions, illustrations and demonstration of your knowledge and understanding of the subject area.

o See the examiner as your potential employer, or ultimate consumer/customer. The whole purpose and culture of marketing is about meeting customers' needs. Try this approach – it works wonders.

o Provide a strong sense of enthusiasm and professionalism in your answers; support it with relevant up-to-date examples and apply them where appropriate.

o Try to do something that will make your exam paper a little bit different – make it stand out in the crowd.

All of these points might seem quite logical to you, but often in the panic of the examination they 'go out of the window'. Therefore it is beneficial to remind ourselves of the importance of the examiner. He/she is the 'ultimate customer' – and we all know customers hate to be disappointed.

As we move on, some of these points will be revisited and developed further.

About the examination

In all examinations, with the exception of Marketing Management in Practice at Advanced Certificate (Stage 2) level, the paper is divided into two parts.

o Part A – Mini-case study = 50 marks
o Part B – Option choice questions (choice of two questions from four) = 50 per cent of the marks (each question attracting 25 per cent)

For the Marketing Management in Practice paper, the same approach is taken. However, all of the questions are directly related to the case study and in this instance the case material is more extensive.

Let's look at the basis of each element.

The mini-case study

This is based on a mini-case or scenario with one question, possibly subdivided into between two and four points, but totalling 50 per cent of overall marks.

In essence, you, the candidate, are placed in a problem-solving role through the medium of a short scenario. On occasions, the scenario may consist of an article from a journal in relation to a well-known organization.

Alternatively, it will be based upon a fictional company, and the examiner will have prepared it in order that the right balance of knowledge, understanding, application and skills is used.

Approaches to the mini-case study

When undertaking the mini-case study there are a number of key areas you should consider.

Structure/content

The mini-case that you will be presented with will vary slightly from paper to paper, and of course from one examination to the next. Normally the scenario presented will be 400–500 words long and will centre on a particular organization and its problems or may even relate to a specific industry. However, please note, for Marketing Management in Practice, the case study is more significant as all the questions are based upon the case materials.

The length of the mini-case study means that usually only a brief outline is provided of the situation, the organization and its marketing problems, and you must therefore learn to cope with analysing information and preparing your answer on the basis of a very limited amount of detail.

Time management

There are many differing views on time management and the approaches you can take to managing your time within the examination. You must find an approach to suit your way of working, but always remember, whatever you do, you must ensure that you allow enough time to complete the examination. Unfinished exams mean lost marks.

A typical example of managing time is as follows:

Your paper is designed to assess you over a three hour period. With 50 per cent of the marks being allocated to the mini-case, it means that you should dedicate somewhere around 100 minutes of your time to both read and write up the answer on this mini-case, leaving a further 80 minutes for the remaining questions. Some students, however, will prefer to allocate nearly half of their time (90 minutes) on the mini-case, so that they can read and fully absorb the case, and answer the questions in the context of it. This is also acceptable as long as you ensure that you work extremely 'SMART' for the remaining time in order to finish the examination.

Do not forget that while there is only one question within the mini-case, it can have a number of components. You must answer all the components in that question, which is where the balance of time comes into play.

Knowledge/skills tested

Throughout all the CIM papers, your knowledge, skills and ability to apply those skills will be tested. However, the mini-cases are used particularly to test application, i.e. your ability to take your knowledge and apply it in a structured way to a given scenario. The examiners will be looking at your decision-making ability, your analytical and communication skills and, depending on the level, your ability as a manager to solve particular marketing problems.

When the examiner is marking your paper, he/she will be looking to see how you differentiate yourself, looking at your own individual 'unique selling points'. The examiner will also want to see if you can personally apply the knowledge or whether you are only able to repeat the textbook materials.

Format of answers

On many occasions, and within all examinations, you will most likely be given a particular communication method to use. If this is the case, you must ensure that you adhere to the requirements of the examiner. This is all part of meeting customer needs.

The likely communication tools you will be expected to use are as follows:

- o Memorandum
- o Memorandum/report
- o Report
- o Briefing notes

- o   Presentation
- o   Press release
- o   Advertisement
- o   Plan.

Make sure that you familiarize yourself with these particular communication tools and practise using them to ensure that, on the day, you will be able to respond confidently to the communication requests of the examiner. Look back at the Customer Communications text at Certificate level to familiarize yourself with the potential requirements of these methods.

By the same token, while communication methods are important, so is meeting the specific requirements of the question. This means you must understand what is meant by the precise instruction given. **Note the following terms carefully:**

- o   **Identify** Select key issues, point out key learning points, establish clearly what the examiner expects you to identify
- o   **Illustrate** The examiner expects you to provide examples, scenarios and key concepts that illustrate your learning
- o   **Compare and contrast** Look at the range of similarities between the two situations, contexts or even organizations. Then compare them, i.e. ascertain and list how activities, features, etc. agree or disagree. Contrasting means highlighting the differences between the two
- o   **Discuss** Questions that have 'discuss' in them offer a tremendous opportunity for you to debate, argue, justify your approach or understanding of the subject area – *caution* it is not an opportunity to waffle
- o   **Briefly explain** This means being succinct, structured and concise in your explanation, within the answer. Make your points clear, transparent and relevant
- o   **State** Present in a clear, brief format
- o   **Interpret** Expound the meaning of, make clear and explicit what it is you see and understand within the data provided
- o   **Outline** Provide the examiner with the main concepts and features being asked for and avoid minor technical details. Structure will be critical here, or else you could find it difficult to contain your answer
- o   **Relate** Show how different aspects of the syllabus connect together
- o   **Evaluate** Review and reflect upon an area of the syllabus, a particular practice, an article, etc., and consider its overall worth in respect of its use as a tool or a model and its overall effectiveness in the role it plays.

Source: Worsam, Mike, *How to Pass Marketing*, Croner, 1989.

Your approach to mini-cases

There is no one right way to approach and tackle a mini-case study, indeed it will be down to each individual to use their own creativity in tackling the tasks presented. You will have to use your initiative and discretion about how best to approach the mini-case. Having said this, however, there are some basic steps you can take.

- o   Ensure that you read through the case study at least twice before making any judgements, starting to analyse the information provided, or indeed writing the answers.

- o   On the third occasion read through the mini-case and, using a highlighter, start marking the essential and relevant information critical to the content and context. Then turn your attention to the question again, this time reading slowly and carefully to assess what it is you are expected to do. Note any instructions that the examiner gives you, and then start to plan how you might answer the question. Whatever the question, ensure the answer has a structure: a beginning, a structured central part and, finally, always a conclusion.

o   Keep the context of the question continually in mind: that is, the specifics of the case and the role which you might be performing.

o   Because there is limited material available, you will sometimes need to make assumptions. Don't be afraid to do this, it will show initiative on your part. Assumptions are an important part of dealing with case studies and can help you to be quite creative with your answer. However, do explain the basis of your assumptions within your answer so that the examiner understands the nature of them, and why you have arrived at your particular outcome. **Always ensure that your assumptions are realistic.**

o   Only now are you approaching the stage where it is time to start writing your answer to the question, tackling the problems, making decisions and recommendations on the case scenario set before you. As mentioned previously, your points will often be best set out in a report or memo type format, particularly if the examiner does not specify a communication method.

o   Ensure that your writing is succinct, avoids waffle and responds directly to the questions asked.

Part B

Each Part B is comprised of four traditional questions, each worth 25 per cent. You will be expected to choose two of those questions, to make up the remaining 50 per cent of available marks. (Again please note that the structure is the same for Marketing Management in Practice, but that all questions are applied to the case study.)

Realistically, the same principles apply for these questions as in the case study. Communication formats, reading through the questions, structure, role-play, context, etc. – everything is the same.

Part B will cover a number of broader issues from within the syllabus and will be taken from any element of it. The examiner makes the choice, and no prior direction is given to students or tutors on what that might be.

As regards time management in this area, if you used about 100 minutes for the mini-case you should have around 80 minutes left. This provides you with around 40 minutes to plan and write a question, to write, review and revise your answers. Keep practising – use a cooker timer, alarm clock or mobile phone alarm as your timer and work hard at answering questions within the time-frame given.

Specimen examination papers and answers

To help you prepare and understand the nature of the paper, go to www.cimeduhub.com or to access Specimen Answers and Senior Examiner's advice for these exam questions. During your study, the author of your Coursebook may have, on occasions, asked you to refer to these papers and answer the questions. You should undertake these exercises and utilize every opportunity to practise meeting examination requirements.

Each of the Advanced Certificate (Stage 2) coursebooks have, at the end of them, some examination questions and guidance provided by the authors and senior examiners, where appropriate, to provide you with some insight into the types of questions asked.

The specimen answers are vital learning tools. They are not always perfect, as they are answers written by students and annotated by the Senior Examiners, but they will give you a good indication of the approaches you could take, and the examiners' annotations suggest how these answers might be improved. Please use them.

Other sources of information to support your learning through the Virtual Institute are 'Hot Topics'. These give you scope to undertake a range of associated activities related to the syllabus and study areas, and will also be very useful to you when you are revising.

Key elements of preparation

One Senior Examiner suggests the three elements involved in preparing for your examination can be summarized thus:

- o Learning
- o Memory
- o Revision.

Let's look at each point in turn.

Learning

Quite often students find it difficult to learn properly. You can passively read books, look at some of the materials, perhaps revise a little, and regurgitate it all in the examination. In the main, however, this is rather an unsatisfactory method of learning. It is meaningless, shallow and ultimately of little use in practice.

For learning to be truly effective it must be active and applied. You must involve yourself in the learning process by thinking about what you have read, testing it against your experience by reflecting on how you use particular aspects of marketing, and how you could perhaps improve your own performance by implementing particular aspects of your learning into your everyday life. You should adopt the old adage of 'learning by doing'. If you do, you will find that passive learning has no place in your study life.

Below are some suggestions that have been prepared to assist you with the learning pathway throughout your revision.

- o Always make your own notes, in words you understand, and ensure that you combine all the sources of information and activities within them
- o Always try to relate your learning back to your own organization
- o Make sure you define key terms concisely, wherever possible
- o Do not try to memorize your ideas, but work on the basis of understanding and, most important, applying them

- o Think about the relevant and topical questions that might be set – use the questions and answers in your Coursebooks to identify typical questions that might be asked in the future
- o Attempt all of the questions within each of your Coursebooks since these are vital tests of your active learning and understanding.

Memory

If you are prepared to undertake an active learning programme then your knowledge will be considerably enhanced, as understanding and application of knowledge does tend to stay in your 'long-term' memory. It is likely that passive learning will only stay in your 'short-term' memory.

Do not try to memorize in parrot fashion; it is not helpful and, even more important, examiners are experienced in identifying various memorizing techniques and therefore will spot them as such.

Having said this, it is quite useful to memorize various acronyms such as SWOT, PEST, PESTEL, STEEPLE, or indeed various models such as Ansoff, GE Matrix, Shell Directional Policy Matrix, etc., as in some of the questions you may be required to use illustrations of these to assist your answer.

Revision

The third and final stage to consider is 'revision', which is what we will concentrate on in detail below. Here just a few key tips are offered.

Revision should be an ongoing process rather than a panic measure that you decide to undertake just before the examination. You should be preparing notes *throughout* your course, with the view to using them as part of your revision process. Therefore ensure that your notes are sufficiently comprehensive that you can reuse them successfully.

For each concept you learn about, you should identify, through your reading and your own personal experience, at least two or three examples that you could use; this then gives you some scope to broaden your perspective during the examination. It will, of course, help you gain some points for initiative with the examiners.

Knowledge is not something you will gain overnight – as we saw earlier, it is not a quick fix; it involves a process of learning that enables you to lay solid foundations upon which to build your long-term understanding and application. This will benefit you significantly in the future, not just in the examination.

In essence, you should ensure that you do the following in the period before the real intensive revision process begins.

- o Keep your study file well organized, updated and full of newspaper and journal cuttings that may help you formulate examples in your mind for use during the examination
- o Practise defining key terms and acronyms from memory
- o Prepare topic outlines and essay answer plans
- o When you start your intensive revision, ensure it is planned and structured in the way described below. And then finally, read your concentrated notes the night before the examination.

Revision planning

You are now on a critical path – although hopefully not too critical at this time – with somewhere in the region of between four and six weeks to go to the examination. The following hints and tips will help you plan out your revision study.

o   You will, as already explained, need to be very organized. Therefore, before doing anything else, put your files, examples, reading material, etc. in good order, so that you are able to work with them in the future and, of course, make sense of them.

o   Ensure that you have a quiet area within which to work. It is very easy to get distracted when preparing for an examination.

o   Take out your file along with your syllabus, and make a list of key topic areas that you have studied and which you now need to revise. You could use the basis of this book to do that, by taking each unit a step at a time.

o   Plan the use of your time carefully. Ideally you should start your revision at least six weeks prior to the exam, so therefore work out how many spare hours you could give to the revision process and then start to allocate time in your diary, and do not double-book with anything else.

o   Give up your social life for a short period of time. As the saying goes 'no pain – no gain'.

o   Looking at each of the subject areas in turn, identify which are your strengths and which are your weaknesses. Which areas have you grasped and understood, and which are the areas that you have really struggled with? Split your page into two and make a list on each side. For example:

Planning and control	
Strengths	**Weaknesses**
Audit – PEST, SWOT, Models	Ratio analysis
Portfolio analysis	Market sensing
	Productivity analysis
	Trend extrapolation
	Forecasting

o   Break down your list again and divide the points of weakness, giving priority in the first instance to your weakest areas and even prioritizing them by giving each of them a number. This will enable you to master the more difficult areas. Up to 60 per cent of your remaining revision time should be given over to that, as you may find you have to undertake a range of additional reading and also perhaps seeking tutor support, if you are studying at a CIM Accredited Study Centre.

o   The rest of the time should be spent reinforcing your knowledge and understanding of the stronger areas, spending time testing yourself on how much you really know.

o   Should you be taking two examinations or more at any one time, then the breakdown and managing of your time will be critical.

o   Taking a subject at a time, work through your notes and start breaking them down into subsections of learning, and ultimately into key learning points, items that you can refer to time and time again, that are meaningful and that your mind will absorb. You yourself will know how you best remember key points. Some people try to develop acronyms, or flowcharts or matrices, mind maps, fishbone diagrams, etc., or various connection diagrams that help them recall certain aspects of models. You could also develop processes that enable you to remember approaches to various options. (But do remember what we said earlier about regurgitating stuff, parrot fashion.)

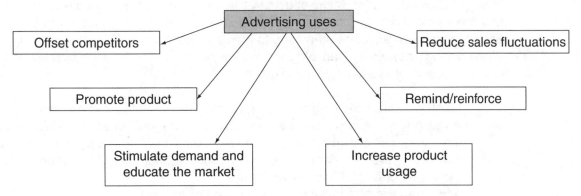

Figure A1.1 Use of a diagram to summarize key components of a concept
Source: Adapted from Dibb, Simkin, Pride & Ferrell, *Marketing Concepts and Strategies*, 4th edition, Houghton Mifflin, 2001.

Figure A1.1 is just a brief example of how you could use a 'bomb-burst' diagram (which, in this case, highlights the uses of advertising) as a very helpful approach to memorizing key elements of learning.

o   Eventually you should reduce your key learning to bullet points. For example: imagine you were looking at the concept of Time Management – you could eventually reduce your key learning to a bullet list containing the following points in relation to 'Effective Prioritization'.

   o   Organize
   o   Take time
   o   Delegate
   o   Review.

Each of these headings would then remind you of the elements you need to discuss associated with the subject area.

o   Avoid getting involved in reading too many textbooks at this stage, as you may start to find that you are getting confused overall.

o   Look at examination questions on previous papers, and start to observe closely the various roles and tasks they expect you to undertake, and importantly, the context in which they are set.

o   **Use the specimen exam papers and specimen answers** to support your learning and see how you could actually improve upon them.

o Without exception, find an associated examination question for the areas that you have studied and revised, and undertake it (more than once if necessary).

o Without referring to notes or books, try to draft an answer plan with the key concepts, knowledge, models and information that are needed to successfully complete the answer. Then refer to the specimen answer to see how close you are to the actual outline presented. Planning your answer, and ensuring that key components are included and that the question has a meaningful structure, is one of the most beneficial activities that you can undertake.

o Now write the answer out in full, time-constrained and written by hand, not with the use of IT. (At this stage, you are still expected to be the scribe for the examination and present handwritten work. Many of us find this increasingly difficult as we spend more and more time using our computers to present information. Do your best to be neat. Spidery handwriting is often off-putting to the examiner.)

o When writing answers as part of your revision process, also be sure to practise the following essential examination techniques:

  o Identify and use the communication method requested by the examiner.
  o Always have three key parts to the answer – an introduction, a middle section that develops your answer in full, and a conclusion. Where appropriate, ensure that you have an introduction, main section, summary/conclusion and, if requested or helpful, recommendations.
  o Always answer the question in the context or role set.
  o Always comply with the nature and terms of the question.
  o Leave white space. Do not overcrowd your page; leave space between paragraphs, and make sure your sentences do not merge into one blur. (Don't worry – there is always plenty of paper available to use in the examination.)
  o Count how many actions the question asks you to undertake and double-check at the end that you have met the full range of demands of the question.
  o Use examples – to demonstrate your knowledge and understanding of the particular syllabus area. These can be from journals, the Internet, the press, or your own experience.
  o Display your vigour and enthusiasm for marketing. Remember to think of the Senior Examiner as your Customer, or future employer, and do your best to deliver what is wanted to satisfy their needs. Impress them and show them how you are a 'cut above the rest'.
  o Review all your practice answers critically, with the above points in mind.

Practical actions

The critical path is becoming even more critical now as the examination looms. The following are vital points:

o Have you registered with CIM?
o Do you know where you are taking your examination? CIM should let you know approximately one month in advance
o Do you know where your examination centre is? If not find out, take a drive, time it – whatever you do don't be late!
o Make sure you have all the tools of the examination ready. A dictionary, calculator, pens, pencils, ruler, etc. Try not to use multiple shades of pens, but at the same time make your work look professional. *Avoid using red and green as these are the colours that will be used for marking.*

Summary

Above all, you must remember that you personally have invested a tremendous amount of time, effort and money in studying for this programme and it is therefore imperative that you consider the suggestions given here as they will help to maximize your return on your investment.

Many of the hints and tips offered here are generic and will work across most of the CIM courses. We have tried to select those that will help you most in taking a sensible, planned approach to your study and revision.

The key to your success is being prepared to put in the time and effort required, planning your revision, and equally important is planning and answering your questions in a way that will ensure that you pass your examination on the day.

The advice offered here aims to guide you from a practical perspective. Guidance on syllabus content and developments associated with your learning will become clear to you as you work through this Coursebook. The authors of each Coursebook have given subject-specific guidance on the approach to the examination and on how to ensure that you meet the content requirements of the kind of question you will face. These considerations are in addition to the structuring issues we have been discussing throughout this Appendix.

Each of the authors and Senior Examiners will guide you on their preferred approach to questions and answers as they go. Therefore where you are presented with an opportunity to be involved in some activity or undertake an examination question either during or at the end of your study units, do take it. It not only prepares you for the examination, but also helps you learn in the applied way we discussed above.

Here, then, is a last reminder:

- Ensure you make the most of your learning process throughout
- Keep structured and orderly notes from which to revise
- Plan your revision – don't let it just happen
- Provide examples to enhance your answers
- Practise your writing skills in order that you present your work well and your writing is readable
- Take as many opportunities as possible to test your knowledge and measure your progress
- Plan and structure your answers
- Always do as the question asks you, especially with regard to context and communication method
- **Do not leave it until the last minute!**

The writers would like to take this opportunity to wish you every success in your endeavours to study, to revise and to pass your examinations.

Karen Beamish
Academic Development Advisor

appendix 2

undertaking CIM assignments and the integrative project

Introduction – the basis to the assignments and the integrative project

Within the CIM qualifications at both Stage One and Stage Two, there are several assessment options available. These are detailed in the outline of modules below. The purpose of an assignment is to provide another format to complete each module for students who want to apply the syllabus concepts from a module to their own or a selected organization. For either qualification there are three modules providing assessment via an assignment and one module assessed via an integrative work-based project. The module assessed via the integrative project is the summative module for each qualification.

	Entry modules	Research & analysis	Planning	Implementation	Management of Marketing
STAGE 3	Entry module – Stage 3	New syllabus to launch September 2004			
		Currently all modules assessed via examination route only			
STAGE 2	Entry module – Stage 2	**Marketing Research & Information**	**Marketing Planning**	**Marketing Communications**	**Marketing Management in Practice**
		All assessed via examination or assignment			*Exam/Integrative Project*
STAGE 1		**Marketing Environment**	**Marketing Fundamentals**	**Customer Communications**	**Marketing in Practice**
		All assessed via examination or assignment			*Exam/Integrative Project*
Introductory Certificate		Supporting marketing processes (research & analysis, planning & implementation)			

Adapted from the outline of CIM 'standard' syllabus, October 2002

224

The use of assignments does not mean that this route is easier than an examination. Both formats are carefully evaluated to ensure that a grade B in the assessment/integrative project route is the same as a grade B in the examination. However, the use of assignments does allow a student to complete the assessment for a module over a longer period of time than a three-hour examination. This will inevitably mean work being undertaken over the time-span of a module. For those used to cramming for exams, writing an assignment over several weeks which comprises a total of four separate questions will be a very different approach.

Each module within the qualification contains a different assignment written specifically for the module. These are designed to test understanding and provide the opportunity for you to demonstrate your abilities through the application of theory to practice. The format and structure of each module's assignment is identical, although the questions asked will differ and the exact type of assignment varies. The questions within an assignment will relate directly to the syllabus for that particular module, thereby giving the opportunity to demonstrate understanding and application.

The assignment structure

The assignment for each module is broken down into a range of questions. These consist of a core question, a selection of optional questions plus a reflective statement. The core question will always relate to the main aspects of each module's syllabus. Coupled with this are a range of four optional questions which will each draw from a different part of the syllabus. Students are requested to select two optional questions from the four available. In addition, a reflective statement requires a student to evaluate their learning from the module. When put together these form the assessment for the entire module. The overall pass mark for the module is the same as through an examination route, which is set at 50 per cent. In addition, the grade band structure is also identical to that of an examination.

Core question

This is the longest and therefore the most important section of your assignment. Covering the major components of the syllabus, the core question is designed to provide a challenging assignment which both tests the theoretical element and also permits application to a selected organization or situation. The question itself will require a written answer of approximately 2,500 words (Stage One) or 3,000 words (Stage Two) in addition to any further information you may wish to provide. This additional information should be in the form of appendices. However, the appendices should be kept to a minimum. Advice here is that there should be no longer than five pages of additional pertinent information.

Optional questions

There are a total of four questions provided for Stage One and Stage Two of the syllabus from which a student is asked to select two. Each answer is expected to provide a challenge although the actual task required varies. The word counts are also lower than the core question at 1,000 words (Stage One) and 1,500 words (Stage Two) respectively.

These are designed to test areas of the syllabus not covered by the core question. As such it is possible to base all of your questions on the same organization although there is significant benefit in using more than one organization as a basis for your assignment. Some of the questions specifically require a different organization to be selected from the one used for the core question. This only occurs where the questions are requiring similar areas to be investigated and will be specified clearly on the question itself.

Within the assignment there are several types of questions that may be asked, including:

o **A report** The question requires a formal report to be completed, detailing an answer to the specific question set. This will often be reporting on a specific issue to an individual.

o **A briefing paper or notes** Preparing a briefing paper or a series of notes which may be used for a presentation.

o **A presentation** You may be required to either prepare the presentation only or to deliver the presentation in addition to its preparation. The audience for the presentation should be considered carefully and ICT used where possible.

o **A discussion paper** The question requires an academic discussion paper to be prepared. You should show a range of sources and concepts within the paper. You may also be required to present the discussion paper as part of a question.

o **A project plan or action plan** Some questions ask for planning techniques to be demonstrated. As such, the plan must be for the timescale given and costs shown where applicable. The use of ICT is recommended here in order to create the plan diagrammatically.

o **Planning a research project** Whilst market research may be required, questions have often asked for simply a research plan in a given situation. This would normally include timescales, the type(s) of research to be gathered, sampling, planned data collection and analysis.

o **Conducting research** Following on from a research plan, a question can require the student(s) to undertake a research gathering exercise. A research question can be either an individual or a group activity depending upon the question. This will usually result in a report of the findings of the exercise plus any recommendations arising from your findings.

o **Gathering of information and reporting** Within many questions information will need gathering. The request for information can form part or all of a question. This may be a background to the organization, the activities contained in the question or external market and environmental information. It is advisable to detail the types of information utilized, their sources and report on any findings. Such a question will often ask for recommendations for the organization – these should be drawn from the data and not simply personal opinion.

o **An advisory document** A question here will require students to evaluate a situation and present advice and recommendations drawn from findings and theory. Again, any advice should be backed up with evidence and not a personal perspective only.

o **An exercise, either planning and/or delivering the exercise** At both Stage One and Stage Two, exercises are offered as optional questions. These provide students with the opportunity to devise an exercise and may also require the delivery of this exercise. Such an activity should be evidenced where possible.

o **A role-play with associated documentation** Several questions have asked students to undertake role plays in exercises such as team-building. These are usually videoed and documentation demonstrating the objectives of the exercise provided.

Each of these questions relate directly towards specific issues to be investigated, evaluated and answered. In addition, some of the questions asked present situations to be considered. These provide opportunities for specific answers relating directly to the question asked.

In order to aid students completing the assignment, each question is provided with an outline of marking guidance. This relates to the different categories by which each question is marked. The marker of your assignment will be provided with a detailed marking scheme constructed around the same marking guidance provided to students.

For both the core and optional questions, it is important to use referencing where sources have been utilized. This has been a weakness in the past and continues to be an issue. There have been cases of plagiarism identified during marking and moderation, together with a distinct lack of references and bibliography. This becomes more important at Stage Two where the nature of the syllabus lends itself to a more academic approach. It is highly recommended that a bibliography be included with each question and sources are cited within the text itself. The type of referencing method used is not important, only that sources are referred to.

The reflective statement

This is the final aspect to each module assignment. The purpose of the reflective statement is for each student to consider how the module has influenced him or her as individuals and reflected upon their practice. A shorter piece of work than for other aspects at 500 words (Stage One) or 750 words (Stage Two), it is also more personal in that your answer will often depend upon how you as an individual have applied the learning from the module to your work and other aspects.

A good reflective statement will comprise a number of aspects, including:

- o Details of the theoretical aspects that you found beneficial within the module, and their reasons. If you have found particular resources beneficial, state this and the reason why.
- o How these concepts have affected you as a practitioner with examples of application of concepts from the module to your work and/or other activities.
- o How you intend to progress your learning further after completing the module assessment.

When looking at the reflective statement, your tutor or an assessor will try to award marks for your demonstration of understanding through the module together with how you have applied the theoretical concepts to practice. They are looking for evidence of learning and application over time, rather than a student simply completing the question because they have a deadline looming. The result of this marking tends to be that students who begin to apply the module concepts early often achieve higher marks overall.

Integrative project structure

The integrative project is designed to provide an in-company approach to assessment rather than having specified assignments. Utilized within the summative module element of each level's syllabus, this offers a student the chance to produce a piece of work which tackles a specific issue. The integrative project can only be completed after undertaking other modules as it will rely on information in each of these as guidance. The integrative project is approximately 5,000 words in length and was introduced from September 2002 at the Stage One level. It will be introduced from September 2003 at Stage Two with the commencement of the new syllabus. The integrative project is marked by CIM assessors and not your own tutors.

Stage Two Assignments – Marketing Management in Practice

This is a new summative module within the Stage Two qualification. This is a more practical module, building on the summative Marketing in Practice module at Stage One. The module is assessed by either an examination or the new integrative project, not by an assignment. The integrative project is designed to be a project-based assessment examining issues within one organization only. The result will be an in-depth investigation into a specific area. Comprising five modules, the Marketing Management in Practice module covers elements of management encountered by most marketers.

Element 1 – Managing people and teams

The first element begins the management process by examining people management issues. Whilst not a critical marketing activity, interaction with people occurs many times each day. These interactions or 'moments of truth' can affect perceptions of the organization and ourselves, personal relationships and performance. A typical question drawn from this element for use within the integrative project is:

Taking your chosen organization for the integrative project, evaluate how relationships are managed within the organization. Make recommendations for improving these relationships, both on a personal and organizational level.

An answer to this question needs to provide a background to the organization whilst leading onto other questions from the module. Therefore this part of the integrative project sets the scene for everything else to follow. An answer would be contained as a report within the whole assignment and would include:

- o   A background to the organization and your own role.
- o   The types of activities and people relationships within the organization. How people are managed, both in theory and in practice in the organization.
- o   A contrast of theory with the reality – how could people be managed better. This evaluation would need to both contain recommendations and link onto future components of the project.
- o   Recommendations need to consider issues of individual and team performance, how conflicts are managed plus issues of change.
- o   The answer forms part of a whole project and would best be presented as a report. Divisions between questions should still be apparent.

Element 2 – Managing marketing projects

The second element of the module goes further into the role and responsibility of management. Although this element forms only a small component of the total module syllabus, issues of project management are vital within marketing management. The element covers the roles of and techniques for project management, together with budgeting and project control/ evaluation. Therefore a sample question would include:

As part of a plan to improve overall effectiveness of marketing activities, there is to be a project comprising two roadshows per location over a period of six months at a cost of £6,000 each. There is an additional budget for marketing communication and other actions suitable for the planned project and this should be no more than the total cost of the roadshows. Produce a project plan and budget, detailing how the project should be managed.

A limited budget is given here, which leaves the decision wide open as to the activities which could be utilized. The roadshows will cover one or several locations depending upon the organization. In addition, the type of activities planned to support the roadshows will vary. An answer needs to be part of the other questions within the integrative project and therefore be based on the same organization.

- o   An answer will continue using the previous organization as a basis and therefore no background is required. In addition, the question forms part of a total report.

- There are two roadshows planned per location. The exact number will differ between organizations. In addition, this will affect the budget; a small organization at one location will have a maximum budget of £24,000 (two roadshows at £6,000 each plus a maximum support budget of £24,000) whilst a major organization with twenty locations will have a budget of £480,000.
- Covering the role and characteristics of projects would help, together with the importance of project management. The techniques for project planning also need covering.
- The tasks involved in the project will require planning, together with a project plan shown (preferably on a Gantt chart). The budget also needs calculating and should be in line with the planned number of roadshows.
- The answer will be added as part of the report covering the whole organization.

Element 3 – Managing knowledge and delivering marketing research projects

The third element of the module draws in aspects of the Marketing Research and Information module. Here, there are components consisting of the planning, gathering, analysis and reporting of research projects. Questions drawn from this element will concentrate on the use of information and/or market research within the selected organization.

Select a particular area within the organization, for example the appraisal or customer service process. Evaluate the use of information within this activity through a market research project. Prepare recommendations resulting from the data gathered.

This question requires the selection of an area that has suitable information available. It will be based upon the same organization as earlier questions, and therefore a background is not required. The research area does not need to be linked directly to the rest of the syllabus. An answer will draw in a research investigation, with its associated plan, plus an analysis and reporting of the research gathered. Research data could be secondary and/or primary data, dependent upon the situation. An answer will include:

- A description of the situation selected for further investigation, together with an assessment of the information currently available.
- An evaluation of potential data sources, both primary and secondary, is required in order to be able to investigate the situation further. The reason for selection of particular information sources will also be needed here.
- A research plan needs to be produced, taking into consideration sampling, data availability, plus data gathering, analysis and reporting timescales.
- The relevant information should be collected and analysed. A series of recommendations would normally be produced and presented.
- The answer (written evaluation of the selection of area, research plan and analysis plus recommendations) would best be shown as part of the overall report, with the relevant presentation attached as an appendix.

Element 4 – Developing and implementing marketing plans

This element draws in the Marketing Planning module as part of the summative Marketing Management in Practice module. This element covers operational marketing plans and draws in the marketing planning process as part of the integrative project and marketing management as a whole. Questions drawn from this element will cover marketing planning as a whole, together with assessing and evaluating the marketing planning activities within a selected organization. A typical sample question would be:

229

Evaluate the role of marketing planning within your selected organization. Take into account how planning is used and consider its effectiveness. Make suitable recommendations for the improvement of the planning process together with any implications this may have.

An answer to this question will continue the theme of the selected organization for the whole integrative project. It will need to draw in an investigation into the planning process and make recommendations that are relevant and in keeping with the evidence shown. An answer will include:

- Continuation of the organization used for earlier questions.
- An investigation into the level, type and effectiveness of marketing planning within the organization. In addition, evaluating whether the actual level of planning differs from that intended is useful here. For example, rather than a continual plan being created and followed, is there an annual plan which is simply left on the shelf, updated and put back down each year. The use of data from the research exercise in element three would fit here as part of a cohesive whole.
- The answer should then progress onto a series of recommendations for improving the marketing planning process and its overall management within the organization.
- An answer will fit in with the rest of the integrative project and therefore it will form part of the whole report, although references are needed at the end of the answer.

Element 5 – Delivering communications and customer service programmes

The final element within the Marketing Management in Practice module brings into this summative module the Marketing Communications aspects drawn from elsewhere in Stage Two. A question here would complete the integrative project process by examining communications within the organization. This is designed to link to other activities and form a whole project through questions such as:

As part of the integrative project, consider how the organization undertakes its marketing communications inside and outside the organization. Investigate the effectiveness of this communications process and make appropriate recommendations.

This question comprises both internal and external communications leading to a consideration of the entire marketing communications process. Therefore, internal marketing should not be ignored. The same organization is used as a basis as per earlier answers. A good answer will provide an in-depth perspective of organizational marketing communications and include the following:

- A description of the communications process in the organization. This will include internal and external marketing communications.
- Evaluation of the effectiveness of marketing communications. It is useful to draw in the research from element three if not used for an investigation into marketing planning, therefore creating a more cohesive assignment whilst also gaining additional value.
- A series of recommendations drawn from the investigation and coupled with theory on best practice in marketing communications.
- The answer then again forms part of the whole integrative project and is submitted as such, although a bibliography is needed within the answer.

Assignment regulations

There have been a number of changes to the assignment structure compared with previous years, timed with the introduction of the new syllabi. These have been designed to provide consistency in approach for a student whether they are completing the assessment for a module by examination, assignment or integrative project. The more significant changes include:

o   For the current academic year tutors at CIM centres will mark assignments. These are then moderated by CIM assessors. An integrative project is marked by CIM assessors only.

o   No resubmission of assignments, as per an examination. In previous years a range of assignments were being submitted. Where a student does not achieve the 50 per cent pass mark, they were requested to re-take the assessment for the module through examination or assignment/integrative project.

o   Whichever assessment route is selected is fixed rather than having the option to change at the last minute. Past history has shown that students sometimes begin on an assignment route, change to an examination at the last minute due to not meeting the deadline and then score badly in the examination. The paths to an assignment or examination are different and therefore it is unadvisable to switch, which is the reason for the change of rule.

o   In the 2002–3 academic year word limits for questions and assignments were introduced. This was introduced due to assignments being submitted which were of a wide variety of lengths. These ranged from under 2,000 words to over 25,000 words. Where a student is completing four modules by assignment this would equal over 100,000 words – the equivalent of a medium-sized textbook or novel. As such, it became impossible for two assignments to be considered together. Therefore the word limit guidance was introduced in order to provide equality for all students undertaking the assessment by assignment.

o   Two sets of assignments per year as with the examination route. With this change, students are required to complete the assignment aimed at the nearest examination session. Previously students had between 3 and 9 months to complete an assignment depending upon whether it was given out in September for a June deadline or in March for the June deadline. Therefore a decision was made to follow the examination route with the intention of giving all students equal time to complete an assignment.

These summarize the key changes which have occurred due to the introduction of new syllabi with the assignment/integrative project route in order that there is parity of assessment at all levels and using all formats. Some of these changes have been significant, others minor. However, all the changes have been considered thoughtfully and with the best intentions for the students in mind.

Use of case studies

For anyone who is not working or has difficulty in access to information on their or another organization, there are a number of case studies available which allow the completion of a module using a case-based approach rather than basing it upon an organization identified by the student. These case studies are provided on a request-only basis through your accredited

CIM centre and should only be used as a last resort. Using a case study as the basis for your assignment will not mean an easier approach to the assignment. However, they do provide an opportunity to undertake assignments when no other alternative exists. Each case study comes with a certain amount of information which can be used specifically for the completion of a question. Additional information may need to be assumed or researched in order to create a comprehensive assignment.

Submission of assignments/integrative project

The following information will aid not only yourself and your tutor who marks your work and but also the CIM assessor who will be moderating your work and moderating the integrative project. In addition, the flow diagram represents the process of an assignment/integrative project from start to final mark.

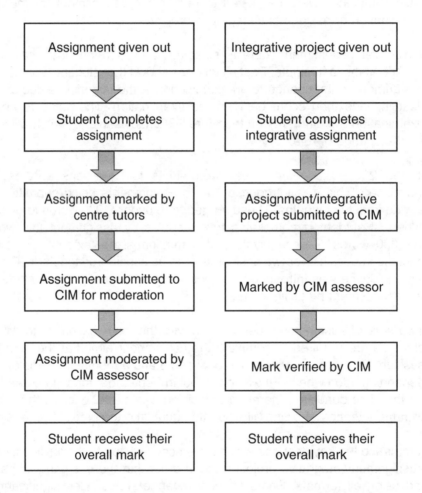

When completing and submitting assignments or the integrative project, refer to the following for guidance:

- o Read through each question before starting out. Particularly with the core question there will be a considerable amount of work to undertake. Choose your optional questions wisely.
- o Answer the question set and use the mark guidance given regarding the marking scheme.
- o Reference each question within the assignment and use a bibliography.
- o Complete all documentation thoroughly. This is designed to aid both the CIM and yourself.

○ Ensure that the assignment is bound as per instructions given. Currently, assignments are requested not to be submitted in plastic wallets or folders as work can become detached or lost. Following the submission instructions provided aids both the CIM administrators and the CIM assessor who will be marking (integrative project) or moderating (assignments) your work.

○ Complete the candidate declaration sheet showing that you have undertaken this work yourself. **Please note that if you wish the information contained in your assignment to remain confidential you must state this on the front of the assignment.** Whilst CIM assessors will not use any information pertaining to your or another organization, CIM may wish to use the answer to a question as an example.

An assignment will be marked by a tutor at your CIM centre followed by moderation by a CIM assessor. The integrative project will be marked by a CIM assessor as per an examination with moderation by the CIM. To ensure objectivity by CIM assessors there exists a mark-in meeting prior to any marking in order that standardisation can occur. The senior assessor for each subject also undertakes further verification of both examinations and assessments to ensure parity between each type of assessment.

David C. Lane
Senior Moderator (Advanced Certificate)
February 2003

appendix 3

sample exam questions and answers

The exam

The exam is based on a midi case study. The section A questions are compulsory and account for 50 per cent of the marks for the paper. Two questions must be selected from the four section B questions (25 marks each). The midi case study gives you a role and a context within which you can demonstrate your knowledge of the relevant theory and the skills in applying the techniques to a specific area.

Study Guide

The successful application of marketing theory is like driving a car. You can read many books on the subject but this is no substitute for getting behind the wheel and practising under guidance. Marketing demands the application of theory. The way to develop this skill is to work with your tutors' guidance through relevant case studies. Practice at specimen questions and comparison with outline answers will develop your skills to pass the exam.

Before the exam

Knowledge of the theory is vital, so go over the various models well before the exam date to ensure that you fully understand them and you have practised their application. The Chartered Institute of Marketing is a professional exam, and on qualification, employers will expect you not only to know the relevant theories but also to apply them creatively to real situations. To gain this level of skill it is not sufficient to sit in class or passively read textbooks. Work on case studies and study of real marketing situations is vital. Marketing is a fast-developing area so there is a need to read the current press. Exams require specific skills so do not make your first practice the actual exam. Work through specimen case studies and questions under simulated exam conditions, and discuss your answers and approaches with your tutor. In a busy life there may be a temptation to question spot and 'cherry pick' in the hope that your favourite questions will turn up. Questions will be set across the entire range of the syllabus and in a variety of contexts such as service, not for profit and b2b marketing.

In the exam

Do not repeat the question or complete long environmental and SWOT analyses. These waste valuable time without gaining much marks. What is required in the exam is a structured answer demonstrating the knowledge and application of theory to the specific context of the midi case study. Brainstormed ideas without structure and application of theory are likely to yield a marginal fail mark. Theory without context-specific application will also be likely to not gain a pass mark. Report format (unless otherwise indicated in the exam paper) is required in your answers.

Take care to answer the entire question and spend appropriate time on all aspects, e.g. on a question including some cover of the marketing mix, consider all aspects of the service-extended marketing mix with case study relevant points. Standard template answers with little or no context are not acceptable. It is vital to plan your answer so take a few minutes considering your answer structure. Take care to leave enough time for the last question.

Marketing Management in Practice

Time

Date

3 Hours Duration

This examination is in two sections.

PART A – Is compulsory and worth 50 per cent of total marks.

PART B – Has **FOUR** questions; select **TWO**. Each answer will be worth 25 per cent of the total marks.

DO NOT repeat the question in your answer, but show clearly the number of the question attempted on the appropriate pages of the answer book.

Rough workings should be included in the answer book and ruled through after use.

Marketing Management in Practice

The Eden Project – The eighth wonder of the world

In the 90s there was a vision to turn a disused industrial site in Cornwall into a world centre of plants with the largest conservatory in the world – 200 m long and 100 m wide. Even before completion, the project captured the world's imagination and the Eden Project has become one of Europe's most visited attractions and has placed Cornwall well and truly on the map. In 2000, 200,000 visitors were anticipated, but more than double the number came. At present visitors average 1.8 m a year.

The project is owned by The Eden Charitable Trust, a registered charity. It is not a green theme park. Some pre-eminent academic staff have joined the project to develop the academic excellence on site and achieve the educational objectives of the trust.

The world media have acclaimed the project, and in its short life the Eden Project has become in its sector a global brand. Not content with this success, the trust has imaginative ideas for future developments for 2004 and beyond.

Disclaimer: The factual information contained in this case study has been taken from the Eden Project's published sources. The management issues below have been written for the needs of the Chartered Institute Qualifications and are not intended to reflect the detailed management plans of the Trust. **Candidates are specifically requested not to contact the Eden Project's management.**

March 2003

Your Role

You are James Smith, a marketing consultant. The CIM scenario is that given the ambitious expansion plans, the Eden Project is considering retaining you as a marketing consultant.

Appendix One

James Smith's fact file

The Eden project is located in Cornwall in the West Country of the UK, 270 miles west from London. It is located close to major roads but the outstanding success has caused some congestion at peak visiting times. Buses link the project to nearby towns and the main rail station. The 'green' platform consideration has been given to provide good access by coach and bicycle (the Eden Project is on the UK National Cycle Network).

The existing attraction consists of the Humid Tropics Biome, the Warm Temperate Biome and the outdoor landscape. Towering rainforest trees are included in 100,000 plants representing some 5,000 species, a truly world class attraction.

There is, at present, no hotel as part of the complex. Plans are being developed to build a conference-based hotel to host major international conferences.

The Project has a good shop and it is possible to buy Eden Project merchandise. Appropriate facilities are provided for refreshments with two restaurants.

The Eden Project has had a major impact on the local environment. The Eden Trust is concerned to take full account of the legitimate concerns of local stakeholder groups.

Education is a major aim of the Eden Trust providing a resource for learning, a living curriculum for schools and college.

As a not-for-profit organization, maximizing profits is not the key objective. However, to finance the scientific and education activities, the Eden Project must generate significant earnings. The original project cost £86 million. Although a charity, an effective and efficient commercial operation is needed to generate the cash flow to fund the not-for-profit activities.

The Eden Project has been successively used to host major events such as concerts.

The Eden project can be used as the ultimate in Corporate Entertainment and has been hailed as the 8th wonder of the world. It provides clients with an unforgettable experience.

Appendix Two

Future plans

Additional space has recently been purchased to provide room for extra facilities such as the Education Resource Centre.

Designs for a third 'semi-arid' Biome have been developed.

Plans are under consideration for a 'Meeting House' for conferences and seminars.

A hotel is also included in the potential new developments.

Appendix Three

Private functions

The Biome Link is situated between the giant conservatories. There is an impressive open area with a first floor viewing gallery. This has been successively used for a variety of events such as banquets and award ceremonies.

Visitor centre gallery

This spectacular location overlooking the Project is available for evening use for receptions and meetings.

Eden as a leading live music and theatre location

The Summer 2002 season established the Eden Project as spectacular setting for special performances.

PART A

Question 1

a. Corporate events and concerts can generate vital revenue to fund the plans. If the Eden Project was to consider appointing a Marketing Manager with specific responsibility for marketing the project for corporate events and concerts, what advice would you give on the recruitment, selection and induction of this person?

(25 Marks)

b.   Outline a marketing plan to develop profitable corporate business for the project. Lengthy environmental analysis and SWOT analysis are NOT required.

(25 marks)

PART B – Answer TWO Questions Only

Question 2

What Marketing Information System would you implement to monitor and develop visitor satisfaction of the Eden Project experience? What information would you collect, and how would you obtain it?

(25 Marks)

Question 3

The Eden Project is concerned to be sensitive to the needs and wants of the local stakeholder groups. Outline the marketing communications activities you would undertake for the Eden Project locally.

(25 marks)

Question 4

Clearly with almost two million visitors a year, the Eden Project has got off to a spectacular start. However, maintaining interest and visitor numbers will be key to the future. Using Relationship Marketing and other relevant marketing techniques, what initiatives would you consider appropriate to maintain and grow visitor numbers?

(25 Marks)

Question 5

You have decided that you wish to produce a new brochure for the corporate hospitality business, and complete a direct mail shot in the UK to expand this business. Using appropriate project management concepts, outline an action plan for the production of this brochure.

(25 Marks)

The outline answers provided are not intended to be the only appropriate treatment, and do not cover all possible points and approaches. Research on past high-mark earning answers written under exam conditions indicates that some 600 to 900 words provide scope for an appropriate treatment in the time available. These answers have been kept to this length to indicate approaches that are practical under actual exam conditions.

Answers

Question 1

a.   Corporate events and concerts can generate vital revenue to fund plans. If the Eden Project were to consider appointing a Marketing Manager with specific responsibility for marketing the project for corporate events and concerts, what advice would you give on the recruitment, selection and induction of this person?

(25 Marks)

To   Marketing Manager – Eden Project

From   James Smith

Date   March 2003

Appointment of Marketing Manager for Corporate Marketing and Concerts

Introduction

This will be an important revenue-earning activity, working with high-profile clients and delivering exciting events. This is a critical appointment demanding an able operational manager who will be able to creatively exploit the potential but with ability to manage the details as well. The issues will be considered under the headings below:

- o Drawing up the specification
- o Finding the right candidates
- o Short-listing
- o Selection process/event
- o Induction.

Drawing up the specification

The secret as always for successful management action is pre-planning. Actions that need to be resolved before the candidate search gets underway include:

- o Senior management agreeing how the new manager will fit into the organizational structure, reporting relationships and responsibilities
- o Agreement at senior management regarding level of pay and overall benefits package to be offered
- o Working with the Personnel Manager, a job description needs to be drafted
- o Again personal specifications need to be drafted including 'Must Haves' (e.g. relevant experience) and desirables (e.g. attainment of Chartered Institute of Marketing qualifications)
- o Agreement of the selection process
- o Agreement reached as to who should be involved in the selection process
- o A plan agreed to attract suitable candidates (see below). As this is a relatively senior position, a national search may be appropriate. In which case any re-location package to be offered should be agreed
- o The candidate package should be agreed with the wording of any intended advertisements

Note: There are many legal implications in this process. Use of Personnel experts is essential. It is assumed that standard rules exist for the payment of candidates' expenses.

Finding the right candidates

The problem of finding the right candidates for more responsible positions which demand experience is that many attractive candidates are not actively searching for work and thus not scanning the recruitment pages.

   o Given the costs of advertising in the national press, and the likely situation that many strong candidates are not in active job search (i.e. not looking through the jobs pages), this option should be rejected

   o A marketing recruitment specialist should be appointed. This is not a low-cost option but may be a more certain way of getting a range of suitable candidates for interview

   o The job should be posted on the website

   o The job should be advertised internally (there may be suitable candidates and an open process is needed to maintain a good working atmosphere)

Short listing

   o The use of a standard application form is recommended. This makes the checking for 'must haves' easier. Candidates that fail to satisfy these criteria can be eliminated

   o The 'desirable' characteristics can be used to rank the remaining candidates to draw up a long-short list

   o The candidate information for the long-short list can be circulated to the selection panel and the final short list agreed

   o The candidates can then be contacted regarding the arrangements for the selection event. It is advisable to also note a couple of 'reserves' in case at this stage a candidate should decide to withdraw

Note: All candidate information should be treated in the strictest confidence.

Selection process/event

   o Candidates should be given an appropriate briefing and a tour of the facilities

   o In consultation with the Personnel Manager, appropriate aptitude tests can be used to contribute information for the panel

   o It is suggested that candidates should be asked to make a presentation on an appropriate marketing topic (in the corporate selling situation this will be a key skill). In consultation with the Personnel function, other activities that might provide useful information are a group activity and an in-tray exercise involving writing some marketing copy

   o The formal interviews should be conducted in a friendly and supportive atmosphere

   o Candidates should be informed of the outcome as quickly as reasonably possible

Induction

This can be considered under three headings:

Formal induction process
There are legal requirements such as the Health & Safety Act, and full use should be made of the Personnel Management to ensure that all the legal issues are properly covered.

Induction to the job role
Cover of the full range of roles and responsibilities, and relevant organizational procedures, etc.

Informal induction
Introductions to others in the management team and people working in support roles.

Conclusion

Of necessity the above is an outline only. Good preparation, and clear objectives and processes should ensure that the position is filled by a good marketing person, who can rapidly make a full contribution to the organization.

Guidance notes The above is a structured review of the issues and processes. Candidates are not expected to be full experts in Employment Law (this is for the Human Resource specialists and Lawyers) but are expected to have a general awareness of the issues, in particular, when there are specific legal issues that need specialist involvement (e.g. contracts of employment). The rejection of press advertising may be seen as controversial by some people. It was introduced here to make the point that sometimes it is appropriate for a candidate to propose a negative action. A good answer could use press advertising as an alternative approach. These outline answers are intended to be indicative not prescriptive. Other issues could be considered such as a probationary period. Clearly, in the exam timescale, candidates cannot be expected to cover every possible issue. What is required is a demonstration of a balanced professional level of understanding of the issues.

b. Outline a marketing plan to develop profitable corporate business for the project. Lengthy environmental analysis and SWOT analyses are NOT required.

(25 marks)

To   Marketing Manager – Eden Project

From   James Smith

Date   March 2003

Outline Marketing plan for Corporate Business

Brief situation analysis

There is great scope to generate revenue to support our educational and other charitable activities by the sympathetic use of the facilities for corporate use. A lengthy environmental analysis is not given here but in brief we need to note the following focused SWOT issues.

Strengths

- o One of the most exciting locations in Europe
- o Perceived as new and where it is happening

Weaknesses

- o Somewhat outposted from London
- o Full facilities required for corporate users – still not fully in place, e.g. hotel yet to be built

Opportunities

Chance to exploit the unique platform and brand, not just another Disney theme park or another 5 star 'bed factory' hotel chain.

Threats

- o Economic downturn reducing corporate hospitality spend
- o Crowded market with many other offerings

Mission

To bring the Eden experience and values to the corporate sector.

Aims

To develop a profitable corporate activity for national and international clients.

Objectives

At this early stage, detailed objective is yet to be formulated but the working objective is to achieve one profitable corporate event a week after one year.

Segmentation

In the detailed future development of this outline plan, the following segmentation variables need to be considered:

- o Size and location of company (e.g. small and national – large and international)
- o Nature of the event such as: product launch, corporate hospitality, management conference, training events, etc.

Positioning

In a crowded market place, it is suggested that we maximize the unique attributes and position of the Eden Project. We will of course accept 'normal' activities but will actively promote green theme corporate events as our competitive advantage. This is also in keeping with the not-for-profit part of our agenda.

Research

- ○ **Secondary research** To identify event organizers from trade directories, etc.
- ○ **Primary research** Interviews with potential clients to see needs and validate projected mix offering. Research of the mix including price of other event locations

Provisional service extended marketing mix

Product
All the normal conference facilities (we will need to check out when a client requires special facilities such as three-phase electricity supply).

Given that we do not have our own hotel accommodation at present, we will have to form strategic alliances with local hotels for this part of the offering.

If required, we can offer expert speakers on 'green' issues to clients.

Price
We need the revenue to support our other activities so a market-based price based on the 'going rate' for good national locations as indicated on the positioning map.

Place
Access by car is satisfactory.

For delegates arriving by rail etc. we need a contract with a local taxi company for personal pick-up.

Promotion
In this b2b context, the identification of the key decision makers in the clients' DMU will be key. To conclude the sale, skilled personal selling will be essential.

Target stakeholder publics will include:

- ○ DMU in potential client organizations
- ○ Media publics (vital for our publicity-driven strategy)
- ○ Local publics (e.g. local partner hotels)
- ○ Internal publics (we must keep all the employees informed as they are a critical part of the service offering)

Advertising
Limited to key trade magazines and trade directories.

Publicity
Work with early clients to gain publicity as 'the' place to hold your company event.

PR
Press releases to get the above publicity.

Internet
Need to maintain a lively section on our website for this aspect of our activities.

Personal selling
This will be key to close the sale. We should seek to recruit a person who has past experience in selling to the corporate event sector.

Direct mail
Rejected as probably expensive and lots of other 'junk mail' are cluttering up the desks of key decision makers in the major companies. We will rely on a pull strategy with clients attracted by good publicity and then gaining further information from our website.

Physical evidence
The buildings speak for themselves.

We should have a good event organizers' pack to convey our professionalism in this type of activity.

Process
Personal service. Single person to call on to organize things and resolve problems.

People
Briefing session with all front line staff in the special needs of these clients to develop empathetic client care.

Availability of top 'Green' experts to speak at events to add status.

Other clients: post list of top companies who have used the facilities on the website, 'If it is good enough for BT, it is good enough for us to use'.

Outline action plan

- o Research
- o Recruit manager and develop mix elements
- o Have promotion literature printed and website up-dated
- o Place advertisements
- o Launch
- o Ongoing marketing support

Budget

Too early to draw up a formal budget. To do this, we will need estimates for the printing and other media costs. We will need to recruit a person for this role and this must also be in the budget. Revenue can be estimated after the primary research.

Feedback and control

Normal plan against budget.

Key in relationship marketing terms will be a good debriefing process with event organizers to build on success and eliminate bugs.

> ***Guidance notes*** Writing an outline marketing or communication plan is a frequent task within the CIM exams. The above is suggested as one suitable framework for this. This answer takes a specific view to focus on the green platform. Taking this specific stance is not intended to indicate that this is the single 'right' answer. What is needed for a good pass mark is a practical self-consistent plan that could be developed into a full operation plan. In a midi case study context, it is not possible to give all the figures to draw up a detailed budget. Some indication of the information is needed to start to construct a budget of appropriate size.

Question 2

What Marketing Information System would you implement to monitor and develop visitor satisfaction of the Eden Project experience? What information would you collect and how would you obtain it?

(25 marks)

To   Marketing Manager – Eden Project

From   James Smith

Date   March 2003

Report for Marketing Information System for Visitor Satisfaction

Introduction

Kotler (2003) defines a Marketing Information System to consist of the people, equipment and procedures to gather, sort, analyse, evaluate and distribute needed, timely and accurate information to marketing decision makers. Components identified by Kotler are:

- o Marketing research system
- o Internal records system
- o Market intelligence system
- o Marketing decision support system

This report outlines some approaches for such a system to monitor visitor satisfaction and identify directions to improve the Eden Project visitors' experience.

The aim will be to identify what features contribute to a positive experience, and what aspects cause dissatisfaction. In addition, also to provide some pointers to developments and management policies that would enhance a visit.

Research

Secondary research is used to establish general factors in the marketing environment that affect visitors and primary research to gain specific information of the quality of the visit.

Secondary research

General information on the PEST environment such as:

o Political/legal: Issues such as disabled access, what is the law so we can work within both the letter and the spirit
o Economic: Spending on leisure activities and prices expected for comparable leisure activities
o Social: demographic information about regional tourism. Who comes to the region? Where do they come from? How do they travel to the region?
o Technical: developments in Internet, how is penetration progressing, what use are people making of the new technology for planning and booking trips

Information will be available from government sources and regional tourist organizations.

Primary research

Ongoing quantitative research to track satisfaction and qualitative research to probe issues further.

Quantitative research

A questionnaire to a sample of visitors, on an ongoing basis, to track visitor satisfaction with the attractions and other relevant information such as:

o Visitor demographic information such as age, etc.
o Travel and access to the project (e.g. by coach. Also 'satisfaction'; for example, 'Is access satisfactory for groups with small children?')
o Queuing time/issues
o Length of stay
o Satisfaction with facilities such as restaurants and the shop
o Overall satisfaction
o Would they visit again?
o Value for money

Qualitative research

Focus groups from target groups to probe 'deeper' issues such as attitudes to green issues.

Observation research to see how people move round the site, and time spent in specific attractions.

Internal information

Tracking all the normal sources of information from the commercial systems such as:

o Ticket purchase (how many, where purchased, advance purchase, collaborative travel and entry packages, e.g. group purchase). Numbers and trends
o Spend levels and patterns in restaurants and shops

Other sources of information

- Front line staff on questions (an indication where there may be issues such as poor direction signs)
- Tracking formal and informal complaints (tracking formal letters of complaint is vital but getting front line staff to report informal expressions of dissatisfaction will be useful to identify irritating aspects not sufficient to cause a formal complaint).

Market intelligence

Tracking press cover as this affects people's attitudes prior to their visit.

Satisfaction is a comparative issue. What are other attractions such as zoos and theme parks doing to provide a good day out?

- Visits to other centres
- Web-based research
- Review of press cover of competition
- Analysis of advertising platform of competition

Marketing decision support system

Detailed analysis of the data from all the sources is necessary to convert data to useful marketing management information such as:

- Statistical analysis of data, for example, to appraise if certain user groups are more or less satisfied (e.g. families as against adult only groups)
- Analysis to evaluate if time (e.g. day of week or time of day) or weather conditions have an effect on enjoyment
- Tracking of trends, both internal and external, against other parameters such as general level of holiday activity (e.g. visitor numbers to other attractions)
- If queuing is identified as an issue, modelling of queue lengths under different conditions and marketing strategies (e.g. modelling the effect of a promotional offer for pre-purchase of tickets to avoid on-site queuing for entry)

Conclusion

The above system will identify negative issues to be resolved (e.g. if facilities do not provide a good day out in wet weather) and provide pointers to new developments that will enhance the visit and encourage repeat attendance.

Guidance notes The answer illustrates an appropriate structured approach. Various writers indicate slightly different structures and classifications. The key issue in a good answer is to propose an appropriate range of data with an indication as to how it could be collected and then used.

Question 3

The Eden Project is concerned to be sensitive to the needs and wants of the local stakeholder groups. Outline the marketing communications activities you would undertake for the Eden Project locally.

(25 marks)

To   Marketing Manager – Eden Project

From   James Smith

Date   March 2003

Proposed Local Marketing Communications Activities

Introduction

The Eden Project has a significant impact on the local environment. There is an overall benefit to the local economy boosting the local tourist industry. This is not all good news as this has caused problems with local road congestion on busy days.

The local stakeholders that are relevant to the Eden Project include:

- o Media: local radio, TV and papers
- o Political Publics: Local elected representatives
- o Local services: e.g. Police
- o Supplier publics: local suppliers of products such as catering products to the restaurants
- o General public
- o Friends and relations of people working at the Eden Project
- o People seeking employment
- o Given the educational aims – local schools and colleges
- o Given this is a charity with not-for-profit aims, potential donors and volunteers (existing volunteers covered in our internal marketing plan)
- o Visitors to the Eden Project who live locally

Note: Internal stakeholders are excluded as they are covered by our internal marketing activities.

Key issues are considered first and then some specific activities are suggested for each of the above stakeholders.

Media: local radio, TV and papers

Their need is for news and to service the needs of their readers. A positive attitude from this group is vital, especially in the event of a PR disaster such as an accident to one of the visitors. Key to build relationships with local journalists:

- o Special briefings to provide background information
- o CD fact file including images to provide resource material
- o Press releases and invitations to special events
- o Make certain that the local press publics are not ignored when national press events are taking place
- o Have a contingency crisis management PR plan

Political publics

This group shape and respond to local opinion. The legitimate concern is that the international stature should not be built at the expense of the local community. A key influencer group for the local general public. Key to build relationships before there are problems.

- o Meetings to brief them with the senior management to solve problems before they become major issues

Local services

Large events need security. This group will have a legitimate concern that large numbers of visitors do not cause public order problems (e.g. as has happened in the past at rock festivals).

- o Relationship-building to ensure effective communications when there is an issue (e.g. larger than normal visitor numbers for an event)
- o E-mails to provide up to date information about plans that might affect their activities

Supplier publics

Modern supply chain management invites the organization to make suppliers part of the extended structure. As a major local buyer, we must be sensitive not to be seen to be exploiting this Porter-type power (e.g. recent controversies with supermarkets and small food producers).

- o Build relationships in a Relationship Marketing context, e.g. catering manager to visit food suppliers to build relationships
- o Local newsletter sent to suppliers to make them feel involved and part of the extended team
- o An invitation to the 'local friends' evening (special open evening for key local publics to be invited to)

General public

Local pride in the new attraction is balanced with concerns about traffic congestion. Key that we appear sensitive and responsive, and do not become a local 'Big Brother'.

Local general public will, of course, use the website, so make certain it has any special information that might be relevant.

- o Key activity will be communication through publicity generated through the press releases. As a charity, we have a limited budget
- o A responsive attitude to local people when they complain; communication is also about listening

Friends and relations

Simply an extension of the internal publics. We wish to gain and retain the reputation as a local 'family-friendly' employer.

- o Invitation to the 'friends evening' outlined above
- o A friends' newsletter.

People seeking employment

The unemployed are vulnerable, and we must be seen as fair and caring in our treatment. Poor procedures here could damage positive attitudes built up by other activities.

- Job section on the website
- Relationship marketing view of the recruitment process. Even if we do not employ, we wish applicants to still view us as fair and a good local corporate citizen

Given the educational aims – local schools and colleges

Education is a key objective of the Trust. An ideal opportunity to build deep and positive links with the local community. Good attitudes from students are likely to be shared by their friends and families.

- Special educational visits to the site
- Local education resource pack to complement the general education resource pack
- Education visits by research staff to schools

Potential donors and volunteers

Many charities use voluntary assistance to reduce costs and widen local participation in the broader objectives.

- Information pack for prospective volunteers
- Special web pages for prospective volunteers

Visitors to the Eden Project who live locally

Key to a service is gaining use at off-peak times.

- Loyalty passport for entry all the year for local people
- Concessionary rates for out-of-holiday season visits

Conclusion

We should monitor local attitudes by periodic surveys. We should subscribe to a 'clippings service' so that we are fully aware of media cover.

With the above actions, we should build and maintain good relationships with our local stakeholders.

Guidance notes The above structure considers the publics, some issues and then some action points. Clearly, this is not the only possible structure. These outline answers are not intended to be prescriptive. An alternative approach would be to consider communications actions and then consider their impact on various stakeholders.

Question 4

Clearly with almost two million visitors a year, the Eden Project has got off to a spectacular start. However, maintaining interest and visitor numbers will be key to the future. Using Relationship Marketing and other relevant marketing techniques, what initiatives would you consider appropriate to maintain and increase visitor numbers?

(25 marks)

To   Marketing Manager – Eden Project

From   James Smith

Date   March 2003

Relationship Marketing Approaches to Building and Maintaining Visitor Numbers

Introduction

Gummesson defines relationship marketing as 'marketing seen as relationships, networks and interaction'. The traditional marketing focus tended to:

- Focus on short time-scales
- Be product-driven
- Have sales as the objective
- Have discontinuous customer contact

The relationship marketing focus tends to move marketers:

- To longer time-scales and lifetime value of the relationship
- To focus on customer benefits and value more than just product
- To see sales as part of the broader issue of customer orientation and relationship building
- To pursue more frequent customer contacts not restricted to just sales interactions

This can be expressed in Payne's relationship ladder. Traditional marketing takes people from step one (a prospect) onto step two (a customer), the so-called 'customer catching'. The relationship ladder seeks to move people through the full five steps:

- Prospect
- Customer
- Client
- Supporter
- Advocate

The marketing activity changes from simply selling to developing and enhancing relationships, customer retention.

In the context of the Eden Project, we need to move people from a single visit to repeated visits by suitable promotional activities (e.g. discount price for a second visit). Ultimately, we wish to move people to advocates not only of the Eden Project but also in the context of the overall green movement. Marketing activities could include a 'Friends of the Project' scheme with a newsletter and a special section of the website to maintain and develop relationships. Thus, drawing people into the deeper not-for-profit objectives of the Eden Project.

Morgan and Hunt propose that it is not only the buyer partnerships that are important but also:

- o Supplier partnerships
- o Internal partnerships
- o Lateral partnerships

In this discussion, I will focus on the lateral partnerships.

Competitors

One can regard competitors as strategic partners. We could consider a packaged ticket, which provides entry to a number of attractions and engage in collaborative marketing communications.

Non-profit Organizations

Other not-for-profit organizations are not so much competitors but partners. We should ensure good web links from such organizations and again consider collaborative marketing communications such as a 'save the rainforest week'.

Government

Given the expansion plans, a favourable view is needed by national and regional government for support such as local infrastructure development, e.g. improvement of the access roads. Good strategic PR to lobby key political decision makers will be important.

A visit to the Eden Project is a leisure activity in a service marketing context. Services have four main characteristics:

- o Intangibility
- o Inseparability
- o Perishability
- o Heterogeneity

These characteristics are addressed by marketers by the use of the service-extended marketing mix. However the quality of 'people – people' interactions, etc. are much more difficult to measure than the weight of a bag of sugar. The SERVQUAL model seeks to address these issues. Gap analysis can help the Eden Project consistently achieve a quality experience for visitors.

Gap 1: Consumer expectations – managers' perceptions of consumer expectations. Need to research that we are creating the right service experience for our visitors

Gap 2: Managers' perceptions of consumer expectations – service quality specifications actually set. Again research that service level specifications such as target queuing times are appropriate

Gap 3: Service quality specifications – actual service delivery. We must ensure that internal records systems monitor levels of performance and flag up when these fall below specification

Gap 4: Actual service delivery – external communications about the service. We must conduct research to check we are not creating expectations – visitor expectations, which we later fail to deliver

Gap 5: We must check from our internal systems, where resources have to be adjusted such as additional attendants at peak periods

Conclusion

By integrating a range of these actions, we should ensure that we build up long-term relationships with our key stakeholders; ultimately, converting a casual visitor to a supporter of the Eden Project and an advocate of the green movement.

> ***Guidance notes*** The above provides a structured outline using some appropriate approaches with selective use of the theory. Candidates in the exam setting are not expected to cover all the theory and use all the elements of all the possible tools. Good answers will indicate selective use of the theory to address the practical issues in the case study situation.

Question 5

You have decided that you wish to produce a new brochure for the corporate hospitality business and complete a direct mail shot in the UK to expand this business. Using appropriate project management concepts, outline an action plan for the production of this brochure.

(25 marks)

To   Marketing Manager – Eden Project

From   James Smith

Date   March 2003

Project Management for New Brochure Production

Introduction

There are many methods of project management such as critical path analysis (e.g. activity-on-arrow or activity-on-node) and Gantt charts. Such approaches are vital to Marketing Managers as many plans have time-critical events. A new summer brochure published in the autumn will not achieve much. Even a modest marketing initiative involves a group of people and a failure of one of the supporting staff can have a knock-on effect. This can provide a fatal delay in project completion much later. Explicit methods of project management allow the identification of 'pressure points' and prompt the project manager to provide appropriate communications. This will co-ordinate the activities of the extended project team and bring in the project on time.

For a relatively simple project such as the production of a brochure, the activity plot against time format (Gantt chart) may be all that is required. For increased complexity, a network-type approach such as activity-on-arrow with critical path analysis will provide an analysis of the logic sequence and identify the critical path. Therefore, focusing management time and energy on critical activities, where modest delays could affect the completion of the whole project.

For convenience in this report, the brochure production will be considered under the following headings:

- o   Pre-planning
- o   Collection of material
- o   Integration of material

- o Production of brochure (it will be assumed an external printer will be contracted for this)
- o Distribution and post-production

Pre-planning

It is vital to start the process early, and to establish key parameters and responsibilities. Issues that need to be considered include:

- o Setting of publication deadline
- o Setting budget and identifying budget responsibilities
- o Establishing house style (possibly with design consultant)
- o Guidance on must haves (e.g. good images) and must not haves (e.g. things outside the house style)
- o Appointing project leader
- o Establishing communications objectives
- o Defining the theme for authors to work to
- o Establishing outline structure (e.g. number of pages and images, size of sections)
- o Budgetary estimates should be obtained from printers, etc.
- o The nature and costs of any copyright should be established
- o Legal experts should be consulted about any contracts that are to be used like contract for photographers (e.g. who will own the copyright of the images)

Collection of material

This can be an 'explosive' phase of the project with many different people involved. Firm briefing and good project management skills are required, as there is no such thing as 90 per cent ready material. Either you have it or you do not. Actions that need to be managed include:

- o Firm briefing instructions to authors and photographers
- o Checking that where contracts are needed for providers, they have been agreed and signed
- o Milestone checking with the contributors that work is progressing satisfactorily
- o Checking that where library resources are to be used (e.g. an image bank library), the material is of adequate quality, if an appropriate format and establishing if copyright clearance may be used
- o Once a firm definition of what is required is established, firm tenders can be sought for printing and the contract placed

Integration of material

Here the diversity of material has to be checked and assembled. It is assumed that the final process of producing the files will be completed by a printer. Issues to be considered and actions to be completed include:

- o Checks that images are acceptable and are in the required format for the printers
- o Check that texts to be integrated are correct for factual content, typographical errors and house style issues
- o Integration of texts into appropriate file format for the printer
- o Where work is completed ensure fees are paid

Production of brochure

The physical production will be the responsibility of the printer but the project manager still has work to do including:

o Checking that the printer has received all the materials and files in good order
o Distribution of the proofs to the various authors for final proofing
o Checking that all proofs have been 'signed off' by the appropriate responsible people (note the need of cover for sickness or holidays)
o Authorizing the print run

Distribution and post production

The project is not over until the brochures are in the hands of the intended recipients. Actions in the final lap include:

o Checking that all stock points have received the number of brochures required
o Ensure that all remaining bills have been paid
o Ensuring that authors and other relevant people have their courtesy copies
o Most importantly, a review of the process to see what areas caused problems (was a particular contractor poor on quality or consistently missing deadlines, etc.)

Conclusion

Project management of even a modest project is a demanding challenge needing the ability to see both the big picture (the completed product) and meticulous attention to detail where one small error (e.g. failure to gain copyright clearance) can cause a disaster. Modern software for project management helps the busy operational marketing manager in this process.

Guidance notes It is impossible in the exam setting to cover every detailed point and it is suggested that in the time allowed detailed construction of networks or charts is too time-consuming. What a good answer needs to demonstrate is an appreciation of project management tools and a practical understanding of actions and their control in a typical project situation that an operational level marketing manager may be faced with in their day-to-day job.

---

appendix 4
answers and debriefings

The answers that follow are indicative and are not intended to be complete. Some of the answers to the activities are embedded in the course materials, the essential text, in websites or simply in the mind of the reader.

Unit 1

Activity Debriefing 1.1

Managers are likely to differ in how they perceive demands, choices and constraints, and they may have more choices than they perceive. Different perceptions arise out of a combination of personal factors such as personality and previous experience, cultural factors such as views about how managers and other staff should interact and who has the authority to make decisions, and job factors relating to the work context and the people with whom the manager interacts. In some contexts, such as retailing, it can be very important for front-line staff to have the discretion to respond to customers and clients rather than to apply a rigid set of rules. 'More than my job is worth' is the embodiment of a lack of both choice and responsiveness to customers. However, in some other areas of work, the rigid application of a set of rules is necessary to ensure that people are treated fairly or that health and safety procedures are followed. Therefore, whether or not different perceptions about demands, choices and constraints is a problem or not depends on the context.

Activity Debriefing 1.2

Most managers have strengths and weaknesses, and few managers are strong in all respects and an awareness of personal strengths and weaknesses is an important aspect of management. Different management styles can be effective and efficient, and views about what makes an 'effective' manager might vary depending on your role where you 'sit' in the organization. Being popular and being effective are not the same. The television series 'The Office' provides a humorous example of the embarrassing consequences of a manager who feels that being 'a chilled out entertainer' is what people are looking for in a 'boss'.

Activity Debriefing 1.3

In looking at the time you spent on interpersonal roles, decisional roles, informational roles – does this match the priorities of your job? After completing your chart are there any less developed management roles you need to improve? If you were promoted tomorrow what roles are you likely to have to perform in addition to those you have already?

Activity Debriefing 1.4

The Spiderman website is more geared up for advertising the merchandise that is available. The Lord of the Rings site seems to focus more on providing in-depth information about the characters and the films. However, whilst the Spiderman website looks to be more sophisticated technologically is it as quick to navigate this site compared with the Lord of the Rings site? – What is your view? Which site is the most effective from a marketing perspective is a matter of opinion but criteria to look at are, for example, ease and speed of navigation, how well different parts of the site are signposted and how straightforward it is to find what the site is marketing. You might think of other criteria that could be used to compare marketing effectiveness.

Activity Debriefing 1.5

Likely problems:

For managers – supervision and control, communications, understanding employees needs/concerns, etc., building and maintaining relationships, motivation, evaluating performance, etc.

For employees – isolation, lack of interaction, home distractions and protecting work space (both physical and mental), personal development, lack of sense of belonging, etc.

Implications for the business – Insurance, health and safety, also redesigning/reducing office space, providing space for team events/meetings, ensuring steelworkers have the necessary equipment and maintain this equipment, use of technology, e.g. videoconferencing, intranet, fostering the work ethic and protecting reputation and brand.

Activity Debriefing 1.6

In many organizations, functions such as sales and marketing are combined in one role but in some organizations, sales and marketing departments can work against each other, with each group planning their strategy, training their team and implementing their plan without considering each other's plans, gathering their input, providing feedback or gaining support from each other. If co-ordination is a problem in your organization, what are the causes of the problem and how could they be improved?

Activity Debriefing 1.7

One of the benefits of the site are the Special Reports on CRM but there are other benefits as well. However, you may find that the site is too specific to the USA and the ideas that are discussed may need to be adapted to your own context.

Activity Debriefing 1.8

The USA site has information about campaigns such as child labour in the chocolate industry but the UK site does not seem to contain similar information. Maybe this is based on a view of what is important in the USA compared to the UK, or maybe it says something about the use of social causes in marketing. You decide.

Activity Debriefing 1.9

It should be clear that in many organizations, the effective performance of marketing roles requires good working relationships with a wide range of people inside and often outside the organization. This means that there is also a need to develop a range of other social skills as well as marketing expertise. Marketing managers need skills in the following areas:

- o Communication
- o Project Development
- o Team leadership
- o Delegation
- o Time Management
- o Working across organizational boundaries
- o Negotiation and conflict resolution
- o Project Planning
- o Managing people
- o Performance management
- o Coaching.

Activity Debriefing 1.10

1. Definition
Your answer should begin with a definition of service marketing, for example, Kotler, 'Any activity of benefit that one party offers to another, which is essentially intangible and does not result in the ownership of anything'.

2. Characteristics of services marketing
Heterogeneity – Service provision varies.

Intangibility – A need for tangible proxy evidence such as environmental quality, friendliness of staff, etc.

Perishability – A service cannot be stored like a product can be kept.

Inseparability – Service and consumption cannot be separated.

3. Explain the 7 Ps

- o Product
- o Place
- o Promotion
- o Price
- o People
- o Process
- o Physical Evidence.

Mention the need for good training and development to help make the service have some standardized components but also leave room for staff to add their individual flourish to the service.

Point out the need for physical evidence – stationery, uniforms, the general environment and ambience.

Focus on areas that will help the customer remember the service and help to differentiate it from competitors' services.

Process is important because needs have to be anticipated and met.

Promotion helps to reduce, for example, under-occupancy, wasted food, etc.

4. Service Quality
Set SMART objectives and try to close the gap between what the service offers and what customers need. Use, for example, Parasuraman's service quality model.

NB - INSERT Parasuraman's model

Identify the factors that can lead to a breakdown in service quality, for example, expectations, perceptions, actual service delivered, the service brief and the way that changes are communicated to the customer.

5. Benchmarking
Explain the concept of Christopher, Payne and Ballantyne to recruits.

6. Service Criteria
Discuss generic service criteria:

Responsiveness – Can cleaning take place at short notice?

Reliability – Does someone turn up at the agreed time?

Empathy – Is awareness shown of busy office practice?

Assurance – Are there SMART objectives?

Tangibles – Are we professional?

7. Conclusion
Conclude by asking recruits to use Parasuraman's model to establish a service performance matrix for the company. Conclude with an opportunity for discussion and questions.

Senior Examiner's Comments:

Answers showed a clear understanding of the five characteristics of services and the extended marketing mix. Better students discussed the GAP model.

NB - INSERT GAP MODEL

They applied the characteristics of the business-to-business cleaning context using a presentation format and a tone that would be suitable for new recruits. Those who failed did not provide enough detail or forgot that the cleaning company existed, preferring to give no examples at all or standard hotel and airline responses.

Unit 2

Activity Debriefing 2.1

Were you able to answer this question easily, or did it take a long time to think about the whole range of stakeholders involved with your organization? Your list should have included internal and external people. In some organizations, the expectations of different parts of the organization will be explicit but, in others it may only be implicit. Sometimes there is a disdainful view of other parts of the organization that contribute to the overheads but whose contribution to frontline activities is not so visible – for example, what is your view of personnel/HRM? finance? – Were you able to identify your key Stakeholders' expectations of your team? Who did you identify as your customers? – Do you see people internal to the organization as your customers?

Activity Debriefing 2.2

In what areas does your team work well and in what areas does it need to improve? If you identified any barriers to effectiveness, how much of this is within the power of the team to overcome? – Usually, teams can improve if one of their goals is to improve how they work together. However, this may not be spoken about even though there may be a recognition that the team does not work well.

Activity Debriefing 2.3

There are many aspects of culture to pay attention to, particularly in marketing activities. The use of language can be a barrier even when the same language is spoken. Unit 1 provided some examples of this but business cultures can vary a lot.

Activity Debriefing 2.4

Employee Specification

Factor	Essential	Desirable
Attainments	Degree preferably in a media or marketing discipline	CAM qualifications to Diploma level
Specific professional skills	Written composition and presentation skills. Media and communications strategies	*
Experience	5 years or more in a media/PR role	Preferably in a non-profit organization or consultancy
Reasoning Abilities	Capacity for strategic media analysis and event management	*
Personality	Calm, proactive, assertive, confident, representative personality. Empathy with NHS values	*
Aptitudes	Networker, promoter, persuader, win rapport with clients. Create and develop promotional material.	*
Physical make-up	Professional, well-groomed image. Stamina & good health	*
Circumstances	Weekend and evening work	*

Essential Attributes essential for adequate job performance. Job cannot be performed unless these factors are present.

Desirable Attributes that are not essential but if present will enhance effective work performance.

This is adapted from http://sol.brunel.ac.uk/~jarvis/bola/jobs/mediajob/perspec.html

Unit 3

Activity Debriefing 3.1

What are your priorities for development? – You could also ask a trusted colleague to complete a form like this about you so that you can compare your responses with his or her perceptions. If there were large gaps in perception you might want to pursue this further to understand why your perceptions are different.

Activity Debriefing 3.2

Were you able to identify your needs and people in the organization that could help? Will you need any assistance to be able to access this help? Is your line manager likely to be supportive or will he or she see this as a threat because they may feel it makes them look like a poor manager – or is your line manager more secure about themselves and likely to be more supportive?

Unit 4

Activity Debriefing 4.1

How easy did you find it to use the model? Do you see any advantages in distinguishing between what is written about approaches on paper and collecting information about what is actually being implemented? Do you have any examples of where there is a gap between theory and practice in your own organization? Would a model like EFQM be appropriate in your situation – or, if you already use such a model how successful is it at promoting improvements?

Activity Debriefing 4.2

It is a self-selecting audience and there must be doubts about how representative it is of a wider population. However, there is no reason to think what interests these women would not interest other women as well, bearing in mind that nothing will please everyone, all of the time. On a limited scale, it is market research and the personal endorsement of some viewers that will encourage other viewers to buy the product.

Activity Debriefing 4.3

Were there any gaps, i.e. information you would like that is not available? How could this information be obtained from other secondary sources?

Activity Debriefing 4.4

A balance needs to be struck between breadth and depth. Usually, it is possible to find out a lot about an issue from a small sample, but not as much from a larger sample. Sometimes different approaches can be combined so that, for example, a focus group can precede or follow a larger survey to probe certain issues in more detail. However, with a large survey, it is important that there is a consistency of approach, and at least some comparative data can be gained. This means that the questioners need to ask the same questions of employers, something that wouldn't happen if in-depth interviews were being held on the shopfloor, not to mention the added expense. A survey of 70,000 employers is a large survey and should enable some useful conclusions to be drawn. The use of the telephone will provide data in greater depth than could be achieved by a questionnaire.

Unit 5

Activity Debriefing 5.1

How easy was it to devise a GANTT Chart? – Did you find it useful? – Can you think of examples of how you could use it at work ?

Activity Debriefing 5.2

There should be a lot of examples where a project management approach may be useful in a marketing context, such as developing a communications campaign or working with external agencies, for example, in market research projects.

Activity Debriefing 5.3

Examples of the key areas could be as follows:

The project timetable, with particular reference to critical event times and potential bottlenecks. There should be feedback on activity times achieved and their effect on the whole project. If network analysis is used, then it is vital that the network is reworked and updated to take into account the actual performance achieved.

The project budget; budgetary control procedures can be used as in respect of any other form of budget.

Quality and performance standards; these need to be monitored against the original project specification subject to changes agreed with stakeholders in the course of project development.

Unit 6

Activity Debriefing 6.1

What kind of issues did you identify? We all need to learn from our experience of being involved in change so that the same mistakes aren't repeated. Gathering feedback after a change has been implemented could be tried providing that the raw feelings associated with change have died down. Otherwise, there is a risk of stirring things up again.

Unit 7

Activity Debriefing 7.1

Are there any conclusions or criteria that you would draw from the campaign that you identified that could be used in other campaigns? What kind of appeal was being made through the campaign? – Was it appealing to 'the rational' or 'the emotional' you? Were you able to associate the product or service with the campaign? Often, we seem to be able to remember advertisements but can't remember the brand that is being sold.

Unit 8

Activity Debriefing 8.1

Case study 1 has rather less detail than the second, and is not organized as systematically. However, the size of the organization is a lot smaller in case study 1 and it could be argued that the type of case study is 'fit for purpose'. Case study 2 is an example of a comprehensive approach and shows how some well-known marketing models can be applied. Gathering the information to do this would have incurred an expense that the company in the case study 1 may have found difficult to emulate.

Activity Debriefing 8.2

Did you manage to construct a GANTT chart to schedule the activities? The GANTT chart should show how complex the scheduling can be and how there are bottlenecks and troughs in activity, i.e. sometimes, everything needs doing at the same time and sometimes there is a lull in activity. The aim is to try and smooth this out as far as possible whilst still keeping to deadlines. What range of people were there in your team? – Did you include finance and human resources – or are these line management responsibilities in your organization ?

appendix 5
curriculum information

Marketing Management in Practice

Aim

The Marketing Management in Practice module practises participants in developing and implementing marketing plans at an operational level in organizations. A key part of this module is working within a team to develop the plan, and managing the teams implementing the plan by undertaking marketing activities and projects. Its aim is to assist participants in integrating and applying knowledge from all the modules at Stage 2, particularly as part of a team. This module also forms the summative assessment for Stage 2.

Related statements of practice

Jc.1 Plan marketing projects and prepare budgets

Jc.2 Manage and report on delivery against plan and objectives

Kc.1 Define measurements appropriate to the plan or business case, and ensure they are undertaken

Kc.2 Evaluate activities and identify improvements using measurement data

Lc.1 Manage a marketing team

Lc.2 Maintain relationships with other functions and disciplines within the organization

Lc.3 Encourage and help others to develop their competencies relevant to a marketing role

Lc.4 Embrace change and modify behaviours and attitudes.

Learning outcomes

Participants will be able to:

- o Explain the roles and structure of the marketing function and the nature of relationships with other functions within various types of organizations
- o Plan and undertake or commission marketing research for an operational marketing plan or business decision

- ○ Interpret qualitative and quantitative data and present appropriate and coherent recommendations that lead to effective marketing and business decisions
- ○ Develop marketing objectives and plans at an operational level appropriate to the organization's internal and external environments
- ○ Develop an effective plan for a campaign and supporting customers and members of a marketing channel
- ○ Use appropriate management techniques to plan and control marketing activities and projects
- ○ Use appropriate techniques to develop, manage and motivate a team, so that it performs effectively and delivers required results
- ○ Define measures for, and evaluate the performance of, marketing plans, activities and projects, and make recommendations for improvements.

Knowledge and skills requirements

Element 1: Managing people and teams (30 per cent)

1.1 Describe the functions/roles of marketing managers and typical marketing jobs and the nature of relationships with other functions in organizations operating in a range of different industries and contexts

1.2 Develop and maintain effective relationships with people in other functions and disciplines within the organization

1.3 Identify and explain the key challenges of managing marketing teams in a multinational or multicultural context

1.4 Explain how you would use the techniques available for selecting, building, developing and motivating marketing teams to improve performance

1.5 Allocate and lead the work of marketing teams, agreeing objectives and work plans with teams and individuals

1.6 Respond to poor performance within a marketing team by minimizing conflict, supporting team members, overcoming problems and maintaining discipline

1.7 Explain the sources and nature of change affecting organizations and the techniques available for managing change

1.8 Evaluate individual and team performance against objectives or targets, and provide constructive feedback on their performance.

Element 2: Managing marketing projects (10 per cent)

2.1 Describe the main stages of a project and the roles of people involved at each stage

2.2 Describe the main characteristics of successful and less successful projects, and identify the main reasons for success or failure

2.3 Explain the importance of, and techniques for, establishing the project's scope, definition and goals

2.4 Use the main techniques available for planning, scheduling, resourcing and controlling activities on a project

2.5 Explain the importance of preparing budgets and techniques for controlling progress throughout a project to ensure it is completed on time and within budget

2.6 Explain the main techniques for evaluating the effectiveness of a project on its completion.

Element 3: Managing knowledge and delivering marketing research projects (20 per cent)

3.1 Explain the concept, and give examples, of the application of information and knowledge management, highlighting the role of marketing and employees within the organization

3.2 Design a research project aimed at providing information as part of a marketing audit or for marketing and business decisions

3.3 Manage a marketing research project by gathering relevant information on time and within the agreed budget

3.4 Make arrangements to record, store and, if appropriate, update information in the MkIS, a database created for the purpose or another system

3.5 Analyse and interpret information and present, as a written report or oral presentation, appropriate conclusions or recommendations that inform the marketing and business decisions for which the research was undertaken

3.6 Review and evaluate the effectiveness of the activities and the role of the individual and team in this process.

Element 4: Developing and implementing marketing plans (20 per cent)

4.1 Develop an operational marketing plan, selecting an appropriate marketing mix for an organization operating in any context such as FMCG, business-to-business (supply chain), large or capital project-based, services, voluntary and not-for-profit, or sales support (e.g. SMEs)

4.2 Use the main techniques available for planning, scheduling and resourcing activities within the plan

4.3 Identify appropriate measures for evaluating and controlling the marketing plan

4.4 Review and evaluate the effectiveness of planning activities and the role of the individual and team in this process.

Element 5: Delivering communications and customer service programmes (20 per cent)

5.1 Plan the design, development, execution and evaluation of communications campaigns by a team of marketers, including external agencies and suppliers

5.2 Use appropriate marketing communications to develop relationships or communicate with a range of stakeholders

5.3 Manage and monitor the provision of effective customer service

5.4 Use marketing communications to provide support for members of a marketing channel

5.5 Use marketing communications techniques for an internal marketing plan to support management of change within an organization

5.6 Review and evaluate the effectiveness of communications activities and the role of the individual and team in this process.

Related key skills for marketers

The syllabus covers the core knowledge and skills for marketing professionals. The 'key skills for marketers' covers the broader business and organizational skills that marketing professionals should also possess. Participants will not be assessed specifically on their ability to perform key skills. However, as professionals working in organizations, they will be expected to demonstrate, during assessment in the relevant modules, their knowledge, understanding and competence in the areas defined by the key skills. Participants should be encouraged to develop and demonstrate the application of relevant key skills through activities, assignments and discussions during their learning.

- o Using ICT and the Internet
- o Using financial information and metrics
- o Presenting information
- o Improving own learning and performance
- o Working with others
- o Problem-solving
- o Applying business law.

Assessment

As the summative assessment at this level, the assessment will require participants to demonstrate knowledge and skills in all areas covered by the four modules of Stage 2. CIM will normally offer two forms of assessment for this module from which centres may choose – written examination (a 'midi' case study) and a project-based assessment. Specimen papers and guidance on the structure, format and approach of these assessments will be published separately.

CIM may also recognize, or make joint awards for, modules at an equivalent level undertaken with other professional marketing bodies and educational institutions.

Recommended support materials

In addition to the texts from the other modules at Stage 2, the following texts and resources are available to support this module.

Core texts

Boddy, D. (2002) *Management: an introduction.* 2nd revised edition. London, FT/Prentice Hall.

Martin, P. (2002) *Getting started in project management.* Chichester, John Wiley.

Workbooks

CIM (2003) *Marketing management in practice companion.* Cookham, Chartered Institute of Marketing.

BPP (2003) *Marketing management in practice.* London, BPP Publishing.

Williams, J. and Curtis, T. (2003) *Marketing management in practice.* Oxford, Butterworth-Heinemann.

Supplementary readings

Adair, J. (2002) *Inspiring leadership.* London, Thorogood.

Belbin, R.M. (1996) *Management teams: Why they succeed or fail.* Oxford, Butterworth-Heinemann.

Brown, A. (1998) *Organisational culture.* 2nd edition. London, FT/Prentice Hall.

Handy, C. (1993) *Understanding organisations.* London, Penguin.

Hilton, S. and Gibbons, G. (2002) *Good business: Your world needs you.* London, Texere.

Trompenaars, F. and Hampden-Turner, C. (1997) *Riding the waves of culture.* 2nd revised edition. London, Nicholas Brealey.

Woodcock, M. (1989) *Team development manual.* 2nd revised edition. Aldershot, Gower.

Marketing and management journals

Participants can keep abreast of developments in the academic field of marketing by reference to the main marketing journals, a selection of which are listed in the Appendix to this document.

Press

Participants will be expected to have access to current examples of marketing campaigns and so should be sure to keep up to date with the appropriate marketing and quality daily press. A selection of marketing press titles is given in the Appendix to this document.

Websites

A list of websites that tutors and participants may find useful is shown in the Appendix at the end of this document.

Additional resources

There are many useful diagnostic tools for those interested in learning more about themselves and the workings of teams, a few of which are mentioned here. Permission should be obtained from the appropriate sources for use of these tools.

- o Learning styles questionnaire, Honey and Mumford
- o Team roles questionnaire, Belbin

- Leadership style questionnaire, Hersey, Blanchard, Reddin, Blake, Mouton
- Work Motivation Inventory, Chartwell Bratt
- Strengths Deployment Inventory, E. Porter, S. Maloney.

Overview and rationale

The Marketing Management in Practice syllabus requires a broad and practical demonstration of marketing at an operational level and an awareness of the strategic context. It provides an opportunity for participants to develop and implement an operational marketing plan, so applying, as part of a team, the theory of research, planning and marketing communications provided in the previous three modules.

This module also provides the final assessment of participants' ability to create an operational marketing plan. As such, it forms an important measure of the participants' ability to meet organization's requirements of an operational marketer.

From an educational standpoint, this module seeks to integrate learning from the full Stage 2 syllabus. As such, it is best suited to delivery after the other modules of Stage 2. It should be lively and fun for all involved. It rounds off Stage 2 and so provides a springboard for Stage 3, which goes on to develop participants for a role in strategic marketing.

Approach

Marketing Management in Practice is about developing and managing teams to add value to the organization's activities and deliver effective results. Like members of other functions and disciplines within organizations, marketers work towards departmental and broader organizational objectives. They work in teams, both within the marketing function and, importantly, with people in other functions.

It is important to recognize that the context within which marketers are operating is continually changing as a result of both external and internal influences. No organization is detached from international influences, even if the organization does not have to deal with international customers. Organizations source materials from around the globe, access international markets from a desk, compete with other organizations from around the world, and imitate global behaviour. It is therefore appropriate in this module to cover international issues as part of everyday marketing life in organizations.

Marketers and marketing managers must be able to work effectively themselves, for example, managing time and problem-solving. They must also be able to manage and motivate people and teams to produce results. Using Adair's model of leadership, effective team performance is contingent on a balance between:

- The needs of the task
- The needs of the individuals within the team
- The maintenance needs of the team as a whole.

Syllabus content

The syllabus for this module uses Adair's concept. It provides underpinning theory on managing teams to help with managing individual needs and team needs to get the most from the team. It also provides basic project management techniques to help with managing the task. These two elements provide the final skills and knowledge for marketers to develop and implement marketing plans at an operational level. The remainder of the syllabus for this module is about the development and implementation of an operational marketing plan, including the management of information, communications and human resources. In other words, participants should apply within a marketing team the theory of marketing research and information, planning and communications covered in the earlier modules. This should be achieved through a project.

A syllabus can contain only so much and this syllabus assumes that, on entry to the module, participants have the skills to manage themselves (defined in the key skill 'Improving own learning & performance') and the principles of motivation, leadership, power and influence relevant to the team context. If participants do not have these skills, then centres may wish to impose additional required learning, or provide additional sessions and materials.

Element 1: Managing people and teams

This element provides the underpinning knowledge required for the selection, development and maintenance of effective marketing teams. It is particularly important to stress the organizational and global context within which marketing teams are operating and how different organizations adopt different approaches to marketing depending on their context and culture. In cases where this subject is taught by a HR tutor, it is important that it is set within a marketing context. This subject is developed further in Stage 3. It is also important to use this element to build on the Key Skills 'Working with others' and 'Improving own knowledge and performance'.

Element 2: Techniques for managing marketing projects & activities

Managing the planning and performance of a marketing task by a team requires skills in planning, scheduling, directing, motivating and monitoring. The techniques of project management equip marketing managers to manage marketing activities and projects effectively. This element provides the underpinning knowledge of the techniques, which are then applied in the marketing activities that make up the rest of the syllabus for this module.

Element 3: Managing knowledge and delivering market research projects

Knowledge management is about people. We need to motivate and enthuse the people we manage with a willingness and desire to share and exchange knowledge. We cannot do this by simply presenting them with a piece of IT equipment. It requires a cultural norm of open communication and informing and sharing knowledge and motivating and rewarding knowledge sharing that benefits the business.

This element builds on the underpinning knowledge developed in the Marketing Research and Information module by providing participants with the opportunity to plan and undertake or commission a research project as a team activity as part of a marketing audit feeding into a marketing plan or business decision.

Element 4: Developing and implementing marketing plans

This element requires effective teamwork and a good understanding of the marketing planning process and techniques to produce successful outcomes. This element builds on the underpinning knowledge developed in the Marketing Planning module by providing participants with the opportunity to develop and implement a marketing plan as a team activity. It is important that the implementation issues are explored in some depth. Apart from providing participants with valuable learning, this will test the realism of the plans they have developed.

Element 5: Delivering communications and customer service programmes

This element builds on the underpinning knowledge developed in the Marketing Communications module by providing participants with the opportunity to manage campaigns or communication programmes as a team activity using appropriate techniques to develop or maintain stakeholder relationships, manage the provision of customer service, provide support for a marketing channel, or deliver an internal marketing plan.

Delivery approach

This syllabus covers approximately 45 hours of tutor-directed learning, usually fifteen 3-hour sessions if delivered face-to-face. As a guide, centres should allocate up to one third of these sessions to cover the underpinning theory and on techniques for managing teams and projects and any coaching required on the assessment. These can, and indeed should, be active sessions with participants using these techniques rather than just lectures.

Two thirds of the sessions should be allocated to a significant practical project involving the formulation and implementation of an operational marketing plan. This should cover the management of information, communications and human resources. It is important that these sessions are of a practical nature. All the necessary theory should have been covered in the previous three modules, so the emphasis in this module should be the application of this theory within a marketing team. The nature of the project undertaken may depend on which form of assessment the participants will use. A typical project will consist of:

- o Planning the project to be undertaken to meet the brief given
- o Undertaking the task. This will involve collecting and analysing information and developing a marketing plan
- o Planning, scheduling and resourcing marketing activities within the plan, identifying and overcoming problems during implementation
- o Measuring and evaluating the outcomes
- o Reflecting on the performance of the team and the individuals in it.

Additional resources

Introduction

Texts to support the individual modules are listed in the syllabus for each module. This Appendix shows a list of marketing journals, press and websites that tutors and participants may find useful in supporting their studies at Stage 2.

Marketing journals

Participants can keep abreast of developments in the academic field of marketing by reference to the main marketing journals.

- o *Corporate Reputation Review* – Henry Stewart
- o *European Journal of Marketing* – Emerald
- o *Harvard Business Review* - Harvard
- o *International Journal of Advertising* – WARC
- o *International Journal of Corporate Communications* – Emerald
- o *International Journal of Market Research* – WARC
- o *Journal of Consumer Behaviour An International Review* – Henry Stewart

- o   *Journal of the Academy of Marketing Science* – Sage Publications
- o   *Journal of Marketing* – American Marketing Assoc. Pubs Group
- o   *Journal of Marketing Communications* – Routledge
- o   *Journal of Marketing Management* – Westburn Pubs Ltd
- o   *International Journal of Market Research* – NTC Pubs
- o   *Journal of Product and Brand Management* – Emerald
- o   *Journal of Services Marketing* – Emerald
- o   *Marketing Review* – Westburn Pubs Ltd

Press

Participants will be expected to have access to current examples of marketing campaigns and so should be sure to keep up to date with the appropriate marketing and quality daily press, including:

- o   *Campaign* – Haymarket
- o   *Internet Business* – Haymarket
- o   *Marketing* – Haymarket
- o   *Marketing Business* – Chartered Institute of Marketing
- o   *Marketing Week* – Centaur
- o   *Revolution* – Haymarket

Websites

The Chartered Institute of Marketing

www.cim.co.uk	The CIM site with information and access to learning support for participants
www.connectedinmarketing.com	A CIM site providing information on current marketing issues and applications
www.cimvirtualinstitute.com	Full details of all that's new in CIM's educational offer including specimen answers and Hot Topics
www.cimeducator.com	The CIM site for tutors only

Publications online

www.revolution.haynet.com	Revolution magazine
www.marketing.haynet.com	Marketing magazine
www.FT.com	A wealth of information for cases (now charging)
www.IPA.co.uk	Need to register – communication resources
www.booksites.net	Financial Times/Prentice Hall Text websites

Sources of useful information

www.acnielsen.co.uk	AC Nielsen – excellent for research
http://advertising.utexas.edu/world/	Resources for advertising & marketing professionals, participants, and tutors
www.bized.com	Case studies
www.esomar.nl	European Body representing Research Organizations – useful for guidelines on research ethics and approaches
www.dma.org.uk	The Direct Marketing Association
www.eiu.com	The Economist Intelligence Unit
www.euromonitor.com	Euromonitor consumer markets

www.europa.eu.int	The European Commission extensive range of statistics and reports relating to EU and member countries.
www.managementhelp.org/research/research.htm	Part of the 'Free Management Library' – explaining research methods
www.marketresearch.org.uk	The MRS site with information and access to learning support for participants – useful links on ethics and code of conduct
www.oecd.org	OECD statistics and other information relating to member nations including main economic indicators
www.quirks.com	An American source of information on marketing research issues and projects
www.un.org	United Nations publish statistics on member nations
www.worldbank.org	World bank economic, social and natural resource indicators for over 200 countries. Includes over 600 indicators covering GNP per capita, growth, economic statistics, etc.

Case sites

www.bluelagoon.co.uk	Case – SME website address
www.ebay.com	Online auction – buyer behaviour
www.glenfiddich.com	Interesting site for case & branding
www.interflora.co.uk	e-commerce direct ordering
www.moorcroft.co.uk	Good for relationship marketing
www.ribena.co.uk	Excellent targeting & history of comms
www.sothebys.ebay.com	New services offered because of advances in electronic technology

Index